THE
Great Undoing
AND
My Journey Home

SUSAN SCHREER DAVIS

LifeRich Publishing is a registered trademark of The Reader's Digest Association, Inc.

LifeRich Publishing books may be ordered through booksellers or by contacting:

LifeRich Publishing
1663 Liberty Drive
Bloomington, IN 47403
www.liferichpublishing.com
1 (888) 238-8637

ISBN: 978-1-4897-0710-9 (sc)
ISBN: 978-1-4897-0709-3 (hc)
ISBN: 978-1-4897-0711-6 (e)

Library of Congress Control Number: 2016903036

Print information available on the last page.

LifeRich Publishing rev. date: 03/28/2016

*To Don,
Nathan, Sam,
and Courtney*

Foreward

This is a story worth reading. There is great depth in this story, brutal honesty, vulnerable questioning, and places where deep will touch deep and soul will touch soul. This is a story worth reading.

This story will take you on a journey. It will take you to churches, hospital rooms, rollercoaster rides, and swimming pools. Most stories will take you there. But this journey will take you beneath the hymnal or diagnosis. It will take you to spaces of great intimacy, and loss, and longing, and the desire not to just be well, but to again be made whole, and to fully come home. This is a journey worth taking.

Susan Davis is a friend of mine. Since the moment I met her I was drawn in. There is no one on the planet like Susan. When she enters the room the room transcends, when she sings the heavens open and when she loves, *and* when she loves wounds heal, hearts mend, and the soul knows it's worth. Susan Davis is worth knowing.

You'll get to know Susan when you read her story. You'll get to know her deeply. You'll probably find yourself in her story. Susan details some of the normalcy of life that we all live, but then there will be spaces where you won't be found. For this journey goes to places so intimate, and so sacred that only Susan can know. But this story also goes to places so dark – even into the valley of the shadow of death – that Susan would do anything for you not to know, but should you go there, because one day you just might, Susan tells her story to serve as light blazing through the darkness.

We all have a story. Many of our stories have great pain, and soul piercing disappointment, but to come to embrace our stories, and not run from them, to find wholeness and healing in our stories is one of the greatest victories in life. This is truth worth believing.

You have a story and your story needs to be told. It could be that your story needs to be written, just like Susan's. But what makes Susan's story unique is not just that it's told, or that it's written down for all the world to see. Susan's story is so beautifully redemptive because she does not just tell the story, or write the story, she lives her story and she is learning to love it. To love her story. Stories are so much easier told than lived and loved. I trust as you read these words you will be encouraged to live and love the story of your life, just as Susan is living and loving hers. If you need some encouragement, I'll bet you'll find it here. Just turn to chapter 1.

Bowler
12/2015

Pastor Craig Bowler
Sanctuary Church
Kennesaw, Georgia

About Ms. Memory and the QR Codes

A friend asked a great question after perusing my manuscript, "How did you remember all of this? Should I be writing my story down so I won't forget it?"

"I don't know," I confessed. "My family often refers to me as *Ms. Memory*—which is not always a compliment. But I do remember a lot of things others don't. At the same time, I kept old journals close while I wrote and looked through them often to keep the timeline and details correct."

My explanation seemed to suffice.

While I'm certain there's no way I remembered everything exactly as it occurred, many of the following stories were burned into my psyche due the poignant nature of the experiences. So having them written down frees a lot of brain space I look forward to using in other ways.

But if my friend asked how I remembered it all, I'm certain others will too. And since I don't want to take my readers for granted, let me reassure you that this is a nonfiction work, written with truth and integrity—not a creative version of my past.

That said, a few months after I started writing the manuscript, I read a book that combined both music and story. The combination not only captivated me, it gave me a vision of how to merge my two loves.

Because I write stories and craft songs, I analyze life with words and pour emotion into music. Inspired, I used both throughout this manuscript.

Most of my songs are available on two CD's that were recorded in 2003 and 2006. However, several of my current compositions aren't available in compilation form. So when my worship pastor, Sonny Lallerstedt, encouraged me to use QR Codes to connect readers to the actual songs, I went to work.

The following QR Code will link you to a page on my website where all the songs from *Life of Love* and *Accepted* are located.

However, if you don't use the QR Code technology, you can also access the songs on my website:

www.susanschreerdavis.com

As to songs that are not currently available on a CD, I added QR codes throughout the book that link to where recordings are located on my website. I hope the interactive potential adds meaning the story.

One

Dead in my sin weary and worn
All of my insides tattered and torn
Father I'm here asking for more
Cause I need the courage to climb
To climb out of this darkened hole

"BRING ME ALIVE"
Accepted, Track 6

My youngest son, Sam, hands me a DVD converted from a video recording taken years ago. Apprehensive, I slide it into a laptop and watch the scene from my past come to life. After viewing only part of it, he exits to do homework, pauses, and quips, "What happened to you, Mom?"

Time suspends as I search for a reply.

"Life ... life happened, Sam—a lot of life. Like your dad dying and you and I ending up with a genetic disorder. Muscle biopsies, spinal taps, surgeries, you know. Crazy stuff happened."

He looks my way only somewhat understanding. His seventeen-year-old, senior-in-high-school self tries on my explanation, but it

1

doesn't quite fit. He can't give in so why should I? He continues up the stairs and I stand alone. Alone with the reality that the hard stuff is winning. That I caved under the pressure. That my tall, blond-haired, blue-eyed son knows who I was, compared to who I am.

A few weeks earlier, my brother-in-law, George, converted the old VCR recording into a DVD. He took the video only months before my first husband, Jason, died of a brain tumor when my boys were three and four years old. Even as a young mom, my faith was strong back then, my hope in God sure. Very sure. We had walked an incredible journey that transformed everything I knew about faith in Christ—and *that* Susan was on full display in the video.

However, by the time I turned forty-two, Sam and I had both been diagnosed with a metabolic disorder, explaining weak muscles and messed up nerves. During our diagnosis process two years earlier, I twisted my ankle on a pine cone and fell. A doctor reattached the torn ligament, but within weeks, intolerable pain shot down the back of my right leg.

Another surgery followed—a back surgery. Once home, I couldn't even lift my leg to roll over in bed. In time, the floor offered comfort, a place of rest. Another reminder that my life was not what it had been.

I turn to our empty living room. The soft carpet beckons me to the floor—my favorite place to sit. Our brown leather IKEA sofa is too soft. The matching chairs tilt, too steep. So I stretch out on the floor with my legs straight in front of me, facing the TV. I slept in this place for more than three months after my back surgery. Huddled against the base of the sofa, I felt safe and warm—and could even roll over.

Some nights I still stretch out on the hard surface, my body unable to relax in the comfort of our bed. So as I sit on the carpet with my back against the front of the sofa, I am home, in my "easy chair," in front of the TV.

My husband, Don, joins me in the living room to watch the video in its entirety. I find the DVD remote, push play, and there we are again. My small family. The family I've missed. The family I've ached to relive. Jason, the father of my children, sits beside me at our kitchen table with disheveled hair and a half-glazed stare. Our little boys come and go as we talk—as I talk—because Jason's speech is slurred and slow.

We explain that this is our *before* video. Not a last will and testament kind of thing. It's our *before* video because we're waiting for a miracle. We're expecting Jason's body to be healed, for the brain tumor to loosen its grip on the nerves in his head.

Miracles happen, you know.

So despite his altered appearance, we preach hope. We talk about God's love. I look calmly into the camera and tell the viewers that I trust the God of heaven to do the unimaginable. I don't cry or fall apart or seem apprehensive at all. I speak as one reassured that all is well. That life is livable in the most unbearable situations.

And I wasn't faking it.

We gather the boys and say Psalm 91 as a family. Even two-year-old Sam could sputter the lengthy syllables. We continue with a passage from the book of Ephesians and put on the Armor of God, with motions.

Fifteen years later, I still know the words by heart, but rarely say them. Heartache has smothered hope. Fatigue has worn down confidence.

As the video ends, I lay in the silence, wondering how I lost my way. A bread crumb trail of memories leads to the place of despair.

It started out well enough. In the beginning, after eight-and-a-half years of widowed life, Don asked me out for coffee. The catch? His wife had only been gone a month.

I was nervous. Confused. But after seeing him briefly the previous Sunday morning, I'd gone home fighting the feeling he would call. My legs worked then. So I walked in a soft summer rain. Four times around the block. I prayed, sought wisdom, and asked for clarity.

Newly-widowed men had hurt me in the past. Deeply. Talking to another seemed unwise, yet destined. I walked up the hill to my driveway one last time and heard, "He's going to call you and ask you for coffee. And it's okay."

"Okay?" I whispered to the still-small voice, "How can it be okay?"

As I stared at a patch of impatiens glistening in the rain, the conversation continued, "You've been alone a long time."

Could it be that simple? My loneliness mattered?

Back inside, I had just started to change out of dripping clothes when my son brought me the phone. I hadn't even heard it ring.

"It's for you, Mom." Nathan handed me the device.

"Hello…"

"Hi, it's Don Davis."

Time suspended—at least in my world. The moment felt surreal, other worldly. A collision with destiny.

Conversation came easily. Don was the first widowed person I'd spoken with who had experienced the richness of heaven in the wake of loss, similar to me. And after almost two hours of rich conversation, he asked me to meet him for coffee the next week.

There was no turning back.

His six-foot-three frame arrived in running shorts and a T-shirt. I wore coral cropped pants and a matching shirt. Calmed by a distinct kindness in his blue eyes, I shared some of my stories that had recently been published. He talked about his family, about his former wife.

And I understood.

Not long after Jason died, I ran into a musician friend I hadn't seen in years. Hope sprang inside. *What if he's the one?*

The music teacher became an oasis of illusion as I fought through grief and loss. I wrote him letters and had lunch with him a few times. His insight helped me navigate long days and nights alone. Having a crush on him didn't change how much I missed my husband though. It simply provided a rainbow of color in the storm. In between bouts of tears, I had hope.

So I understood when Don asked me out again. He wanted to go on walks and talk and show me photo albums of his kids. A hole unlike any other had been drilled deep, straight into his heart, and I soothed the ache, having survived the same.

But everything changed when others found out. They thought I'd chased the older man and was disrespecting his former spouse. While he stood firm and wouldn't cave to others' concerns, I tried to do the same. But my legs grew weak. Literally.

Within six months of our first coffee, I woke to unreliable legs. Some days were fine. Others not so fine. And I didn't know why. Months of tests revealed little, and the descent began.

Don proposed months later, even without a diagnosis. We married just over a year after his first wife died, assuming our love would be enough. But in time, blended family stress polarized our togetherness. When we opened our own business a few months after our first anniversary, the pressure of running a retail store only added to the mix.

Carpet comforts my frame as the question churns with growing fervor. What happened to me? A mound of critical reviews piles up so high that I curl up like a wadded piece of paper, crumpled and torn with little energy to process it all.

Lost community.

Financial strain.

Family stress.

Stiff, awkward legs.

Isolating fatigue.

Abandoned hopes.

Rejection that smothers my soul.

And a business that swallows my husband whole.

It took almost five years, but in time I learned why. Mitochondria power our cells—every single cell throughout our entire body. Tests finally showed that my mitochondria don't function like they should. I was tired due to a metabolic disorder called Mitochondrial Disease that made navigating relational loss almost undoable.

Almost.

Until Sam knew my secret. That there had been a day I had overcome great loss with joy, confidence, and peace with God. The Susan in the video didn't numb her pain by watching crime TV re-runs. She carried her Bible like a purse. It went everywhere. The words offered comfort in doctor's offices. While waiting for MRI reports. And as neurological symptoms took her husband's life one by one.

The Word had been enough. Enough to keep her going as mom, wife, comforter, caregiver, dishwasher, diaper changer, housecleaner, and more. She believed The Word. And her faith kept hope alive. She often danced in her home and sometimes even in church. Unashamed. In love with Jesus.

> *"Praise the Lord, my soul; all my inmost being, praise his holy name. Praise the Lord, my soul, and forget not all his benefits—who forgives all your sins and heals all your diseases; who redeems your life from the pit and crowns you with love and compassion, who satisfies your desires with good things so that your youth is renewed like the eagle's"* (Psalm 103: 1 – 3 NIV).

As I lay on the floor, I realize it's up to me to find her again. I can't blame the faces and words that paralyzed my heart or the verbal darts that caused me to clamber into a shell I didn't know I owned. As the new perspective calls me from complacency, I remember the Sunday I could barely walk forward to take communion.

With no diagnosis, I panicked, embarrassed by my legs—the ones that stiffened and swung forward like wooden puppet appendages on strings. Don was absent, so right before our row was cued, I leaned to my boys and whispered, "After we take communion, we'll walk across the front and exit straight to the back."

I couldn't bear to sit back down again, not after walking clumsily in front of everyone. Fear had created a person I didn't know—one afraid of people and illness, and one who was utterly confused about what had happened to her.

In contrast, when Jason was sick, I had wept on my knees at a televised depiction of the crucifixion one Easter, thankful that the cross had made a way for me to stay more than sane during his illness. Fast forward ten or so years, and I couldn't even walk forward to receive the sacraments without shame—a shame that made me run from the building as soon as I swallowed the bread and wine.

The Susan in the video felt embraced by God. The Susan melting into the carpet feels caged by life.

"What happened to you, Mom?"

The words swirl, a mantra calling me from the depths. They spark hope. If something happened to me that snapped my spirit like fragile bones, then maybe it can heal. Maybe I'm not stuck in the dark, on the floor forever. My fairy tale ending has spun out of control, but maybe there's still a happily ever after to find.

Challenged by my son, I know what I've read for years in self-help books is true. It's up to me—well, me and God. I have to forgive, move on, and set a new mental course. If not for me, for my son. For both of my sons. They need a mom, not a vapor image of who she was. Sam needs to know we can both live above the fray and the threat of chronic disease.

So I start again. I open mental files that have remained closed. I determine to relive the past as I fight through today. Perhaps by recalling the lessons I once learned, I'll find my hope again.

Two

As I'm holding you I'll be holding him
And when I look into your eyes
I'll see the love he lived to give
As I'm holding you I'll be holding him
Touching the love we shared
What an extraordinary gift

"EXTRAORDINARY GIFT"
Life of Love, Track 12

He saw me in a church and pictured marrying me. That's how we met, my boys' father and I.

My life took a unique turn that day and I didn't even know it. Divine hands had been weaving a tapestry with plans to entwine our lives for years. Random moments, simple strands of color in the overall scheme, had seemed purposeless at the time. Yet most of who I am, even twenty years later, hinges on that day—the day the threads of our individual lives were interwoven, creating a new image, a together life, and a love we both desperately needed.

We didn't speak that first day. In fact, we didn't talk for several weeks. But our future began when I walked into St. Philip Benizi Catholic Church shortly after getting my first traffic ticket.

I had missed a shrub-covered stop sign and "failed to stop" while driving in the unfamiliar surroundings. A gruff cop added to my distress. Unsure how my father would react, I was relieved to find him distracted by his duties at the church when I arrived. As the coordinator, it was his job to keep everything running smoothly and on time.

Dad started organizing Lay Renewal events across the country when I was twelve. The five-day events required months of preparation, so he only hosted two or three a year. A pilot by trade, he devoted his off-time to recruiting teams of lay people to travel to churches, where they lived in congregant's homes and shared their faith at meetings spread throughout the week. Similar to a stay-at-home-retreat, evening services topped off coffees and luncheons hosted throughout the day.

As a Presbyterian led ministry, Dad never considered crossing the denominational divide until a Catholic work friend pestered him into action while I was in high school. It took time. A lot of time and determination. But once approved, the renewal at St. Philip's was scheduled for the spring of my senior year in high school—the only year I opted out of the school musical.

I might have shed fewer tears in life if I'd sung my heart out as a lead character in *The Sound of Music* instead of spending the weekend at St. Philip's. But after crying a lot onstage as Ermengarde in *Hello Dolly* the year before—and feeling pushed around by one of the actresses—my interest waned. As the cast took their bows under the lights on closing night, the applause I once craved meant nothing. And I knew then that I wouldn't try out the next year.

Was I sulking? Unable to forgive? Bound by rejection I couldn't shake? I don't know. But having hungered for the limelight since the age of five when I belted tunes through a plastic microphone on the stage I created on our linoleum kitchen floor, I couldn't fully explain the change. An inner longing pulled me to something more. And that something more led me to St. Phillips in early April the next spring— the same weekend as the school play.

I attended the scheduled youth events Saturday night and Sunday morning, but since I wasn't a church member—or Catholic—I spent a lot of time on the back row, unsure of my place. In fact, when I returned home Sunday night, I plopped on my mother's bed and said, "I have no idea why God had me there. I don't feel like I made a difference at all, and I got that awful ticket."

Those emotions started churning when I slid into a pew earlier in the day. After getting the ticket, I joined Grandma for the Sunday afternoon concert. There on the second row, I wiped tears, feeling useless, out of place, and stressed.

And that's when Jason saw me—that's when the artist was intrigued.

"What's wrong?" my grandmother asked.

"I got a ticket for running a stop sign up the street. It was partially covered by bushes."

More tears flowed.

"Oh, don't you worry," Grandma replied as she dug a tissue out of her purse. "It'll be all right."

An unfamiliar voice interrupted us, "Did I hear you say you ran the stop sign not far from here?"

I turned and saw a middle aged woman sitting with a young man on the row behind us. "Cops know that's a hard sign to see." Leaning in close, she continued, "They wait there to fill their ticket quotas for the month. Don't take it personally."

"Thanks," I offered, unaware of what was stirring in the heart of the young man sitting beside her.

The niceties over, I turned back around, and the concert started. A few songs in, my brother, Mark, stood to sing from his Boy Choir repertoire. I followed as his accompanist. When my fingers ran across the piano, the music touched Jason's soul. Many months later I learned he spent the next hour wondering what it would be like to be an artist married to a musician.

He could paint vivid mental pictures—and much more. His eyes saw colors in a blue sky mine could not. He sketched with pencils what I could only see through God-given eyes. Nuances of color and shade opened a dimension of life to him that I often missed. And as he sat enthralled on the wooden pew, he heard and saw something in me I still struggle to see in myself.

Unfortunately, the concert went long, forcing him to leave early to watch his twin nephews. It didn't matter. When his intrigue only grew throughout the week, he took action. Having sung with the Atlanta Boy

Choir years ago like my brother, he decided to send Mark a donation for his upcoming tour. He called the church, asked for Mark's address, and crafted letters to both of us. Within days, he dropped them in the mail.

I was in Nashville the day the letters arrived, auditioning at Vanderbilt's Blair School of Music. As I waited for a return flight, I called home to tell my mom I'd been accepted—with a scholarship. Excited, she added, "A letter came in the mail today with a donation to your brother. It also had an envelope with these words written on it, '*Please give this to whoever played the piano for Mark.*' Do you want me to open it?"

"Sure!" I blurted.

As I stood at the airport pay phone, Mom read, "*I've had some trouble trying to compose this letter so it won't sound too strange. I saw you at St. Phillip's on Sunday and wanted to speak to you—but had to leave early. I sang with the Boy Choir years ago so it was easy to help your brother out. Getting an address was so simple that I had trouble finding arguments not to write this letter, however strange it may seem. I would like to talk to you. Even if I looked for a number I wouldn't know whom to ask for—so I'll give you mine. This really isn't as silly or as much a generic pick-up as it may sound. Please call—it's relatively painless.*"

Relatively painless. The line got to me. I was accepted to college and had a romantic interest waiting at home. The timing of the two events didn't go unnoticed by me. So I knew I would call when I got home from visiting my sister for spring break. After landing in Atlanta, a connecting flight flew me north.

Laura picked me up at the airport and we drove to the College of William and Mary. Excited to spend spring break with her, we made plans: attend a few classes, walk the charming streets of downtown colonial Williamsburg, and meet with some of her friends.

One sunny afternoon, we visited Kyle[1], a good-looking, God-fearing, muscle-toned young man I'd heard a lot about. We sat on his back porch, eating oranges. I don't remember anything else I ate that entire week. But I remember the oranges—and the flirty banter that

---

[1] Name changed

came too easy. Kyle was my sister's good friend, thus the attention was both flattering and unnerving.

The night before I left, he asked if we could go on a walk. Aging cobblestone paths led through charming village shops. He led me down a worn side path where we hopped the Governor's Palace walls. A nighttime stroll through the moonlit garden maze proved most romantic. As water rippled on the lake, he took my hand and told me he wanted to stay in touch.

I'd rarely dated and had not gone north looking for a guy—especially with the letter writer in waiting. So when the college-aged boy said he would drive Laura home when school ended in a month, I wasn't sure what to think. I flew home excited and confused.

Back home, the school routine demanded attention, so it took a few days before I dialed Jason's number. When I couldn't put it off any longer, I nestled on the floor in my upstairs bedroom and leaned against the end of my twin bed. Far from inquiring minds, I picked up my phone.

A female answered, "Hello."

I steadied my voice and said, "Hi. Is Jason home?"

"Yes … May I ask who's calling?"

"My name is Susan," I stammered, not sure if I should go on. "He sent me a letter and asked me to call."

"Oh!" she responded with interest. "I'll get him."

Soon, a lighthearted tenor voice interrupted the silence.

"Hello," he offered in a somewhat breathless tone. "Thanks for calling!"

I launched into an awkward explanation of why it had taken me over a week to call—minus the details about Kyle. Then we chatted for about half an hour.

I learned he attended the Atlanta College of Art and Design and wanted to paint pictures for a living. He was three and half years older than me and planned to complete his education at a highbrow art school in California. Intrigued by his talent, I didn't think twice when he asked if he could call again. Still, graduation and Kyle held most of my interest.

Laura and Kyle arrived the weekend of my senior prom. Before they left, Kyle asked if we could go on another walk. We started up familiar hills in my neighborhood. At the top of the ascent, we turned left onto the sidewalk that led down to the elementary school and playground. The tall swings behind the school remained a favorite place of comfort—a place to fly free.

But Kyle didn't stop at the swings. He led me to the edge of the trees. Hidden under a canopy of leaves, he kissed me lightly before I had time to think.

He seemed like everything I could want—muscular, good-looking, tall enough, and committed to his faith, like me. We walked back to the house knowing we wouldn't see each other for a long time. But I was smitten. Dumb struck.

They left and Jason called, asking to see me. Busy with end-of-the-year events, I mentioned I would be playing piano at the local art center for a program that week. As if on cue, he asked if he could come.

I arrived late for the evening presentation. An unexpected bout with pneumonia had landed my mother in the hospital. Determined to visit her even though pressed for time, I drove the distance after school. Harried and nervous in a knee-length, silk skirt, pink blouse, and navy high heels, I lugged an armful of music across the pavement toward the late-Victorian home.

Balanced precariously, I clambered up the front stairs that led to a wide, covered porch with stately columns. As I hurried through the large, oak door, my heel caught on the threshold and I tripped through the ominous entry. Wind-blown, dirty blonde curls fell across my face as I regained my balance. Mustering up some grace, I walked toward the piano, ignoring watchful eyes.

A friend of mine had been playing, waiting for me to arrive. Diane and I shared similar hair and eye color, but unlike me, she was always on time. Never hurried. Straight forward. As the less confident pianist, though, she was relieved I had finally arrived.

She offered me the bench, and I began to play. An awkward-looking guy approached. I stole a glance and smiled, trying to look calm. Jason introduced himself in between songs and hung around till I had a break.

Ill at ease, I wasn't sure what to think of the artist. Plus, Kyle had called, drawing me in again with his charm.

But Jason didn't seem to mind or notice. Oblivious to my wavering heart, he stood his ground. Months later, I learned why.

After sending the initial letter, he questioned his judgement and whether I was worth the attention. Wanting to double-check his intuition, he pushed his way into my schedule, even though I was busy and preoccupied with school and mom's health.

He arrived at the event much earlier than me and saw my friend Diane. She sat where I was supposed to be, providing the background music he'd expected me to play. With her similar hair color and cut, she reminded him of me in several ways. But there was a stark difference he couldn't explain—until he stood by the front door, and I fell through. Then he smiled to himself and thought, "That's her. That's the one I'm here for."

Safe at the keyboard, I had no idea he'd received divine confirmation when I almost hit the floor, completing his mission before we even spoke. Still, the historic home offered a safe place to visit. So when I left the piano, we made our way to the refreshment room and filled our plates.

While I wasn't uncomfortable, I wasn't awestruck in his presence. Wavy, sandy-blond hair topped off his tall, lanky frame. Soft blue eyes held my gaze. I introduced him to a favorite teacher and a few friends. But we seemed so different, I wasn't sure why we were there—together—sharing an evening.

He was Catholic. I was Protestant. His family lived south of town, and mine much further to the west. While I was enamored with his talent, I was headed to Tennessee and Jason to an art school in California. Pursuing a relationship seemed pointless.

When the event died down, he asked if we could go out. Ready for home, I invited him to stop by my house, instead. Safe at home with Grandma, we sat around our kitchen table, making small talk through layers of awkwardness. When the phone rang, I was grateful to hear my sister's voice, at first.

"Hey! How are you?"

"I'm doing alright, making it through finals," she replied. "What about you?"

She didn't know Mom was in the hospital and I wasn't supposed to tell. But the truth tumbled out.

"Mom's in the hospital, but she should be out soon."

Laura asked a few questions, and I explained what I knew. Then she asked me about Kyle. With Jason at the table, I spoke in code. It took a minute, but she finally caught on. "Is somebody there with you?"

"Maybe..." I stammered.

"Are you okay?"

"Yes, I'm fine, but I should probably go."

Unsatisfied, she hung up only after I agreed to call back.

Turning to my visitor, I offered a lame explanation for my rudeness and tried to resurrect my hostess role. Jason wasn't mad or disgruntled. The artist's soul ran deep. Unfazed, he asked a few questions and then took his leave.

I later learned he got lost driving home that night and pulled over to read the stars. When the clouds cleared, he studied familiar constellations. A divine nudge had led him to me, and God's creation— mere lights in the dark sky—led him home.

While I remained oblivious to the orchestration at hand, the Master Creator was working gently at the loom, weaving Jason in as a strand of gold. The muscle-toned Protestant from up north still held my attention, but God knew I needed the artist most.

Three

I keep tumbling down, falling on my face
Giving all I have I just don't make the grade
Father of mercy come lift me from this place
Hold me tightly in your arms of grace

"ACCEPTED"
Accepted, Track 3

Sweet memories of young love soothe me for a time. Don has long
gone to bed but I know Sam is still awake. Ready to take the first step
toward the old me, I drag myself off the beige, shag carpet and climb
the stairs to where the question that pierced my aged façade originated.
Each step strains my right hip and ankle, but pain is part of any climb.

I knock on Sam's door. "Can I come in?"

"Sure," he replies, since 'no' isn't acceptable.

"You got me thinking. I want to change. I need to change. I need
to find that other Susan again."

My passionate son looks with veiled interest.

"So I'm going to go to First Sunday worship nights with you—to
your church. It's just a step."

16

"Okay," he replies, a crooked smile forming on his lips.

"I'm sorry I've not always been a great example. But I'm going to do better."

With that I turn back to the stairs and descend with renewed determination.

While Sam goes to church with Don and me on Sunday mornings, he attends youth services at the *other* church—the place where I lost the old me. If the church was theologically unsound, I'd have insisted he not go. But it isn't. It's simply full of hurting people, like me, who struggled to process my relationship with Don when I was most vulnerable.

"Hypocrites," some may cry. In a way they're right. Every church is full of people trying to live up to standards they can't master on their own. Even the best are trying to love while overcoming their own personal wounds. So, no, the church isn't perfect. It's a work in progress.

Just like me.

I've nursed my wounds by staying away. By trying to start over and forget what happened. But it's not working. So to connect with my son, I decide to face my wounds head on.

A few weeks later, I pull into a handicap parking space not far from the church's front door, well aware it's the first indication I'm not whole. After turning the engine off, I reach for my teal, speckled cane for added stability. Having arrived late, I hope no one will be stationed to greet me. Successful, I enter the grand foyer alone and traverse the carpeted hall with a weave that throws my balance. Literally. Just like years ago.

About ten months after we married, I was seen at a multiple sclerosis clinic. Even without a concrete diagnosis, a specialist decided to change my pain medicine and increase a few others, hoping to make my legs work. I barely slept and grew incredibly anxious instead.

As unfamiliar emotions churned, Don and I went to church early to pray one Sunday, and the crowds overwhelmed me. While awkward looks were still the norm due to our newly married status, my altered state intensified the effect. The noise echoed louder than before and the bubbly chatter threatened my sanity.

So I stared at the floor as we navigated the corridor, hoping for balance, but the circular pattern kept me from visually grounding each step. Unable to steady myself as we walked, unfamiliar panic erupted into tears when we found the prayer room.

Paper thin—I'd become paper thin. The girl who once danced in church with flags swirling above her head couldn't even offer a simple prayer. So I changed the medicine. Stopped it all together a few months later. While the depression eased and some calm returned, I couldn't stop the flow of rejection and fear, both real and imagined.

It haunts me still.

As I approach the entry to the auditorium alone, my chest tightens. Focused on the pattern beneath my feet, my head swirls—again. The voice of condemnation starts to speak. Once a member, I'm now a stranger. A scared stranger.

I find a seat on a back row on the far side, away from congregants I once loved—whom I still love and miss more than I want to admit. Sam sits rows ahead with others his age and I find solace knowing he's there, up front near the lit stage while I hover in the shadows.

Comfortable on thick, padded seats, my injured leg stretched out, I sing familiar songs. The worship stirs the inner sanctuary of my soul. His presence, or a peace I only know through prayer and worship, wraps around my being. I lean forward. Bent in reverent prayer, I know He is the answer.

He is The One who will help me breathe again.

He is The One who will help me forgive—over and over—till the choke hold I've allowed releases its grip.

Writing empowers me. So I pick up my journal from the seat next to me and put pen to paper. Inner dialogues go to war. Condemnation versus acceptance. Calm versus fear.

For years I served in the church as a young, widowed mom, respected for staying strong. Now the perfect storm of rejection combined with medical mayhem rages inside. Once a rock my first husband leaned on, I feel like a failure as Don's wife as we struggle for common ground. He says we're making history, fighting through the bad to find our marital footing. But his legs aren't nearly as wobbly as mine, figuratively and physically.

Shouldn't it be easier? Didn't I earn a happy ending?

A few months after Jason died, my mom said, "You know, there's a good chance you'll be single for a while."

"That may be true," I retorted, "but I can only accept it in three-month segments at a time right now."

And I wasn't kidding.

I didn't want to be single. I liked being married. I wanted a happy ending in order to make sense of it all. Could that desire still be my greatest stumbling block today?

Don often says God is more concerned about our character than our comfort. But with all that's going on, the notion sends me spiraling more. I can only assume I must have been an especially difficult case if all this trial is necessary to hone my character. So I've asked, *"What's wrong with me? Why did I need all this extra training?"*

For years, a depressing silence followed my cries.

Today, on the back row, I hear:

> *"There is now no condemnation for those who are in Christ Jesus..."* (Romans 8:1 NIV).

Trusting God for provision and healing and even joy had been an adventure in my twenties. Trusting him for the same in my forties makes me weary, which may be the root of the matter. I don't want to work this hard again. I want my version of the Promised Land.

But even the Promised Land held giants.

I've thought about that so many times. After being fed manna in the desert while they wandered for years, the Israelites had to fight their way into the Promised Land. God made a way, but their victories required courage, steadfastness, and determination.

And there-in lays the rub. I've lost my inner fight. Hurt by friends, disoriented by my second spouse, and wearied by medical chaos, I question why God allowed a host of trials right when my second-marriage-happy-ending was to begin.

As that train of thought progresses, the truth bubbles up inside. I'm facing a crisis of faith. I'm back at square one asking, *"If God really loves me, why is he allowing all this hurt?"*

The worship music ends. A pastor stands at the front to lead us in prayer. After mentioning a ministry in need, we pray silently for a time.

When I compare my pain to those across the globe, it pales in comparison. My heartache becomes mere suffering on a cloud. I have good health care, food, warmth, and family, and I'm well aware that the challenges we experience in America don't measure up to what many overseas endure. So I want to be stronger. Far less concerned about what others think of me. Forgiving. But shame clouds my perception, tethered by roots entwined in the deepest place.

Where did it begin?

One of my first childhood memories is running to my room after a spanking and hiding under my bed. Squeezed in the tight place, dark and alone, I longed to purge the wadded-up emotion. I still struggle to do the same. I question why I become undone by a simple reprimand that others can brush off with an air of self-assurance.

I received my last spanking after an argument with my older sister. I hadn't worn the shower cap to keep my hair dry. She threatened to tell. We argued. And since we'd been arguing too much, we both got in trouble. When I entered my third-grade class the next day, I was certain everyone knew I had been punished the night before. A load of shame shrouded me simply because I didn't wear a shower cap.

My parents weren't excessive with force and didn't punish me often. They didn't have to. I was wired to perform. To seek approval. To thirst for affirmation.

Failure undid me. Rattled me to the core. *Has this great undoing been allowed to shake it loose, to force my surrender again at the foot of the cross—or in the sanctuary of the other church?*

When I was ten, I prayed with a visiting pastor to receive Jesus during a family dinner at the first Lay Renewal my dad ever coordinated. Something in the pastor's sermon the night before propelled me to interrupt his meal. As we prayed, a tingling sensation came through the top of my head and settled in my heart. It scared me. So I ran to the bathroom, where I hid and cried. My mom found me at some point and explained I had been touched by the Holy Spirit and shouldn't be afraid.

Comforted, the encounter changed me in a good way. But during my middle school years, when I tried to sleep, a "bad" feeling would often come over me. As crazy as it sounds, the only way I knew to rid myself of the feeling was to rehearse a litany of "bad" things about myself. To ward it off I would say, "I'm stupid. I'm bad. I'm ugly."

In time, I swallowed the accusations whole and didn't need a "bad" feeling to come over me at night to recite the internal litany. The lies had become a part of me. I'd innocently fallen prey to the enemy's favorite pastime—to undermine the very essence of what it means to be a Child of God.

I have since prayed against the curse and spent hours in counseling and prayer. Still the voices echo like a reverb I can't control. Don tells me I still carry shame needlessly. I argue back, certain it's not that simple. Tired of fighting internal demons, I want to believe verbal darts are to blame—his as well as others. But blame isn't making me stronger, only weaker. So I must face it again and run to the crucible of healing one more time.

Why here? Why at this church? Perhaps it's quite simple. When I believe I've failed, I feel shame. And when I feel shame, I want to hide. What better place to confront both lies than in the sanctuary I've run from most?

Sitting on the back row, I open wide my heart with all its failure and shame. Utterly exposed, I join in the prayers offered for others who need His presence like me.

As the service ends, we're instructed to go forward for a time of prayer. I used to bolt for the altar during moments like this. I wanted the corporate blessing. Now I consider whether I'll stick out more by going forward or staying in place. When I'm the only one left sitting, I follow the crowd.

As we huddle together, someone prays for me. Someone I don't know, someone who doesn't care about who I married or whether I made the right choice. She just prays. And while I feel like a foreigner in my home town, her hands hold mine with confidence as she speaks a blessing over my life.

I've entered the scary place and found a friend.

The service ends. I walk to my pew to pick up my journal. Familiar faces approach and we play catch up. They didn't know about my surgeries or my diagnosis. I see concern. I feel empathy. So when I say goodbye to Sam and walk to my car, I'm a little stronger. A concrete step away from my dismal summer existence.

I'll visit the church again.

Four

On and on we must go just like all of the rest
It's a game full of choices each crossing a test
Will we drown in the sorrow of darkness
Or will we fight till tomorrow brings us its best

"LET THE BALLOONS GO"
Life of Love, Track 5

Home after a long day at high school, I hurried to my room with a letter from Kyle. Propped up on pillows on my bed, I reread his scripture filled, lofty words. Since my faith was everything to me—my moral code, the right path—his thoughts left me enamored and wanting more.

While Kyle seemed to share my passion much more than Jason, the artist was patient and persistent—and continued to call. He invited me to the Renaissance Festival and after sorting through dates, we chose a Saturday in late May. After I hung up, though, I remembered I had to play for a wedding that afternoon. So I dialed his number again.

"Hey, it's me. I forgot I have to play for a wedding the day we agreed to meet."

"What time is the wedding?" he asked, nonchalant.

"Three. I need to be there by two-thirty," I explained, biting my lip.

"If I pick you up a little earlier, we can go to the festival and be back in time. Would that work?"

"Sure. That would be fine."

Relived, our first real date was set.

The sun shone bright, and blue skies glistened as we watched knights joust and ate oversized drum sticks. Jason's clever commentary made me laugh. On the way home, I mentioned I needed a summer job.

"I airbrush T-shirts at Six Flags," he shared. "We always need reliable cashiers."

"I don't know. My tall, beautiful sister walked into Six Flags and got a job in the guest relations office. I'm afraid if I apply there, I'll end up on the grounds crew."

"I can get you a job in the air brush shops," he insisted. "The shop owners lease space from Six Flags, so they hire their own people. You don't have to apply through the park."

"Seriously?" I asked.

"Yes, I'll give you a number to call. Wait till early next week, but give them a call."

Within a week I had the job. Shortly after graduating from high school, I put on my first starched navy and burgundy uniform and entered unfamiliar territory. But I needn't worry. Jason not only told his boss to hire me, he asked for us to be assigned to the same shop.

And the tables were turned.

From day one I had an escort and a highly attentive trainer. While I was nervous in the new environment, the artist was relaxed and in his element. He put me at ease, stepping in when I needed help and leaving me hanging when I needed to learn. His gentle, laidback way coaxed me out of my shell and gave me confidence in my role.

Screams from nearby roller coasters and looped carnival music created a jovial background as we worked side by side. He painted cars, hats, T-shirts, and almost anything guests would ask. As I watched colors transform white shirts, I recognized a talent much greater than my own.

When he walked me to my car mid-June and asked if he could kiss me goodnight, however, the truth came out. Stiffened, I mumbled something about Kyle. I wasn't exactly a taken girl, but I wasn't ready for another kiss so soon after the last. In my naïve world, it didn't seem right. After the awkward exchange, I drove home in the dark, hoping I hadn't lost my new friend.

I shouldn't have worried. He called the next day—on Father's Day—and asked if he could come over. No pouting. No distancing. He sounded calm and determined. Sensing it was important, I said, "Sure…"

When he arrived a few hours later, we went for a walk—up the same hills I'd traversed with Kyle.

"I've been thinking a lot since last night." His calm strides led the way. "If our relationship isn't supposed to be romantic, then I have to figure out what it's about. Ever since I first saw you, I felt there was something different about you, and I want to understand it."

I didn't know what to say. No one had ever described me that way. So I kept listening and he kept talking.

He told me about disappointments in high school. A competition lost. Stolen artwork never found. A detention notice turned into a mark on his permanent record. He rebelled by wearing a vampire cape and fangs with his tux to prom, hoping things would change in college.

His story continued as we turned left down the sidewalk toward the school.

During Thanksgiving break of his freshman year in college, his parents noticed a slight pull to his eye. An image study done on one of the first MRI machines in Atlanta weeks later revealed a brain stem tumor. One doctor gave him six months to live but the fear-filled diagnosis was very wrong. After months of radiation treatments, the tumor stabilized. And three years later, he was walking in a light summer drizzle with me, trying to make sense of it all.

I had known Jason for two months at this point and not once had he drawn attention to his past. Even if he hadn't wanted to scare me off, I was mesmerized by his understated manner.

Having never talked to someone who had faced a serious illness, I more than fumbled for words. I asked about treatment and what he'd done about school and he graciously filled in the last few years.

After months of treatment, he finished a second semester of college in the fall. Haunted by the idea his life could be cut short, he then dropped out of school and took a trip to Italy with his church. Squeezed in the plaza square, he shook hands with the Pope. After he returned home, he spent six months in Daytona Beach working as an airbrush artist at a place called *The Rat's Hole*. When he'd had enough, he drove home, enrolled in a local art school, and met me.

As we walked, my head spun. My sheltered, pampered existence wrestled to comprehend his struggle—let alone a place called *The Rat's Hole*! When thick clouds forced us to turn back to my home, I kept listening.

"All I know," he continued, "is that it's like there's a light inside of you—a light that seems to come from your faith. And I want to understand God the way you do."

We stood under a lamp post at the end of my driveway, damp from a heavy mist. Hearts bare, I didn't know what to say. I knew what I believed but questioned if my simple ideology was enough to meet the demands of someone facing life altering issues. Still, it was all I had to offer.

"Faith is simple to me. My family has always gone to church. So believing that God's love is bigger than the problems we face makes sense. I don't know how to make it real for you, especially after the hard things you've faced. But I just believe that when you accept Jesus into your heart, God works things out in the end."

We parted without solving his life dilemma. Thankful our friendship was intact, I sank into a chair at our kitchen table and shared his story with my mom. Concern filled her eyes. The relational risk made clear, I looked forward to more days at the park.

I wore a soft, blue and white striped sweater with matching cotton cropped pants the night I fell in love with him. He had on blue jeans with an untucked, colorful green and blue print shirt.

Our mutual transparency had forged an unspoken bond. Tucked in the confines of the T-shirt shops, I watched as he pulled on a black chemical mask for protection. Fear of a re-occurrence made him vigilant about not inhaling paint vapors. I hadn't thought much of it before, but it held new meaning. Like everything else. When he asked me out again several weeks later, I couldn't wait for our second date.

After a day at work, we changed clothes, climbed into his blue Nissan pickup truck, and went to a restaurant downtown. I well remember the moment I looked over at him and all my reservations melted like wax under a flame. I turned my head away, as if to shake the mirage loose. But when I looked again, a wave of emotion fluttered through me. He'd never treated me unkind for putting off his advances. Our friendship had grown instead. His unwavering devotion captivated me. The artist was mine for the taking, and everything in me suddenly wanted him.

Conversation flowed. We only got lost once. And all too soon we were headed back home.

A white, four-door sedan raced in from behind on the major highway, starling us both. It hit another car and careened toward the front, right corner of Jason's truck. As I braced for the collision, he steadied the wheel. While he maintained control after the hit, the other car sped off. Forced to the side of the road, we got out of his truck and surveyed the damage.

Someone alerted 911 and after a long wait on a dark stretch of highway, a police car showed. Despondent, we waited for a tow truck before climbing into the back of the patrol car for a ride to the closest truck stop.

Knowing the artist was mortified, I reached for his hand. The comforting touch lingered. Our fingers locked till we reached our destination. Stuck in the confines of a sketchy café with bright-orange walls, we called our parents and waited for a ride home. Polite goodbyes, with parents at our side, punctuated the end to our first real date.

A week later, he invited me to his home. When I knocked on the door, he answered with hands covered in soap suds. His gentle nature set me at ease in the unfamiliar surroundings, and he suggested we go on a walk. Under a single, tall oak tree with leaves draped around, he leaned in for a kiss. This time I didn't resist.

The soft touch of his lips left me wanting more and time with the artist became priority.

We worked at the park together and took turns driving the forty-five minutes between our homes. One Saturday a few weeks later, I was about to leave for a visit when the phone rang.

"Hello," I answered in a hurry.

"Hi Susan, it's Kyle!"

His letters had slowed and my interest had waned. But hearing his voice stirred emotion I'd tucked away.

"How are you doing?" I asked, not sure what to say.

"I'm fine. But I'm also in the Atlanta airport for the afternoon. Any chance you can come see me while I'm here?"

I hesitated. Part of me wanted to see him. But I'd made a commitment with Jason. Could I stop by the airport on the way? Would that be fair to either one of them? Thoughts buzzed in a fury. Then clarity spoke.

"I'm so sorry. I'd like to see you but I have other plans today."

After brief small talk, we hung up, and I waltzed out the door to see Jason. Decision made.

Five

Terrorists keep blowing bombs in old Baghdad
And soldiers lose their lives leaving their momma's sad
I'm heavy with this feeling called reality
So Jesus won't you set my broken spirit free

"DREAM IN COLOR"
Accepted, Track 8

A few weeks have passed since my visit to the *other* church, and our blended family has gathered for a meal. A little stronger, I mention an upcoming trip, "We're thinking about taking Sam to visit Yale."

Since Don's oldest son graduated from the prestigious university and Sam makes stellar grades, we've received several pieces of mail encouraging Sam to apply.

"That sounds like fun," my daughter-in-law replies.

"Maybe," I start, "but it's been a long time since I've flown. I get really tired."

"Just use a wheelchair. What's the big deal?"

A tingling anxiety spreads to my limbs as tightness creeps over my chest. Forcing calm breaths, I don't even try to explain that the thought of using a wheelchair stirs panic. It doesn't make sense. To others it's just a wheelchair, but to me it's a public acknowledgement of my disease. When I maneuver at home, I disguise the struggle well. In contrast, long-distance travel takes me far from my comfort zone, and forces me to use mobility aids. My independent self transforms into a disabled soul and makes me squirrely.

As I question my resolve, several good reasons for taking the trip collide at once. While Don encourages Sam to consider going to a far-away college that will challenge him, my grandmother, who lives up that way, experiences a decline in health. When we consider that the weekend after Labor Day is often slow at our store, I cave. Dad reserves our Delta passes, and I try to mentally prep to fly.

I replay my daughter-in-law's admonition, "Just use a wheelchair. It's no big deal."

Yet I can't shake a certain memory from the last time I flew.

A writing mentor offered to pay a significant conference fee for me four years earlier. The catch? I had to travel to California and navigate a hilly conference center to attend. Still clinging to life back then, I faced my fears and dusted off my friend's shiny, red Rollator walker—the one that had been sitting in our garage for months.

After using it once—and becoming undone by awkward glances—I let spiders build intricate webs in its frame. Enticed by the opportunity to travel cross-country, I unburied it from a pile of stuff and wiped down each surface as if waxing a new car. I still hoped I wouldn't need it much, but figured I should bring it just in case.

Early on the morning of my departure, Don dropped me off outside of ticketing where I'd planned to check the cumbersome piece. The large, open space and early-morning arrival made balance difficult, turning my legs to jello. Taking a deep breath to squelch the uneasy feeling, I unfolded the Rollator, set my luggage on the seat, and began my first journey as a bona fide handicapped Susan.

Onboard, I had a row to myself, offering ample room to stretch my legs. Still, they stiffened in route. So I waited until the plane had almost emptied before disembarking. As I made my way to the exit, I steadied my gait by the holding the back of each passing seat.

Parked on the tarmac, away from the terminal, I wasn't sure how to find the walker as I approached the exit. I didn't have to wonder for long.

The California sunshine warmed my skin when I stepped out onto the moveable stairs that led to the pavement. Far below, my red walker glinted in the sun next to other gate-checked items. As I waited high above for the line of passengers to descend, I took notice when baggage men reached for my walker and offered it to a hunched-over eighty-year-old looking Grandma. When she took it, I stiffened. Stunned into silence—and not wanting to claim the device as my own—I stared as she turned toward the covered walk to the gate, maneuvering with the aid of my Rollator walker.

I needn't worry. A flight attendant right behind me noticed the predicament and took action. With her arms waving high and gesturing toward my frame, she frantically yelled, "That walker belongs to *this* woman!"

I wasn't sure what was worse, that the Grandma almost made off with my walker or that the entire city knew that forty-year-old Susan couldn't manage a trip without aid. Embarrassed deep to my bones, I accepted that The Almighty was forcing me to get over myself. "It's no big deal," I imagined Him saying with a smile. "Suck it up. It's just a walker. I created you, your legs, and your heart—and your heart matters most."

I got the lesson but was still mortified. In a somewhat humored way.

An army of strangers watched as I entered the airport, so I stared at the floor. It was easier that way. After weaving through the thick throng of humanity, the masses dispersed and I breathed with greater ease.

When I arrived at the conference center, steep hills met my gaze at every turn. Without hesitation I offered thanks for the metal device that supported my frame. Meeting others as the disabled girl with weird legs still challenged my sense of self. I wanted people to know the real me, or rather the me I once was—a gal who climbed trees and mountains, rode water park rides, and peddled a bike at the beach.

The Susan they met sparked empathy, stirred conversations about potential diagnoses, and maneuvered on stiff legs all week. But it didn't matter. Without the walker, I would never have been able to navigate the daily conference grind. And getting away had been good.

The walker gathered dust again when I got home and was eventually returned to its owner. So as we make plans to see Grandma and visit Yale, a wheelchair ride seems inevitable. But my stubbornness overrides reason.

Sam and I take off for Philly hours earlier than Don. After landing, I choose to maneuver the airport with my cane. However, once we reach my grandparent's retirement home, I borrow Grandma's walker for the long walk from their apartment to dinner, grateful for the added support. I have no choice. My legs need a break.

After picking up Don from the airport, we indulge in ice cream with my grandparents. Grandpa asks about our travel plans and suggests we circumvent New York City on our way north. With bomb threats abounding on this weekend—the tenth anniversary of 9/11—bypassing the Big Apple makes sense.

Logic fades as we drive north the next day. Itchy to see the Manhattan skyline, talk radio warnings have little effect. Magnetic appeal draws me to the city's charm and the pull grabs hold the closer we get to the outskirts of town. So I beg Don to change course, and he happily obliges.

After studying a map, we turn east toward the George Washington Bridge, north of the city. While news blurbs warn of a terrorist threat targeting the overpass, it's the perfect choice. I'll glimpse the skyline while Don avoids playing bumper cars with a string of yellow taxis.

In an odd way, the terror threat adds to the excitement. Since I can no longer ride roller coasters or water slides, getting a glimpse of downtown New York during such a poignant time will provide a much needed thrill.

As we approach our target, I count down the miles and turn up the radio. Sam plugs in his iPod, and worship songs blast through the speakers.

The towering structure comes into view, and we launch out over the river, suspended by steel towers and cables. I throw my hands in the air like I used to on the Scream Machine at Six Flags and sing at the top of my lungs. With windows rolled down and the breeze tossing my hair, we soar across the floating highway that could blow with the push of a button. To my right, the city that never sleeps appears through a slight haze.

I'm not a masochist, nor do I want to die young. But far from home, ensconced momentarily in the place where a madness much bigger than my own occurred, I'm carried above my hurt, my sorrow, and my loss. I feel both big and small at the same time. No longer trapped at home by my body, I'm playing a bit part in the drama called national news.

We reach the other side without a bomb going off and the city quickly fades. The moment ends faster than a roller coaster ride but I feel lighter on the other side. A few cares have flown out the window. The risk paid off. It often does.

Stark industrial buildings line the highway as we continue north. More than an hour later, we approach historic New Haven, and Don navigates us toward the Yale Campus. The famous castle-like dorms appear before we turn toward our hotel. By the time we enter our room, heavy steps indicate my legs won't carry me far the next morning. So we enjoy a short look around after dinner.

While grieved to miss out on the campus tour with my son the next morning, I rest as Don and Sam head out. Hoping the forced togetherness will bridge the awkward distance that remains between my husband and son, I accept my fate and fall back asleep. When they return hours later, I'm dressed and ready to check out, which is a good thing since Don has found a wheelchair and insists on showing me his favorite sites. My personal tour guide wants to take me down memory lane.

Round two quickly tires Sam's feet, but he keeps up. Uncharacteristic enthusiasm shows in Don's stride as he relives cherished family memories. Cobblestone streets and an ensuing bumpy ride soon remind me why I avoid wheelchairs. But I ignore them when Don pushes me through the castle-dorm quadrant. Steeples rise in the enchanting courtyard where a long list of the elite have walked the historic paths. Charmed, I'm grateful for the ride.

We eat lunch in a dining hall straight from a *Harry Potter* scene. From there we cross over to the Beinecke Rare Book & Manuscript

Library, housing a *Gutenberg Bible*. Several displays hold our attention, but none like the glass box housing the Word of God. We accidentally bump the glass and set off a silent alarm, alerting a guard. Not ready to repeat our mishap, we sheepishly make our exit.

An avid runner, Don has set foot on most of the campus more than once. As he pushes me around, he talks about the day he and his first wife left their firstborn at the campus and when they returned to watch him play football. Real life entwines with his memories, making me feel strangely connected to his past—in a good way. We pass several places where family pictures were taken and he chuckles, reliving the good and bad.

Sam is about out of steam when Don says, "I need to show you one last place."

With that, he pushes the wheelchair toward the Grove Street Cemetery, where many who changed our world now lie.

Among tall oaks and aging paths, we find the burial places of Noah Webster and Eli Whitney. Needing a respite from the heat, Sam takes solace under leaf-filled branches. In hushed reverence, we take in the surroundings, familiar with the pain of loss and the stark end of a life that changes the landscape of hearts.

While Sam may not even bother to apply to the school, our day has resonated deep. Step-father and son bonded—albeit just a little. Far from the store, Don revisited and shared the place that changed the landscape of his family. And I've traveled far from the gate in Atlanta to my grandparent's home, across a suspended freeway, to historic landmarks that remind me life is brief, a mere moment in the context of time. As we turn to leave, I long to cherish mine a little more, even if from a wheelchair.

Back on the highway, we head south toward New York City again. We discuss taking the same route back to Philadelphia, but as the miles' fade, I want more. I want to see the hustle and bustle right outside my car window. Sam moans, not needing a close-up view while Don suggests we circumvent the city to avoid downtown traffic. I agree, hoping to navigate us on a highway that runs around the outskirts of Manhattan.

Our approach from the east side requires an unexpected amount of tolls. Don never balks as he hands over five and ten dollar bills every time we enter a tunnel or cross a bridge. A wrong turn takes us toward Queens, away from the city, until I realize my mistake.

Sam moans again. Don patiently drives. My excitement grows as the skyline finally approaches.

We enter the Queen's Midtown Tunnel, thinking we can take an immediate left toward the Brooklyn Bridge once we surface. When daylight indicates our turn is close, we realize there's no way to get into the necessary lane and Don is forced to drive straight into the city. Sam moans again, Don starts dodging taxis, and a rush of adrenaline surges through me.

We're in downtown New York City, and despite the fact I traveled a great deal in my youth, I never set foot in the Big Apple. I rode through it once with my aunt, but never stood on the pavement. So I soak in the magnitude and search for another way out.

While it seems we've made a serious mistake, I'm confident we'll remedy the situation in good time. We stay south on a street lined with serious high rises before seeing signs for the highway we need. I study the map in between frequent glances out the window, and know we're making progress. And right before we duck into one last tunnel that will lead us out of the city, we realize we're passing the World Trade Center construction site and catch a glimpse of the memorial.

On the actual tenth anniversary of the event, we are here, passing by. Only for a second, but that second counts a lot in my world.

After exiting the tunnel, we turn onto the Brooklyn Bridge, heading back to Philadelphia for a return flight in the morning. The moon is rising while the Statue of Liberty glimmers in the bay to my right. I've seen the postcard image on TV, but never in person. So I peer out the window, craning my neck till the view fades, and the skyline sinks into the horizon.

Piercing nerve pain shoots through my feet when we enter the airport the next morning, causing tears. It's time to go home. But that's okay. Deep down I'm changed. When offered a wheelchair, I accept without reservation. Touching the national tragedy roused me from self-absorption. My soul feels alive, stretched wide beyond itself.

Six

Live a life of love
Won't you, live a life of love
Dance in the river that rolls with forgiveness
And live a life of love

"LIFE OF LOVE"
Life of Love, Track2

Home from our jaunt north, I feel close to Don in a new way. Reliving his past heightened our sense of togetherness. Reliving my own continues to stabilize swirling emotion.

The present and past—they tie together like shoe strings to hold us intact.

Several important milestones occurred during the first year I dated Jason. With Kyle no longer a distraction, time with the artist took precedence. While summer days slipped away and our coming separation grew imminent, unexpected conversations knit our hearts together. The first occurred on a beach in the moonlight.

Another air brush artist, Janice, also worked as a youth group leader. In need of chaperones for a retreat, she asked if Jason and I could come. The invitation didn't surprise me since I knew how much Janice respected Jason. My parent's approval did.

After dinner the first night, everyone gathered for team-building games. As the sun set, we divided into two groups with instructions to pass our team across a high rope stretched several feet wide. Jason knelt on the bottom of a pyramid while the largest guy in his lineup tried to crawl over the high rope. Unsuccessful, he landed hard on Jason's foot. The appendage swelled and turned colors.

An X-ray confirmed it wasn't broken, but the severe sprain slowed him down. So when the group left to ride go-carts the next evening, Janice encouraged us to stay behind. Alone at the ocean, we spread a towel on the beach and watched the moon rise.

Soothing waves crashed on the shore as moonlight danced on the water. With only weeks before my departure for school, conversation went deep. No matter how much Jason loved on me, part of me pushed back. Inner shame from a myriad of sources kept me bound.

A few years before, I'd been involved in a relationship with the older brother of a friend of mine. Their mom had died in a tragic accident during Thanksgiving break. When I visited with the family, the older sibling wasn't there. He was at the funeral home. Alone. I offered to hunt him down and his dad seemed relieved.

Upon entering the funeral parlor, I found my friend trying to unlock his mother's casket, which was already closed due to the horrific nature of the accident. Not knowing what to do, I watched in vain as he tried to see her one last time. When he gave up, I listened as he talked about his underappreciated mom.

In time, our relationship evolved into a romance that ended abruptly when he went back to college a few months later. A postcard offered a final goodbye. Due to physical interaction that involved more than mere kisses, a new kind of rejection rattled my confidence. I'd always been guarded with boys, but the older guy broke through barriers I hadn't known to erect. Naivety was to blame. But of course, I internalized shame.

There on the beach, safe with the artist, I laid it all out. I told him every detail that caused me pain, almost certain it would push him away. But it didn't. Jason listened intently, waiting till he knew I was done. And then simply said, "Susan, I love you and nothing can or will change that."

The first of many chains broke free.

Back at the park the following week, we stood side by side in the shop on a slow weekday morning. Jason leaned on the high counter not far from me, folded his hands, and looked my way. "Do you remember me telling you I planned to return to Arizona this fall?"

"Yes..." I offered, knowing he'd dreamed of attending a famous art school in California after completing core classes at Arizona State University. The brain tumor had derailed his plans for a few years, but he was finally ready to hope again.

"Well, I've changed my mind," he began, "and you're the reason— but there's no pressure with that."

Surprisingly, I didn't feel pressure.

Standing up straight, he turned my way, "Here's the deal. I could go out to California and chase my illustration dreams, or I can stay here and see what happens with you."

He paused, waiting for my reaction, but I was still taking it in, wondering how I could be more important than his lifelong dream?

"Ever since the brain tumor scare," he explained, "having a family has mattered to me more than having a degree. So as long as I don't freak you out, I'm going to attend Georgia State and work toward a degree in graphic design—and maybe visit you some in Nashville."

Utter peace enveloped me. I wasn't freaked out and didn't feel coerced. His humble persistence came with no strings. Just possibility. And surprisingly, I could live with that.

Even so, when we parted a few weeks later, I left without promising a forever commitment. I felt too young to make such a big decision, especially with so much change ahead. Still that hesitation didn't stop me from accepting my parent's offer to call him halfway through move in day.

And the calls didn't stop.

My roommate and hall friends knew I talked to a guy back home. Not comfortable with the term "boyfriend" I referred to him as "just a friend." It didn't matter. In time, their suspicions grew.

Six weeks into the semester, I invited him to visit. We met on the open lawn in front of the massive library when my philosophy class ended. The first few hours felt awkward, but we soon found our step and merged into the couple we'd been at home. While he stayed in a friend's dorm across campus, we spent as much time together as possible, enjoying the crisp, fall weekend. When he left, my friends called me out.

"He's not just a friend," Dottie quipped with a smirk. "Or at least not like any friend I've ever had."

She lived two doors down and always seemed to know me best. Hesitant to broadcast an unavailable status, I simply smiled.

Not long after, a young man I'd met at a campus ministry event asked to see me. We walked a short distance from my dorm and sat on a bench outside the courtyard. As he fumbled with a tall umbrella he brought in case of rain, he asked if I had any interest in pursuing a relationship.

As I listened to his offer and thought about a response, the importance of my friendship with Jason became uncannily clear. Another juncture had come. Another choice had to be made. I could entertain a relationship with a Vanderbilt student or choose my guy back home.

I chose the guy back home.

Jason visited again in mid-November and we spent our last morning in the chapel balcony. Perfectly content, we dreamed of our future, one with no more good-byes. Years of school kept us practical about a time line, but I put myself out there and blurted, "You know, someday I might like a ring from you—not necessarily an engagement ring just yet—but I've never wanted a ring from someone before. It just feels right."

Never swayed by my emotion, he just smiled. And all too soon we parted ways.

In spite of the distance, Jason always felt close. How could he not? The artist valued the very essence of me. He saw something in the depths of my soul that took me years to understand. He spoke of my sensitivity as a strength instead of a weakness. I could cry a bucket of tears and never throw him off guard. Free to be me, I grew less afraid of my emotions and began to harness them as an asset. My feelings had purpose, and as I grew more confident in myself and our relationship, he began to open up more about his medical concerns.

A friend of a friend had asked him to visit another young man battling a brain tumor. The late-teen patient wasn't doing well, and Jason wasn't sure he wanted to stop by. What would he say? How could he offer encouragement? What if the young man's fear triggered his own?

While most people didn't know Jason had an issue, he was reminded of it every time he looked in the mirror. Compressed nerves had slightly altered the right side of his face, pulling it up, non-symmetrical. When he looked at his reflection, most mirrors distorted the disfigured side.

Due to the perceived damage combined with myokymia in his neck (an involuntary quivering of muscle), he daily fought for peace. Stress or lack of sleep made the symptoms worse, which of course intensified nagging worry. Our relationship was a great distraction, but the reality was never far from his mind—though he rarely admitted it.

During a visit in early spring, we climbed our favorite tree in Centennial Park near the Nashville Parthenon and later collapsed onto a nearby bench. Cooled by a slight breeze under a clear-blue sky, we contemplated the heavy truth. The tumor could return. And Jason wasn't sure how he'd respond.

Would he lose hope? Fall into despair? Get angry with God?

Questions loomed large with no easy answers—except faith—which was all I had to offer. And so I did. I assured him that faith in God would get us through, one day at a time—even if deep inside, I didn't exactly know how.

Jason visited the sick teen but never felt like he helped him much. Still, the discussions provoked by his visits mattered to us. An acknowledgment of the uncertainty served as an important milestone for our future.

Spring break arrived and with it, the awareness that we'd almost known each other an entire year. Ironically, Kyle traveled to my home with Laura for their break as well. At home together, his good looks and charm lit up the room—and a tiny place in my heart.

He'd called me once during the year, keeping our friendship alive. But I didn't realize more stirred inside until Jason and I sat across from each other at my favorite yogurt shop late in the week. As I savored each bite, he looked my way casually and said, "You still like him, don't you?"

His words stung. Snapped into a reality I didn't want to face, I cringed at my own betrayal, "I guess I do."

Although I wasn't sure what that meant.

Jason didn't flinch or fuss and continued on as if nothing had changed. I cried, and the tears fell harder the closer we got to home. Certain we were about to break up, I dreaded our goodbye.

"What do we do now?" I asked.

"We don't have to do anything." He put the car in park, turned my way, and asked, "Do you want to break up?"

"No."

"Then let's keep going and see what happens."

And so we did—and I never thought much about Kyle again. In fact, I'm not even sure I ever heard from him again. Facing the truth set me free—free to embrace more of the artist.

The next six weeks flew by. As summer approached, my dad encouraged me to consider a job as a bank teller instead of a supervisor at the park. I interviewed for the position with feigned interest and got the job. Three days in, my misery was apparent. The thought of counting money in quiet quarters instead of working with Jason at the park wreaked havoc in my soul. When I left in tears that wouldn't stop, I quit. And my dad accepted my resolve.

Back at the park, I worked as a store supervisor which meant we didn't have as much time together during the day. So we made up for it in the evenings. As we drove home together one night, I thought it would be endearing to share all the things I really liked about him. I spoke without interruption for about twenty minutes, unaware that mounting fear burned in his heart.

After he pulled into the driveway and turned off the ignition, an awkward silence hung between us.

"Is that it?" he asked.

"Well, yeah," I replied, confused.

"So you're not breaking up with me?"

Shocked that my well-meaning diatribe had gone so wrong, I stammered "No ... No, I'm not breaking up with you. I just wanted you to know why I love you."

He burst into tears. Right there in the car. The artist wept while I reached for his hands in stunned silence. When he calmed down, we soaked in the quiet and then walked inside. Despite all that we went through in the coming years, I never heard such deep sobs emanate from him again.

In early July, he rode with my family to a church conference in Montreat, NC. Having attended for years, I was excited to explore familiar territory with him. We strolled around Lake Susan after the evening assembly the first night. Tucked behind a tree on a secluded bench, he pulled something out of his pocket. I don't remember what he said. But I still have the ring—a blue sapphire center with tiny diamonds on a gold band.

We'd made it an entire year. And I had a ring to show for it.

Seven

Bring me alive, set my soul free
I want you living in all of me
Bring me alive, help my heart soar
Keep me believing I'm waiting for more

"BRING ME ALIVE"
Accepted, Track 6

September has turned to October. Fall leaves dot the landscape as I drive home. On this particular Sunday afternoon, Don is busy at the store. Sam, a year-round swimmer, is returning with his team from an away swim meet. And I'm driving home after visiting Nathan, my oldest son, at college.

While I've put on a brave face, I miss him.

We're cut from the same cloth. When he graduates, our family will boast a third-generation music major, since both my mom and I studied the same. Aware of his talent from early on, I initially discouraged him from pursuing a career in the arts. It's not an easy choice. But his voice stood out when he joined a college choir and within a semester, he changed majors.

He entered college as a psychology major because even as a young child, he had an uncanny knack for interpreting life. I benefitted from his wisdom often. While Sam cuddled close on the couch and needed a mother's touch, Nathan and I verbally processed events.

A void still lingers. But after watching him perform last night, I'm grateful that Don's presence in our lives allowed him to launch unencumbered by concern for me. As I drive in the autumn sun, sadness entwines with motherly pride.

Halfway home, my tank registers empty. So I pull off the highway and into a gas station. My phone rings as the tank fills. It's Sam.

"How'd the meet go?"

"Not good," he shares. "My hands and feet turned purple at the end of the races. Even the coach says I look bad."

My heart sinks. A weight settles onto my shoulders. I feel the added pressure, right there, standing on ugly cement, breathing fumes.

"Tell me more," I reply, not sure I want to hear more.

"I don't know. I was pale and shaky after my swims and really don't feel well."

"I'll call the doctor tomorrow."

Familiar mom emotions swirl. They calm at times, but not for long. When I think about the possible ailments my son could face, like childhood cancer, I know things could be worse. Still, my mother's heart doesn't settle for long—not when he pushes himself like he does with a diagnosed mitochondrial disorder.

And yet that's the very issue. There are no set rules in the world of mitochondrial disease. Each patient exhibits their own unique symptoms. Certain characteristics abound, no doubt. But the cellular level energy disorder can send any organ or body system into chaos, exacerbating doctors and patients alike.

So I never know what symptoms to take seriously. I doubt my instincts, even though they're often right. They haven't led us astray yet. But when medical mystery trails each moment of insight, fear gnaws continually. Purple hands and feet don't help.

I climb into my van, onto a cloth, tan seat, paralyzed by child worry. I want to sleep. Drift away. But I turn the ignition instead.

Settled in an open lane on the highway, I set cruise control and remember.

About the time Nathan insisted on taking tap dance lessons in first grade, Sam started nagging me about sports. I was a musician. Not an athlete. But as a single mom, I determined to do some of the things his dad would have done. The practices. The sidelines cheering. The at-home training. So when team practice schedules didn't conflict with the music lessons I taught, I signed him up.

He tried a lot of different sports, and I bought a lot of gear. Stretched far from my comfort zone, I longed for him find his place and succeed.

However, over time, physical challenges slowed progress—his and mine.

His shoulder hurt when he threw a ball. My wrists hurt when I played the piano. His hips and ankles ached when he ran too much. Over time, my legs grew wobbly and unstable. By fall of his eighth-grade year, he was in pain, and I needed a cane. And no one knew why.

The memories cascade into a swell of emotion as I drive. How can this be God's best for our family? How can continued struggle be part of a divine plan?

I remember the night four years earlier when Sam found me in the stands after a long day that included a cross country meet and a marching band festival. When the band performed earlier in the evening, Nathan had directed the group as drum major while Sam marched with his trombone. Beaming with pride as both boys stood on the field to represent their school during the award ceremony, I had no idea Sam was in pain. Finally connected, he said, "Mom, my ankles and feet really hurt."

The discomfort showed in his eyes.

"I'll call the doctor tomorrow," I promised. And his pediatrician finally listened.

A few days later, an orthopedic doctor explained Sam had weak hips and tight hamstrings. We juggled physical therapy appointments for over a month, and Sam improved some. But when he finished, the therapist accused Sam of not working hard enough. He hadn't done his exercises every day, but I certainly didn't agree with the specialist's perception.

As I merge onto another highway, closer to home, confusion haunts me now just like it did then. Thoughts collide. Do I let him swim? Do I demand he slow down? Don tells me he's old enough to make his own decisions, but I don't want to watch my teenage son run himself into the ground.

Other kids with mito are often hospitalized after a "crash" or metabolic meltdown, where infections reign and stomachs stop working. I've heard the stories. If he pushes too hard, he could make things worse.

Or maybe he won't. He survived a season of high-school JV lacrosse.

Despite the pain, he spent hours throwing a ball off the side of our house, determined to play. Nervous, I drove him to offseason practices. My husband told me he was fine. But deep down, I had a sense that I would be diagnosed through him—that the journey wasn't over.

Shoulder pain sent him back to physical therapy months later, around his fifteenth birthday. Same therapist. Same concerns. Weak and tight muscles. Six weeks of therapy helped some. But after a month of pre-season training with the team, he opened up during Christmas break.

"Mom, my knees hurt. Pretty bad. It's hard to climb the stairs, and I think they're swollen."

His knees were swollen. And now his hands and feet turn purple in the pool. He's taken my breath away so many times. And it doesn't get easier.

I exit the highway near Kennesaw Mountain, a Civil War landmark near my home. Don often chides me for taking the long route home. But I like the forestry, non-commercial path, especially when fall leaves render the mountain alive, vibrant. Unlike me.

Bare oaks trees and spotty pines dotted the same mountain in mid-January, the day the orthopedic explained, "Sam's leg muscles aren't holding his kneecaps in place when they rotate. If we took the kneecap off, you would see a bloodied, roughed up underside."

Since the doctor still didn't see a connection between our symptoms, Sam left with braces and pain relievers that he used to play lacrosse. I walked out in disbelief.

When we stopped for school supplies a few hours later, clarity came. "Hey, Mom," he called out, "when you buy me pens, will you get the expensive, fat kind? My hands shake when I write with skinny ones."

"Your hands shake when you write with skinny pens?"

"Yeah," he replied, "it's no big deal. They've always been that way."

A memory flashes through my mind. One afternoon when both boys were in elementary school, Nathan forced me to stop vacuuming.

"Mom, Sam's crying."

When I didn't run upstairs right away to soothe the tears, he pressed me again. "Mom, Sam's crying and tearing up all his drawings on his desk in the playroom because he says he isn't a good artist."

I turned to Sam, who had sulked into the living room and collapsed on the sofa in a lonely stream of afternoon sunlight. His tears glistened in the glow as he explained that someone at school said one of his latest airplane drawings had "squiggly" lines. I held back a chuckle at the time, but now wonder if his hands have always shaken?

Within an hour of calling the pediatrician's office the next day, he was scheduled to see a neurologist. While it took over six months, that neurologist diagnosed our problem.

I drive through my favorite wooded area, watching for deer. The familiar stretch away from subdivisions and strip malls offers a respite from the grind; God's creation a beckoning lighthouse in suburbia land.

The glowing, autumn leaves remind me that the seasons have cycled twice since Sam gave up lacrosse and started swimming. A muscle test, called an EMG, indicated our muscles aren't healthy, which led to the muscle biopsies and spinal taps. While we waited for results, swimming proved a natural fit, since it was easy on his muscles and joints.

Watching him compete made me nervous. But he loved it. After years of searching, he'd found the perfect sport. I hoped for simple medical answers so we could get on with life, but I lived through the blur of medical activity instead.

The official diagnosis, Mitochondrial Disease with Cerebral Folate Deficiency, came right before Christmas his sophomore year. Weak Muscles. Messed up nerves. Supplements and medicines help, but don't offer a cure.

After a few months on the medicine that treats the folinic acid deficiency, Sam took off in the water. In March of his junior year, he broke his personal records at the championship meet and made his first state cut in the hundred breast stroke event, meaning he could compete with the elite at the state event next fall.

I danced—even with wobbly legs. Nathan was finding his footing at school as a music major, and Sam finally felt successful in the water. All was well, for a moment.

But since I was about six months ahead of him on the same medicine, I fought concern. Having felt stronger after starting it, I fought disappointment when I had to pick up my cane again six months later. My muscles hadn't been able to keep up with the change and pain had slowed me down. Sam was performing way beyond his doctor's expectations, so I prayed in earnest for just one normal year—his senior year—especially during the swim season.

But those purple hands and feet changed everything.

I pull into our driveway, nestled high on the crest of a flood plain. No one is home, so I open my laptop and search the internet. Certain his doctor will order an echocardiogram of his heart, I dread another round of appointments. The kind that never seem to end.

Hovered in the night under the safety of my covers, sadness permeates my being, feeding the inner ache I know too well. I miss Nathan and worry about Sam. As the darkness starts to weary my soul, Don comes home, crawls into bed next to me, and I know I'm not alone.

Eight

Challenges come we don't understand
But we must walk on holding His hand
Through perils of doubt and nights full of fear
We must remember He's always near

"HE WILL CARRY US THROUGH"
<u>Accepted</u>, Track 1

Young love held the artist and musician together while they were apart. Though the distance grew tiresome, their devotion remained. The blue sapphire ring never left my hand as Jason drove to Nashville and I flew home on Delta passes. Yet our season of innocence passed much too quickly.

On the professional front, things progressed well. Design professors recognized Jason's unique talent and gave his name to ad agency directors. Soon, work came easy, especially with his ability to draw marker comps for advertising campaigns on the fly. By using over four hundred shades of markers, he added nuances of color that set him apart.

While he worked and designed layouts for school, I studied classical music. Classes in advanced theory and music history enhanced my understanding of the arts. Monthly concerts and listening assignments broadened my knowledge of composers. Surrounded by talent, I inhabited a world that stretched my soul.

Jason expressed concerns about his health on occasion, but stress remained the trigger for symptom fluctuations. So we set aside worry, focused on school, and when summer finally arrived, met up for a third season at the park.

At ease together, we shared life. One evening in early June, Jason showed up at work with a radio so we could listen to reports about the Tiananmen Square massacre. Set against a background of carnival music, we mourned the dismal news. On the flip side, when I showed up with a new perm that needed a few days to chill, Jason fluffed the curls with his fingers and smiled at the change. Whether the topic proved heavy or light, he put me at ease.

As our two-year anniversary approached, he insisted I ask for the evening off. When he didn't show up on time for our morning shift that day, I wondered if he might be with my parents asking for my hand in marriage. The thought sent shivers down my spine but I dismissed it when he arrived with an explanation for his tardiness.

We dispersed after our shift, but later that afternoon he picked me up and we headed downtown. When he parked near a newly built sky scraper, curiosity reigned. He led me to the building entrance with a picnic basket in hand and gave his name to the security guard. The guard led us to the elevators where we rode to the top floor.

Upon exiting the elevator, we walked onto a slab of concrete covered with studs and wires. While the unfinished surroundings may not have been splashy, the floor-to-ceiling windows offered a wide open view of the city. Jason spread out a table cloth near the glass wall and opened the basket.

Perched high in our own nest, we enjoyed the city lights. Hidden in the secret place, our future seemed as bright as the shimmering landscape below. Jason had taken me to the heart of busy Atlanta, yet created a unique experience, alone—above the fray. And that's what it felt like to be with him on the ground. No matter the chaos, noise, traffic, or stress, with Jason by my side, I felt carried away and safe—my heart protected from the onslaught.

He didn't propose up near the stars. The ring was pinned in his pocket and he considered the option. However, in true Jason form, he waited till we were home, on my back porch, where the memory would linger. There he knelt on one knee and asked for my hand in marriage. And I whispered, "*Yes!*"

Before I left for school in the fall, we set a date for our wedding—a week after his college graduation the following summer. My junior year slogged by as we passed through each season with growing anticipation.

Exams over, I searched for an apartment near campus for us to live in. When I forgot to set the parking brake on my friend's car and it coasted backward into a pole, denting the door, a young couple kept me calm. Landlords for several houses on the street, they offered a tour of the small apartment on the second floor of their aging home. It wasn't fancy, but I liked them. So I signed the contract and went home to get married.

In front of a host of family and friends, I joined my life with Jason in my home church. After a week-long honeymoon on the Island of Eleuthera, we packed a moving truck and headed north. Initially appalled with my choice of housing accommodations, my gracious spouse kept his opinion to himself. In time, the dilapidated character took on historic charm.

A rickety, metal stairway led up the side of the home into a small living room. Avocado-colored kitchen appliances sat on torn, brown linoleum. Bright red, shag carpet covered our bedroom floor. And the ceiling in what became Jason's home studio office slanted on each side, forcing him to watch his head.

It certainly wasn't fancy. But it was close to school. And when we held spaghetti dinner parties for friends and bonded with neighbors, it became home. Our home.

Jason drew and painted pictures for advertising agencies, often running out the door late to mail overnight deliveries. I finished classes and applied for master's degree programs. We lugged our first Christmas tree up the rusty stairs and set up the shimmery ceramic nativity set his father made. By early spring, we'd traveled to several cities where I auditioned for graduate schools. Upon my acceptance to Arizona State

University, we began making plans to move west, to his favorite part of the country.

As graduation neared—and with it our first wedding anniversary—I felt certain we had much to celebrate.

A few weeks before graduation, we attended another Lay Renewal event in Philadelphia, at my grandparent's home church. The trip allowed time with family and a short walk down memory lane. Since we met at a renewal event, it seemed apropos to attend one as team members. However, when Jason gave his testimony mid-week, the trip took on new meaning.

As I listened from the second row, he referred to being in remission. The word use jolted me but I wasn't sure why. Before I could ask him about it, we had to separate for after-glow meetings in members' homes. As I sat in a nicely decorated family room with people I'd never met, anxiety built to free flowing tears—the embarrassing kind.

The lead team member, a grey-haired beauty with deep southern charm, asked everyone to introduce themselves. When they came to me, Liza asked if I was okay. Thankful for the opportunity to explain my odd state, the group listened as I expressed my irrational concern about my husband's health due to his word choice. The group prayed and I calmed for a time.

But when I met up with Jason in a church hallway about an hour later I blurted, "Are you all right? You've never used the word remission before."

His answer? "We need to talk."

We rode with my grandparents back to their home, acting like everything was fine. Jason held my hand reassuringly but his eyes were filled with apprehension. Suspended in time, I didn't want the ride to end.

When we reached the privacy of the oversized upstairs bed room filled with childhood memories, Jason finally spoke, "I have double vision. It started in January when we climbed that mountain outside of Sedona—remember?"

"Yes," I recalled, "you were taking my picture and felt like you had vertigo."

"That's right," he continued, "that was the first sign. But it's gotten worse and I probably need to have an MRI."

My world as I knew it stopped spinning. We'd known all along that balance or vision issues could indicate tumor growth. With viable treatment options exhausted, growth would mean a terminal diagnosis.

Tears fell—again. But Jason had to catch an early morning flight, and I had meetings to attend. The early wake-ups forced us to try for sleep.

Once home, we scheduled an MRI and took off for the weekend. A state park offered affordable rates so we holed up in a rustic hotel where I sobbed in my best friend's arms. Fear paralyzed rational thought. A torrent of tears fell like the rain outside.

In between sobs, Jason said, "I can't imagine God letting you hurt this much."

While I valued his concern and even liked his theology, we both knew that my inability to cope would not put an end to our crisis. At the time it sure seemed that the easiest answer was for God to solve the problem at hand by healing Jason and thus making Susan's pain go away.

Unable to imagine life without him, I cried to exhaustion. When my eyes grew puffy and tissues became scarce, we attempted prayer, found dinner, and scheduled a horseback ride for the following morning.

After a quick breakfast, I climbed up on a chestnut mare as fog lingered in the forest green. Our guide led the way so I was soon alone with my fearful thoughts, longing for a way to cope. A favorite hymn came to mind, *"My hope is built on nothing less than Jesus' blood and righteousness. I dare not trust the sweetest frame but wholly lean on Jesus' name."*

My voice quivered as I sang under my breath, *"On Christ the solid rock I stand—All other ground is sinking sand. All other ground is sinking sand."*

"His oath, His covenant, His blood; Support me in the whelming flood. When all around my soul gives way, He then is all my hope and stay. On Christ the solid rock I stand—All other ground is sinking sand. All other ground is sinking sand."[2]

The words took on new meaning. No longer just a familiar hymn I'd sung a lot in church, the song became a life force. The lyrical truth something I could bank on.

---

[2]   Mote, Edward, *The Solid Rock*, 1834.

"You can trust me, Susan," the Spirit whispered, *"I'm the rock you can lean on."*

My heart was calmer as we drove home—not quite strong—but calmer, more trusting, ready to face the week. And much to our surprise, the first MRI didn't indicate tumor growth. The doctor even suggested radiation damage may have caused the vision change. With no definitive answer, another MRI was ordered three months later and the first of many long waits began.

Nine

You say you are my shelter in these troubled times
You say you are a refuge where I can hide
Underneath the shadow of your mighty wings
You say my heart can rest, my soul can sing

"HIDE AWAY WITH YOU"
Life of Love, Track 9

Solving the crisis of the purple hands takes precedence in my life. Forget colored foliage and pumpkin patch fun, I need to know that my son is okay.

First thing Monday morning, we're led down the carpeted hallway to a pediatric exam room. While Sam's blood oxygen levels register above normal, finger monitors don't always compute oxygenation levels deep in the muscles. So I still wonder what's causing his purple hands and feet.

The nurse leaves and we wait, in the room. Sam stretches out on the exam table while I lean into a chair near the door. He can tell I'm worried. I'm often worried. It's a mom thing.

Ever since their dad died, I've been trying to make things right, to keep life happy, as if enough consistent cheer could undo the catastrophic blow. But even when he was young he knew better.

"I don't want a new daddy," he once declared from his booster seat in the back of the car. "I just want our old daddy back."

At four years of age he was calling my bluff. A new daddy wouldn't fix things the way I promised. And he knew it. He liked the old daddy—the one who played red-light games at the stoplights when he was two.

He trumped me then so I know better than to offer platitudes now.

"God's got this, Mom," he says with resolute calm. "This swim season is His. Whatever happens, it's in His hands."

I respect my son more than he knows—especially in this moment. He doesn't need me to fix anything. He's leaning on The One who knows best.

The pediatrician enters. He sees obvious signs of congestion and gunk, but doesn't hear wheezing—at least right now. But he's not sure what to think about the purple hands.

Most doctors we encounter know very little about Mitochondrial Disease. Our pediatrician is the same. So we leave with antibiotics, a new asthma medicine, and a referral for a stress-echo. He wants Sam's heart checked during exercise.

Sam tells me his sinuses clear when he swims. So he takes little time off. I worry he's not resting enough to recover. He argues he'll lose speed if he lets up at practice. Reality is probably somewhere in between.

So I schedule the stress echo a week out. Before the test, we head to another swim meet. I watch for him at the warm-down pool to see how he's doing after each race. A purple hand grabs the wall where I stand. His pale face meets mine and I know he's struggling.

The big fancy aquatic center stresses me out. It shouldn't. I know there's so much more to life than race times. But gathered with abled body performers, I lean on my cane, not knowing how to let go of the anxiety that churns.

It's one thing to process my own issues. It's another to know my Sam could end up where I am physically in a matter of years. I'm driven by a desire to stop his disease progression before it begins—while he's a teenage boy on the cusp of manhood wanting to fully live.

How can I deny him that? How can I tell him to back down because of a whole host of "what ifs"? We butt heads more than I want to admit over this very struggle. My fear versus his need to fly—to just be free to grow up, regardless of the cost.

A week later we learn that the results of the stress echo offer little explanation for the purple hands. His heart looks great, meaning I should let go of whatever it is I hold onto. The stress should dissipate. The worry lines ease.

But they don't fade on their own. It's an act of my will—a choice to ignore their tethered barnacles that wrap around my soul. I want to feed him better, provide nutritional aid. But I can't always get through a grocery store. I want to pull up the carpet in his room in case it's causing an allergic reaction, but he balks at more money spent on the unknown.

Our daily supplement regimen exhausts our finances as it is—a common struggle for all families dealing with mitochondrial disease. Since choice treatments are rarely covered by insurance, the out of pocket expense creates a struggle all its own.

Sam knows this and tells me to leave the carpet. So I do. Instead, I pick my nails, wondering if I'm being a bad mom.

I've started saying Psalm 91 out loud in the morning, when I remember.

> *"He who dwells in the shelter of the Most High will rest in the shadow of the Almighty. I will say of the Lord, "He is my refuge and my fortress, my God, in whom I trust"* (Psalm 91: 1 – 2 NIV).

There was a time when I envisioned myself hidden in that fortress, a God built protection around my heart. Safe there, I could let Him take the blows. But that was a long time ago. Before I lost my mind and built my own shell, a burdensome weight.

"Surely he will save you from the fowler's snare and from the deadly pestilence. He will cover you with his feathers and under his wings you will find refuge" (Psalm 91: 3- 4 NIV).

As a child I once read about a woman in a carjacking in New York City who shouted, "He will cover you with his feathers," over and over till the thief jumped out of the vehicle. I never forgot the story. And finally learned where the phrase came from. If I shout it enough now will Sam swim faster?

"For the word of God is alive and active. Sharper than any double-edged sword..." (Heb. 4: 12 NIV).

When Sam was five months old, he spent four days in an oxygen tent after contracting the RSV virus. It developed quickly. In the morning I held an infant with a mild cold. By mid-afternoon, he made a clicking sound when I tried to feed him a bottle. The severity of his illness became clear when a nurse placed him on oxygen within minutes of our arrival at the ER.

We prayed. Back then. His dad fasted and prayed. We asked for bold things. Healing. Divine healing. And right when it seemed he was getting much worse, he turned a corner, smiled, and became our Sammy again.

We prayed many more times for our boys. We fought off colds with prayer. We knelt in the middle of the night when coughs wouldn't cease. And we experienced breakthrough.

Yet now I stifle my Sam. I speak limits on his life. I tell him to slow down when he wants to speed up. I try to hold him in place, in a shelter I've erected, one I can watch over—not grasping my role is coming to an end. He needs the feathers. And they're enough.

"You will not fear the terror of night, nor the arrow that flies by day, nor the pestilence that stalks in the darkness, nor the plague that destroys at midday. A thousand may fall at your side, ten thousand at your right hand, but it will not come

*near you. You will only observe with your eyes and see the
punishment of the wicked"* (Psalm 91: 5- 8 NIV).

My friend, Ann, and I meet at Starbuck's for coffee. Her husband is
weakening day by the day, battling pulmonary fibrosis. Without a lung
transplant, he won't survive the holidays. He's suffocating before her
very eyes and there's nothing she can do about it. Except pray.

I open mental files from long ago and share my stories. Offering
her comfort takes me back in time. As I speak life to her fears, my past
collides with my present again, melding the two even more. Safe in a
Starbuck's on a cloudy day, warmed by a pumpkin spice latte, I'm saved
by my own memories.

I was once a healthy spouse nursing a dying mate. And I survived.

I tell her about the Susan in the video. The Susan who belted Psalm
91 every day.

"God's got this Ann," I promise as she points to a rainbow filling
the sky.

However, not long after I return to the confines of my home, the
churning begins. He held me once, but I struggle to feel His firm grip
in the reality I face in the walls of my home. I know He's got Ann. I
know that from past experience. But I'm not sure about me.

> *"If you make the Most High your dwelling—even the Lord
> who is your refuge—then no harm will befall you, no disaster
> will come near your tent. For he will command his angels
> concerning you to guard you in all your ways; they will lift
> you up in their hands, so that you will not strike your foot
> against a stone. You will tread upon the lion and the cobra;
> you will trample the great lion and the serpent"* (Psalm 91:
> 9 – 13 NIV).

The question lingers: What happened to me?

It was one thing to lose the father of my children; another when a
metabolic disorder slowly drained my energy reserves. But learning my
son has the same, buckled my knees. Fighting for all of us takes more
effort than I have. Preparing breakfast is a monumental task.

But I long for peace. I want to wake with joy. So I will claw my way up one praise after another—one scripture after another—until I am whole. Until I truly trust again that God's got me too.

> *"'Because he loves me,' says the Lord, 'I will rescue him; I will protect him for he acknowledges my name. He will call upon me and I will answer him; I will be with him in trouble, I will deliver him and honor him. With long life will I satisfy him and show him my salvation"* (Psalm 91: 14 – 16 NIV).

Only a few weeks later, we're back in the doctor's office for another round of antibiotics. Sam's not better. But he still swims. He's driven to. It's high school swim season—his senior year.

I've got to let him fly—covered with the feathers.

Ten

Lord, send me a touch of You in this darkest hour
My heart feels so unsure but I know you're the God of power
My sin so clear and never ending keeps me on my knees
Oh Lord have mercy, Your touch is all I need

"TOUCH OF YOU"
Life of Love, Track 6

The unremarkable MRI results gave Jason and me time to regroup and consider our options. With another MRI scheduled in three months and graduation behind me, decisions had to be made.

Not wanting to move across the country with lingering uncertainty, I called the head of the Choral Music Department at Arizona State University and turned down my acceptance into their master's program. Then we scoured local papers and found a small duplex with a beautiful backyard and even purchased an upright piano for me.

Not long after the move, we munched on nachos in a Mexican restaurant and discussed whether or not we should start a family. Jason loved kids and had always wanted to be a father but we certainly hadn't planned on making such a monumental decision with a brain tumor clock ticking in his head.

Waiting was an option. But I couldn't imagine trying to get pregnant if an MRI confirmed growth. When we combined my concern with Jason's deep desire to be a dad, a gentle resolve filled us both. We left knowing we would give it a try.

Next, I wanted to learn what it meant to step out in faith, to leave my comfort zone and rely totally on God. So when we sat in church a few weeks later and a pastor announced the next mission trip— smuggling Bibles into China—I elbowed Jason and said, "Let's go."

By the end of July, I held a positive pregnancy test and we were making plans to head to China in November. The distractions proved invaluable. Compelled by an elder's testimony, we began raising funds. The way-out-of-our-comfort-zone challenge offered a perfect opportunity to enlarge our faith, and ours needed stretching.

MRI results came back inconclusive again the next month, lightening our load further. Jason's doctor still ordered another test three months out, but we focused on the life growing in me instead of the tumor that might be growing in his body.

Jason continued to draw pictures. I started adjusting to life without classes and tests. And autumn leaves began to fall. I was four months pregnant and Jason's vision was still an obstacle when we boarded a plane to the other side of the world.

The sights and smells of Hong Kong unnerved me at first. Flat, dried duck hung outside local shops. Barrels of dried bugs made my nauseous stomach churn. Laundry stretched between windows and children wandered in the streets. Not sure what we'd find when we crossed the border into China, we were thankful to spend our first day in the prayer room.

Away from the norm, brain tumor fears crept to the forefront— especially for Jason. With time to talk and pray, he shared concerns he'd kept to himself, "The double vision is getting worse. I don't know how much longer I'll be able to drive."

His confession startled me.

"And if I can't drive," he continued, shifting in his seat, "I don't know how I'll be a good dad. I can't even throw a Frisbee."

Fear hung on him like moss on a southern live oak. More questions surfaced.

How would he make a living?

How would he play with his child?

How could he know God loved him when he might be fighting for his life?

There, on the other side of the world, his fears stirred my own. So we held hands and prayed, or rather we sat in that prayer room and tried to pray for hours. Our minds drifted a lot. Fears came and went. And while I'd like to tell you we left changed that day, we didn't. In fact, we didn't even feel like our prayers had been heard.

But they had. It just took time for the answers to be made real.

Before we went to bed, we filled our backpacks with pocket Bibles and prepared to cross the border the next day. After breakfast, our host missionaries explained the border crossing routine.

Our team would travel by subway to the border and then separate. We would pass through several checkpoints individually that culminated at the large x-ray machines. Dispersed, we would place our bags on the conveyor belt, hoping a distraction would keep the border agents from seeing our books on the screen. If we were caught, our bags would be confiscated yet left where we could retrieve them once we returned to Hong Kong.

Directions made clear, our group of ten walked to the local station. As we rode north on the subway to the border city, we chatted like regular tourists. However, everything changed when we entered the customs area. The sheer volume of people made it easy to split up.

Lines were non-existent. Crowds moved like cattle. Chinese verbiage echoed loud in the concrete building.

Startled by the mass of humanity, I shrank into my skin. So I prayed and grew calm when a presence wrapped around me—the invisible kind that makes you feel heaven is close. Comforted, I felt bigger than normal me, more confident than afraid, as if carried through the crowd.

One by one, I passed the checkpoints and eventually stood in line at the x-ray machine. Once there, I couldn't imagine how any Bibles passed through. Yet right as my backpack rode down the conveyor belt, the agent on duty stood from his stool and walked away from the screen.

In no time at all, my bag appeared on the other side of the machine and my Bibles were free to go.

I hesitated—like I should have been caught. Then remembering to veil emotion, I stifled the sense of awe and picked up my bag.

Not one to break the rules, distinct tentacles of panic squeezed the sense of wonder when I walked across the Chinese border. It was one thing to be caught with Bibles at the border. It was an entirely different matter to be caught in the communist country with the same.

Tall, blonde, and pregnant, I stood out in the Asian crowd. Not sure where to go, I drifted to the side, squatted on my bag on a dusty path, and waited till another team member went by. Relieved, I followed at a distance till the group appeared up ahead—on concrete steps in the open air, in front of a large building.

As we walked to a restaurant for lunch, Jason and I noticed that China felt very different than Hong Kong. Tense. Busy. Dirty. Car horns honked as drivers merged on their own terms. Bikes filled overcrowded sidewalks. A young burn victim and her children lounged in a dusty ditch.

Oppression hung in the air like low lying clouds. I'd never felt anything like it.

My pastor, Craig, recently spoke about his two week stay in China while adopting his young daughter. His observation rang true, "I saw millions of people with no life in their eyes—no fight and no life in their eyes."

Eye contact was scarce; smiles, a rare encounter. Until I heard my pastor's description, I'd wondered if I harbored a warped perception since we'd been carrying illegal material. Now I know better. My experience lined up with his. So I can honestly say it felt like we encountered a mass of humanity, who led lives of drudgery, with little hope or reason to smile.

Seated around a large circular table in the back of a restaurant, we ordered food. While we waited, those of us who got Bibles through passed them under the table into one large suitcase. That suitcase was later checked into a hotel storage room near-by.

While my hands carried a bag that made it across, I was well aware I had little to do with my own success. I had lived a miracle. That miracle didn't specifically address our brain tumor concerns, but it reminded me of who was in control. And that reminder sufficed—at least for a day.

When we arrived back in Hong Kong later that evening, the difference was striking. What had seemed foreign only hours before now served as a sweet taste of home. Dry ducks still hung in shops and vendors sold unusual fare, but the air was clean and the people were free. The spiritual heaviness I felt across the border lifted, as if we'd walked through heavy smog into clean, filtered oxygen.

We woke the next morning prepared to go back to the prayer room but our plans changed when the ministry leaders pulled us aside after breakfast. Bags of stored Bibles needed to be picked up in hotels and carried further into the country. Our team leader asked if we would be willing to travel back into China to assist a missionary from New Zealand, named Alexey.

Alexey was born in China and spoke fluent Mandarin. But since his father was Chinese and his mother Russian, his family had been forced to leave China during a purging when he was young. His genetics allowed him to blend in with ease, making him perfect for the task at hand.

Hesitant, yet excited, we soon learned we weren't what Alexey expected. The weathered servant knew the work that lay ahead. A pregnant semi-blonde and her double-seeing spouse didn't jive with his idea of reliable help.

We doubted our abilities as well, but with everyone on board, Jason and I stuffed a small duffle with clothes and filled my backpack with snack food and toiletries. Opting for the all or nothing approach, Jason deliberately packed all the pocket Bibles and Christian literature in his shoulder bag.

The next morning, we traveled by train to the border city and dispersed. After navigating each station in the crowded border crossing, we arrived at the x-ray machine. There I placed my bag on the conveyor belt again.

My bag, filled with juice boxes, granola bars, toothpaste and such, rolled toward the x-ray machine. When the screen displayed the small, rectangular shaped items, the border agent started yelling in rapid-fire

Chinese. Reaching for my bag, he motioned to me and demanded I empty the contents. As I placed each item on the metal table, I nervously explained that there was nothing illegal in my bag.

It didn't matter. He didn't speak English. Ironically, as he scolded me with a sternness that left me feeling like an elementary school girl, Jason entered China with his bag full of Bibles.

Another miracle. Another divine touch. We weren't alone.

We met up with Alexey not far from the border and walked to another train station. There he found a waiting area free of locals. As I sat my pregnant-self down he explained that I was to sit in the station while he and Jason separated. They would collect the stored Bibles and bring them to me one by one.

Quite surprised, my thoughts swirled, *"I'm supposed to sit alone in a train station with a growing pile of Bibles?"*

Without a dress memo, my pink, pregnancy pants and flowered print shirt stood out among the plain-clothed locals. Undeterred, Alexey pulled out a wad of tickets and handed a few to Jason. Then, they left me with only a magazine to hide my face.

I had no idea where they went, how long they'd be gone, or where I was. As they came and went, the luggage pile grew from two suitcases to about fifteen. With each addition, I sank lower and lower behind the printed page.

Hidden there, I prayed. I didn't log onto Facebook or check email on my cellphone like I would now. Alone with awkward prayers, I talked with the God of the Universe—the only one who knew right where I was and how to keep me safe. Together, we managed my fear. With His help I remained composed. Not fear free—just settled. But that was enough.

After a few unnerving hours, the job was done and Alexey purchased more train tickets. Then, we headed deeper in, to where our faith would indeed be stretched.

Eleven

By your stripes we are healed
By your stripes we are healed
Every longing fulfilled
By your stripes we are healed

"BY YOUR STRIPES"
Accepted, Track 9

Comfortable in my "easy chair" on the living room floor, I stare at cornball TV. Sam's cough has abated, allowing me to focus on something other than his health. Christmas lights, wound tight around each branch of our fake tree, create a magical effect. Finals distract both boys and holiday retail hours' demand Don's attention, so I escape holiday stress with a lighthearted, happy-ever-after type film.

My cell phone rings, interrupting a commercial break. When I see Ann's name, I straighten up, accept the call and blurt, "Did you get a lung?"

"Yes," she replies with pilot-trained control, "There's a lung waiting for Jon."

I flash back to the rainbow we saw as we left our recent coffee. The promise has been made real. Hope rushes through me.

"Do you need anything? Can I come to the hospital?" My heart races.

"No," she continues, "I'm fine. But I do need you to help me find Grace. Can you call Nathan and see if he knows where she is? She lost her phone this week and I can't reach her."

"You got it."

Nathan and Grace, our oldest kids, are only a year apart in school. Not only did they attend the same high school, they now attend the same college and share mutual friends. Relief floods in when Nathan answers his phone.

"Hey! Sorry to interrupt your Friday night but Grace's dad got a lung and Ann needs you to find her. She lost her phone."

"I'm on it," he assures me as we hang up.

I call Ann back and let her know Nathan is searching for Grace. When I offer to meet her at the hospital again, she explains she would rather rest and spend the long hours with the quiet of her thoughts. My leg has been giving me trouble so I don't argue much. An all-nighter would put me back a few days, but I'm willing.

We hang up and Nathan calls. He found Grace through a friend so she knows what's going on. Ensconced in my quiet house, I stare at the TV, unable to rest till I know my friend has safely arrived at the hospital across town.

TV chatter fades into the background as the real life drama unfolds. Safe in the comfort of my home, I know that across town one life is being traded for another. While we silently celebrate, others grieve— our Christmas miracle, their holiday nightmare.

A twinge of sadness wells up but I push it aside. Having grieved my share, I remind myself it's okay to relish a miracle. The father and husband whose lungs have filled with fibrous tumors, leaving no space to breathe, may soon inhale with ease. And that's a good thing.

A text arrives, informing me that Ann and Jon arrived safe and are waiting in pre-op. I send prayer texts in return, knowing the couple will soon part ways. While we never really know what goodbye will be our last, heartfelt sentiments shared in stale hospital corridors allow for a rare breed of goodbye.

Ann calls one last time, letting me know Jon's in the operating room. Still calm, she asserts that she's ready for the long night. Her spouse has withered away for months, unable to breathe on his own for over a year. Now the moment has come, the juncture is clear. Healing is on its way—on either side of eternity.

I turn off the TV and crawl into bed, unable to imagine spending the night alone in a similar situation. Amazed by her strength, I remember she flies airplanes for a living and I struggle to walk. Her training demands calm in turbulence while I wobble on solid ground.

Safe in bed, I picture Ann curled up in a straight back, plastic chair, eager for Jon to cross from inevitable death to a life of possibility. Hospital stays stir those emotions—hope, fear, longing. You enter in need of a fix, expecting to come out stronger, but wait in discomfort for the outcome to be made real.

I know this well.

Last Christmas Eve, Sam and I woke in the children's hospital. A small leak in his spine from a spinal tap five days earlier had caused a serious headache. Expecting the local children's hospital to offer a blood patch fix, we drove to the ER on December 23rd. They admitted him instead, insisting he lie flat for another twenty-four hours before offering the cure.

So instead of enjoying last-minute shopping and thinking festive thoughts on Christmas Eve morning, I stumbled to the hospital cafeteria in search of coffee and cream, hoping we'd be home before sundown.

And thankfully, we were.

An anesthesiologist rushed the procedure after lunch. After drawing Sam's blood, he injected it into his back where the original tap had been done. The blood adhered to the spinal opening and the headache stopped.

Home by dinner, we ate store bought appetizers and pizza. Later, I stuffed stockings with grocery store trinkets and gladly spent the night at my sister's home where lit candles flickered around cookie trays on marble countertops.

The year before that, I had ankle surgery three weeks before Christmas, moved the day after Christmas, and then landed back in the hospital three weeks later for that unexpected back surgery—the one where my leg never really recovered.

Having experienced my share of holiday hospital stress, I feel for Ann. While the whole world seems to celebrate, you're tied to moment to moment wondering.

How will you finish shopping? Will the kids feel slighted? Will the holiday pass without time to sense the holy hush we long to feel, if just for a fleeting moment?

I drift asleep praying for divine intervention for Ann, Jon, and their family.

When I wake, the sun is up and I realize Ann hasn't called. Hoping no news is good news, I grab my phone. When she answers, I ask, "How's Jon?"

"Surprisingly well," she offers. "There weren't any complications."

A wave of wonder rushes through me. Dressed in faded checkered flannels and an old T-shirt complete with morning breath, I truly feel wonder. Jon is alive—hooked to a massive amount of medical equipment—but very much alive.

I later learn that a few weeks before the procedure, a doctor told Ann that they never lose patients on the operating table due to the use of ventilators and other life stabilizing machines. If they lose them in the short term, it's due to acute rejection or infection. So inserting the new lung for the surgeon was about as routine as Ann landing a plane full of passengers in inclement weather.

Still, the surgeon landed the plane well. The lung connected to Jon's body in record time—with no complications. And as the weekend goes by, Jon defies the odds and leaves the ICU within days, breathing with his new lung. A veritable lung transplant poster child.

Their miracle buoys me. It's December after all. The time for miracles, lights, angels, wonder—and stress.

Balancing families during the holidays stirs angst, and it's evident by my bloodied cuticles. We're not *The Brady Bunch*. Not even close.

In fact, it often feels we're like Spain merging with Japan or Germany with Sierra Leone.

Don's a farm boy at heart. I'm a city girl. He likes cats and I favor dogs. While I grew up with silver and china on the table during the holidays, Don doesn't seem to notice if our plastic cups match.

Our differences challenge us—and our blending families. So I struggle and often don't know how to act. While I long to create a cozy, *Hallmark* © Christmas, complete with homemade cookies, candles, and connected souls, I feel more like a stranger when we're all together.

So in the midst of our planning, Ann's plight brings perspective.

The fact that Jon came through the surgery well was just the first step. Even if he shows no signs of rejection, he won't be allowed to go home for over a month. Instead of enjoying time around their tree, her family will move into The Mason House near the hospital, where transplant patients live for at least a month post-surgery.

Ann longs to pull her kids close and create ideal holiday moments like me. But she's in a hospital. Not a shopping mall or concert hall.

We continue to touch base by phone almost every day and Jon's recovery remains miraculous. In less than two weeks we pray for an opening at The Mason House that will accommodate their family. Within a day, the one room suite opens and soon they begin life in semi-posh surroundings, focused on breathing treatments and a complicated array of medicine. It's better than the hospital, but still far from the holiday norm.

So a few weeks before Christmas, I act on an idea that requires the help of my musical family. Since Jon, a Classical music buff who buys season tickets to the symphony, can't soak in the live sound any time soon, I suggest we pick a date and bring the music to him.

Mom and Dad buy into the plan since we've often caroled as a family at Christmas. Far from your everyday carolers, though, we carry pedigrees. Mom sings with the Atlanta Symphony Chorus and Dad with the Big Chicken Barbershop group. Nathan and my brother both have vocal training. So when we combine styles and my piano skills, we have a decent repertoire of music for a live, impromptu, Christmas concert. With everyone on board, we wait till Ann gives the go ahead.

She asks and receives permission for us to come. So when Jon's routine stabilizes and he seems strong enough, we put our plan into motion. Mom, Dad, my brother, Mark, my boys, and I make the long drive.

The stone front Mason House looks more like a bed and breakfast than a medical haven. Nestled in the woods near the main hospital, the two-story foyer is decorated for the season. Garland on the banister offers a homey feel. But when Jon enters the living room area—complete with a baby grand piano—his emaciated frame reminds me that this isn't a typical get away. Hunched over with an oxygen tank in tow, the father of two smiles meekly, surprised by our presence.

Not wanting to get his hopes up in case we had to cancel, Ann kept our visit a secret. Only when he sinks into the sofa does he realize he's entered a concert arena.

We stand side by side, and the music begins. Hark the Herald Angels Sing. Joy to the World. Silent Night. We fill the faux living room with Christmas tidings.

Wooden floors and a high ceiling amplify our sound. A tall, lit tree and a decorated hearth add a festive backdrop. As we close with O Holy Night, our voices soar in ascent. And the holy hush—the one that's normally reserved for the moment we raise our candles high at our Christmas Eve service—rushes through me.

"A thrill of hope, the weary world rejoice, for yonder breaks a new and glorious morn…"

The words tether me to the divine. They always do. But I haven't performed them in over two years. Maybe even more.

I can tell by the look on Jon's face that we've more than dislodged him from the day's routine. In the richly ornamented room, we've all experienced a moment of living unlike most moments allow. While Jon's learning to breathe with someone else's lung, we're using ours to share music we love; music that speaks over and over of God's divine entrance into man's depravity.

"Long lay the world in sin and error pining, till he appeared and the soul felt it's worth…"[3]

---

3   Placide Cappeau de Roquemaure, "O Holy Night", 1847.

That's it. My soul feels worth. And part of me awakens; a part I haven't felt stir in a long time. Due to the confines of my energy disorder, I haven't sung with a choir or group during the holidays for years. The holiday rigor requires all my reserves, leaving little energy to do what feeds my soul most.

Jon's miracle has changed that. Stirring hope for him has done the same for me. I didn't perform for crowds like my mom and dad. But singing for one who needs it most proves enough for me.

Jon retreats to his room to rest after my parents and brother leave. My boys and I head to the dining area with Ann and her kids and play games while indulging in take-out food. We laugh and carry on like family. Real family. Cause in this moment, our hearts are knit together by all that is Christmas.

My blended family will gather next week and I'll fight feeling odd, like outdated, silver icicles hung on a tired tree. So I soak in the feeling around that table. The sense of belonging. The heightened awareness of joy. The sweetness of hearts buoyed high above medical mayhem.

Being a catalyst for joy in their unusual year is changing mine. Having treaded water through the past several holiday seasons, barely keeping my head above the fray, finding family in The Mason House has lifted me above the waves and I might just swim to shore.

Or rest in the water of life.

Twelve

I am letting go; I am letting God
I am trusting in my Father's love
Cause this world can't own what belongs above
So I'm letting go and letting God

"LETTING GO, LETTING GOD"
<u>Accepted</u>, Track 7

A rare kind of trust walk began as we maneuvered through the Chinese train station. The further in we traveled, the less Alexey shared about our journey. We didn't know where we were headed or what we would do once there. We simply followed our guide, lugging heavy bags with the aid of two flimsy, metal luggage carts.

Early on we developed a routine. I stayed in place while Jason and Alexey strapped several suitcases onto the wheeled devices and rolled them to another location. One of them would then stand guard over those bags while the other shuttled more between us. We took turns with the various roles, although I usually didn't haul heavy loads.

With no elevators, we climbed up and down several flights of concrete stairs while rolling the bags on steep inclines located on each side. When I reflect on the trip, the ginormous stairs come to mind first. Steep, unforgiving, and tiresome, they were unlike anything I've encountered while traveling. But my legs worked back then. So even though I was pregnant, I carried bags up and down those steps for days. Locals offered to help, but Alexey always shook his head no.

Unable to trust anyone, we lugged those bags like donkeys.

A mound of suitcases surrounded us on the train as we traveled to a major city two hours away. Once there, we unloaded, using the same routine to navigate the stairs, and then followed Alexey to a cab. The taxi driver swerved through unmarked lanes, forcing an adrenaline rush. Thankful to be alive, we unloaded at a five-star hotel, but wasted no time in the lobby. Packed like sardines in an elevator we rode up several floors.

Alexey exited, walked straight down the hall, and knocked on a door. A young man answered and let us in. We entered the small apartment room filled with piles of Bibles and Christian literature. Only then did we understand that we'd entered another staging area for the ministry.

Surprised by the find and full of questions, Alexey quickly told us to keep conversation light and off topic. Someone could be listening, having bugged the room. Caught in a real-life drama, we watched Alexey and his comrade repack our bags with Chinese TV masking the noise.

A few hours later Alexey booked a room for us in the hotel across the street. Again he warned us not to talk about God or Bibles or anything we'd done that day—which made for a very awkward evening. Longing to verbally decompress once alone in our room, we felt strangely constricted.

While Christians across the globe live under that kind of scrutiny every day, we felt like actors in a mini-series and questioned the seriousness of the restrictions. However, three weeks after we returned, Chinese officials stopped another missionary traveling further north and interrogated him. Alexey's name was compromised, meaning he could no longer travel freely in China, and the ministry shut down the apartment staging area.

Only then, safe at home, did our James Bond Jesus flick seem real.

The next morning, a waiter brought us partly scrambled eggs after we ordered an American breakfast in the hotel café—an attempt at something normal. It almost worked. The austere insides of the upscale lobby shimmered like hotels at home. The runny eggs and undercooked bacon provided a hint of familiarity. Unable to talk freely, though, our stilted conversation undermined the endeavor.

In time we checked out, ate a late lunch, and met up with Alexey— and ten tightly packed bags of books. After another harrowing taxi drive, we trudged back into the train station. Crowds slowed progress. Mile long stair cases wore us out. Sweat dripped from our brows.

The constant disorder provoked an unease I couldn't shake. Deeper in with a large number of books, fear rose. As we neared the train, I finally asked, "Do we need to be concerned about the green army guys that we see everywhere?"

"Not really," Alexey explained, "The plain-clothed officers who blend-in pose more of a problem. They have the authority to search our bags."

Relief flooded in. I didn't have to fight nerves every time a soldier walked by. I felt safer than I had in a while. But the feeling didn't last long.

As we slogged our way to the waiting train, we passed a car with a black interior and exterior. Alexey mentioned, "That's the food car. You can order meals from there."

While crazy enough to smuggle Bibles when pregnant, I wasn't prepared to eat Chinese junk food from the scary black car. Our granola bar stash would have to suffice.

Soon, Alexey finally stopped between two train cars, looked at our tickets once more, and then climbed the steep, metal stairs. We turned into the car on our right and awkwardly maneuvered down a narrow left-side aisle with our heavy bags. Our luggage barely fit under the bunk beds in our compartment, but after everything was stored, we sank in to the bed and wiped sweat from our brows.

But not for long.

When another passenger stopped at our seats, Alexey realized we were in the wrong compartment. More than tired, we dragged the bags down a few more sections, stuffed them under another a set of bunk beds, and collapsed again. Only then did I take in my surroundings.

On the left side of the narrow aisle, a small fold out table and chairs sat below each compartment window. Two sets of three-high bunk beds lay across the walkway, perpendicular to the windows. Another table folded out from below the opposite window, close to the bottom bunks.

By the time the train pulled away from the station, eight travelers filled our compartment, both locals and tourists. As we settled in, shanty towns came into view. Lean-tos made of flimsy material lined one against the other. Black kettles sat over open flames as ethnic minorities cooked their evening meal. Mesmerized, I watched the stark, real-life faces of poverty pass by our open window.

The dismal site eventually gave way to unusual country scenery and the rhythm of the train relaxed me. Jason and I struck up a conversation with two female tourists from England while Alexey chatted with three locals. Having been told to share that we were students on our way to study at a local college, we probed the travelers, hoping to talk less. Headed into a long night, we enjoyed listening to English speaking folks who traipsed, worry-free.

When we settled into our bunks to try for sleep, Alexey got our attention and whispered, "You need to pray. The Chinese passengers I've been talking to are city officials. They've asked about our luggage and where we're going. I told them that you're going to the university to study. But they could still ask to search our bags."

Curled up on a thin mattress far from home, I did what he asked. I prayed, "Father, we ask for mercy and protection. Silence their concerns and watch over your Bibles."

Familiar fear kept me from sleep. I knew it well, having battled it all my life. I hated staying at home with my siblings as a child and avoided being alone at night as an adult. I required nightlights and hall lights in my teen years. And when I went forward at church for prayer in college, I listened as a woman I didn't even know kindly said, "You have too much fear in your life."

It haunted me.

Yet there I was on a train in China, with an entire night of uncertainty ahead—much like the uncertainty Jason's brain tumor threat brought to our lives. With nowhere to hide, I tried to tame unwanted thoughts by replacing them with God's truth:

> *"Be strong and courageous. Do not be terrified; do not be discouraged, for the Lord your God will be with you wherever you go"* (Joshua 1: 9 NIV).

> *"But we are not of those who shrink back and are destroyed, but of those who believe and are saved"* (Hebrews 10: 39 NIV).

> *"Find rest; O my soul, in God alone; my hope comes from him. He alone is my rock and my salvation; he is my fortress I will not be shaken"* (Psalm 62: 5 – 6 NIV).

Sleep finally came. When I woke, I was still me, fighting fear, dressed in colorful pregnancy clothes with morning breath and no way to brush my teeth. Jason still had double vision and the locals continued to grill Alexey through the morning hours. When he left to get food, the trio even tried questioning us.

But they didn't speak English and we didn't speak Mandarin. So after an awkward exchange, they left us alone. By midday, they disembarked uneventfully and we whispered prayers of thanks. Alone in our car, we relished the rescue.

Hours later, when granola bars and crackers no longer satisfied, the train started to slow and Alexey told us it was time to disembark. Nearly twenty-four hours after we boarded, we pulled the heavy bags out from under the bunks and cranked up our game of follow the leader.

After maneuvering through another crowded station in an unknown city, Alexey walked up to a Swedish couple and gave them a big hug. Since earlier in the trip, he'd indicated that he didn't know our plans once we disembarked, I was shocked. In fact, I laughed out loud.

Living moment by moment following another was foreign to me. Very foreign. I didn't consider myself a control freak, but I usually lived aware of the day's plan.

Deep in China, we trusted another for everything. Food. Lodging. Travel. Safety. Everything.

Stripped of control, we leaned heavy on Alexey—and God.

And wasn't that what the trip was about? Learning to lean on God? The Almighty longed for us to journey with Him through a medical foreign land, one with double vision and drastic unknowns. But relying on Him every minute of every day—though a basic tenement of our faith—just wasn't the norm. Trailing Alexey as donkeys along for the haul, allowed us to experience that heightened daily dependence. Understanding our need and what it meant to depend on another was truly the answer to our prayers.

There in the station, Alexey and his friends greeted each other with genuine care. As I watched, I felt part of big plan—one I didn't even need to know. I could trust. Walk. Carry bags as donkeys. And wake to another day.

With that, we traveled to several hotels in search of a room, and once settled, killed several large bugs, and fell fast asleep.

Thirteen

There was a man with a child
That brought fulfillment to his dreams
After a lifetime of waiting
The promise finally came to be
But high upon a mountain
He stood beside his chosen one
And prepared to make an offering
Of the precious one he loved

"LAYING DOWN MY ISAAC"
Life of Love, Track 3

Sam sits at our kitchen table, munching a bowl of cereal in between coughing fits. Home from the first night of the county wide swim meet, he sounds terrible, and feels worse, since his race times still rank below state meet standards.

The high school swim season races to an end mid-winter. As temperatures dip low and ice storms loom, swimmers run around in bathing suits on wet concrete—indoors, at least. The County Championship Meet is held in late January, two weeks before the state meet, offering one last opportunity for high school swimmers to make a qualifying time to attend the state wide meet. Sam has one more shot, tomorrow night.

I stare at my pale teen, hunched over his cereal, "Do you think I should take you to the doctor in the morning?"

"I guess so," he mumbles.

His answer lets me know he feels as terrible as he sounds. Another round of antibiotics helped some last week, but not enough to stave off the infection. Worried, I remember his words from the doctor's office, *"God's in control, Mom. This swim season is his. If I get better, great. If not, well it's His."*

Ever since his major upswing in the spring, his times have lagged behind. Some say it's the normal ebb and flow of the sport. If his hands didn't turn an off shade of purple at the end of races, I might agree. Grateful that senior swim night has passed, complete with top hats and photos, I count down the days to the end of the season banquet. What will be, will be, and we will finally move on—after the next two weeks.

Weekend office hours prove convenient. So a nurse calls his name early Saturday and for the first time all season, his blood oxygen levels register a little low, causing concern. As we wait in the exam room, he lays on the table, pale and exhausted and states, "Well, I finally know what this feeling is."

"What do you mean?"

"This lightheaded, crappy feeling—I've had it off and on during this swim season. Now I know that it means I'm not getting enough oxygen."

My body freezes so I take deep breaths, trying to expunge overwhelmed mom emotion. It doesn't work. So I mentally rehearse the good: *Sam has never been hospitalized, never needed IV fluids, and still swam well enough to make finals last night. He's okay. Really okay. Not as healthy as I'd like, but definitely above average considering he swims hard with a metabolic disorder.*

"How often has this happened, Sam?" I finally ask.

"Maybe three or four times. Not a lot."

His typical nonchalance shouldn't surprise me. But it does.

After a thorough exam, our pediatrician prescribes steroids, new asthma medicine, and another round of antibiotics. Sam needs rest, not exercise. But the doc knows better. He doesn't tell him not to swim. He understands the importance of the meet.

And so do I. Deep down I get it.

However, when we enter the aquatic center hours later, I'm grateful they need help at the ticket table. While Sam warms up in the pool, I make change, offer silent prayers, and prattle on about our day, his sickness, and my strung-out mom nerves. Another mom rushes to our table to ask if we have medicine she can borrow. Her daughter is throwing up in the bathroom. I'm not alone.

A young female sings The National Anthem and the meet begins. The medley relay is the first event so I make my way to the far end of the pool and hold my breath as he dives in. It's only a 50-meter free style swim, one of his best strokes. But it's a test. A test of will and physical stamina.

The water parts with each stroke. He glides forward with seeming ease—even after the flip turn. His pace remains steady as he races back to the starting block. When he touches the wall, another teammate dives in. All four swimmers perform well and they make the state cut, meaning they will compete again in two weeks.

The pressure's off. Relief floods in. Sam's even smiling when I find him in the warm down pool.

I head back to the front table, more at ease, and make change while waiting for the 100-yard breast stroke event—Sam's last chance to make a high school state cut in an individual event. I know he'll start strong because he usually does. But when he struggles, his pace slows during the second half of the race.

The race won't start for a few hours, giving him ample time to recover from the first swim. But rest alone may not help. His unpredictable body has surprised us all season long, stirring constant disappointment for Sam.

At his peak last spring, Sam swam the 100-yard breast stroke event in 1.06.6 (just over one minute and six seconds). But during this season, he hasn't broken 1.10.00. The four second difference counts a lot in the world of swimming and he needs to post a swim time of 1.08.5 to get the state cut.

As his race draws near, I walk to the far side of the pool, as close to his lane as I can get. After climbing over feet and towels, lining the first row of metal bleachers, I pause near the tall wooden lifeguard stand that sits at the end of the racing pool. Officials patrol the walkway to my right. The bleachers ahead are full.

So I huddle near the wooden structure, away from the crowds and pray. In fact, I begin praying the kind of prayer that feels as if the Father's presence has come to whisper his plan into my soul—a plan I become a small part of as I lift it back to Him in earnest petition.

The whistle blows, Sam dives in, and I begin, *"Father, you said you are strong when we are weak. Will you please be strong for Sam tonight?"*

His stroke looks good, but it's the last 25 yards I'm worried about. So I keep praying, *"Let your power be made perfect in Sam's weakness, Lord. Let your grace be sufficient for his every need."*

Sam doesn't waver. And I never stop praying. After his first flip turn, he surges on to 50 yards, then to 75 yards, and one last turn. As his hands reach the wall at the end of the race, I look at his results and a surge of tears fill my eyes. He made the state cut. The time falls short of his personal best, but he made the high school state cut.

I want to shout to everyone in the stands. But they won't understand. Sam's time is good, but not as impressive as others. Still, after months of struggle, something different happened in the pool. After a long, discouraging season, we both feel victory one more time.

"Thank you, Jesus," I whisper back to the One whose presence held me as my son swam.

The noise fades and I sink into myself, realizing I just watched Sam surge with a power not his own. I remember again that my son belongs to the Father of Lights who came down from heaven to make the weak strong and the broken whole.

Years ago I imagined that I parented with God, that I was my boy's mom and The Almighty, their dad. Plain and simple. My confidence in His role waned when I lost focus but when I needed a reminder tonight, He came near

Samuel belongs to God. Every cell. Every mitochondria.

When we drive to the State Meet two weeks later, Sam is still sick. Antibiotics and a second asthma medicine roam his system, even after a breathing treatment two days ago. So I slip into the stands in the large aquatic center with our family, hoping he holds his own.

When the 100-yard breaststroke event begins, he dives into the Olympic pool and takes off. I wait for him to slow, certain he will, but his pace never falters. His split times show on the score board and they look good. Very good. Strong to the end, he breaks his record, coming in at 1.05.73.

I turn to find Papa, Jason's father, in the stands. As a certified swim official, he's worked most of Sam's meets and knows his struggle well. Both thrilled, we share a knowing glance and pump our fists in the air.

After warming down, Sam finds us in the stands. Having placed 38th in the state for the 100 breast stroke event, even he feels cause for celebration. His satisfied smile makes the fight worthwhile.

Though tonight feels epic, the reassurance I needed came two weeks ago at county finals—a reassurance that allowed me to enter the aquatic center tonight with a peace and trust I didn't have throughout the fall. The lesson has little to do with race times. No, it has much more to do with my ability to let go of worry, to stretch my soul wide, and to lean into God's plan and purpose for our lives, no matter where they lead.

Sam has a path to forge. And I need to let him go—to trust Him to the One who made Him and loves Him more than me.

Fourteen

There's a fire burning bright in many hearts
People just keep reaching out to play their part
Though paradise has washed ashore and broken down
Together we can turn this crazy world around

"DREAM IN COLOR"
Accepted, Track 8

While our sojourn as Bible smugglers came to an end, life changing experiences continued during our stay in China. Local believers delivered our materials since discretion protected them. With the pressure of transport past, Alexey interacted with us more. As he opened up, we glimpsed true sacrifice—the first testimony of two that made landing in America a stomach churning ordeal.

After a day of rest, Alexey led us from our hotel to a government sanctioned church not far away. As we walked, he explained that while anyone can legally participate in the Three-Self Patriotic Movement, restrictions force compromise.

Pastors cannot preach from the *Book of Revelation*, teach about the Second Coming, or evangelize to minors. Members are required to officially register their involvement with the church, potentially causing backlash from employers. Government printed Bibles remain available through the twenty or more registered churches allowed, but many Christians choose to attend underground gatherings in order to worship free from man-made rules.

So while some questioned why ministries went to so much effort to smuggle Bibles when other versions were available, Alexey wanted us to understand the importance of our time and task. Even now, over twenty years later, the underground church provides the preferred place of refuge for the growing Christian population in China.

By late afternoon, the Bibles and books were delivered so we joined the Swedish couple for dinner. We fellowshipped until fireworks diverted our attention and then woke the following morning to the news that Alexey had purchased plane tickets for our departure that afternoon.

With several hours to spare, he took us to a local park. The path led to panoramic views of the city but locals preferred taking our photo. When the crowd grew at one point, Jason and I stood like caricatures in an amusement park as a group of Chinese minorities took turns with their cameras.

Alexey seemed annoyed, but stayed close. So when we returned to our hotel and waited on a taxi, I sought to understand the man and his walls. Surprisingly, he opened up and shared more of his story.

As a young adult and father of two, he surrendered his life to Christ, but his orthodox leaning wife didn't approve. She left with their children, divorced Alexey, and allowed little contact. So in time, he decided to use his Chinese looks and fluent Mandarin skills to help get Bibles into China.

He went on to explain that he didn't open up with visiting ministry personnel like us because visitors come and go so quickly. Friendships form only to be followed by life-long goodbyes. Ironically, he finished his explanation only minutes before we had to leave.

Humbled, I sat quiet. We'd traipsed through inner China protected from his deep pain. Yet the wall, meant for our safety and his, tumbled down just as our taxi arrived. Forced to say goodbye fully aware we might never see him again, we got his address and promised to write.

Tucked away in the taxi I questioned my inquisitive nature. On the one hand, I scolded myself for having pressed him so much. On the other, I was simply thankful to have gained a greater appreciation for those who surrender much to serve God in obscure ways.

His story added poignancy to our trip that forged a deeper understanding of personal sacrifice. We had a brain tumor to battle. He longed to see his children.

Deep down, it all required trust.

Our plane landed in Guangzhou and we caught another taxi to meet up with our group. After ten days of mission work, a sightseeing tour would offer a respite before we traveled home. While we appreciated the down time, visiting historic landmarks paled in comparison to the evening we spent at an underground church with another true believer—Pastor Samuel Lamb.

Samuel Lamb was featured in a prominent American magazine not long before we left for China. My mother had read the article so I knew some of his testimony before he shared it in person.

When China sanctioned the Three-Self Patriotic Movement, many house church pastors refused to join due to the restrictions imposed. Pastor Lamb, one of the first pastors imprisoned for not following protocol in the mid-fifties, chose obedience to God over compliance with the government. Wanting to serve in a God-centered church, rather than a sanctioned rendition, Pastor Lamb stood his ground and paid the price.

As we navigated dimly-lit neighborhood streets, our eerie journey offered a mere taste of the precautions many believers face every day. Walking quietly alongside apartment homes with dimly lit interiors added to the obscurity. While a roof kept the renters dry, the black interiors of their homes reminded us of another age—far from current standards of living.

We stopped at a three-story apartment building on our right and climbed several flights of stairs. Overhead lights shown bright in comparison to others we passed. The top floor opened into a large room where former walls had been knocked out to create space for church gatherings. Backless, wooden pews lined the floor and as we filed in, Pastor Lamb welcomed us.

He was small in stature, skinny and unassuming. But when he told his story, he spoke with boldness, defying the law of the land. Born the son of a Baptist minister, he preached his first sermon at the age of nineteen. By his mid-thirties, he had been sentenced to—and was serving—twenty years in prison for maintaining his churches independence.

Assigned to clean the sewer at one point, the prisoner grew to value his task. The repulsive smell kept guards at a distance, giving him freedom to sing and worship as he worked. The unassuming cleric turned a veritable cesspool into a sanctuary, a place of holy surrender.

At the risk of further harassment upon release, he opened his church again. Hard labor and years away from his family didn't deter his faith.

As our service ended, the aging pastor posed for pictures and agreed to pray for Jason. While he didn't pray as boldly as I had hoped, his words made sense because he espoused to what he considered the holy principle, "*more persecution, more growth.*"

He wasn't afraid of our discomfort. He wasn't afraid for us to suffer. He understood that most spiritual growth comes through trial. While he may have wanted Jason healed for my sake, he knew first hand that staying true to God's calling and growing in our faith mattered most—whether healing occurred on earth or in heaven.

Between Alexey's life story and Pastor Lamb's testimony, we left Guangzhou the next day aware of how little we understood about true abandon to Christ—a life that worships in the cesspool.

Could we do the same once home? Would we do the same if the tumor started to grow?

As we approached the Hong Kong border, sidewalk construction forced a detour. A dusty path led to a long tunnel where amputees and burn victims crowded the entrance, making us both uncomfortable. Once inside, however, the begging took a dire turn.

Huddled on all fours, face to the ground, a young man exposed a tear in the backside of his pants. The split cloth revealed a deep, unhealed wound, almost to the bone. Scattered coins invited us to drop our own.

Stunned, we walked past, unsure of what to do. A slow rhythmic clank of metal hitting metal echoed as we exited the dark tunnel. Jason and I wanted to stop, to turn around and help the man in some way. But our team kept moving and we didn't know the first thing about medical care in the foreign, communist country.

Huddled on the subway, we considered our options. But after earnest discussion we accepted our limitations, fully aware our plight paled in comparison to the man's desperation. So we prayed. Right there on the subway. We prayed that our Bibles would meet someone's deep, spiritual need and asked God to send help to the injured man.

Smuggling Bibles and witnessing stark poverty would have changed us alone. Walking past the man in the tunnel further punctuated the breaking. So when we landed in America, the commercialism we once valued overwhelmed us. For months, our way of life inundated our senses. I entered several large homes, convinced I could never live in plush comfort after witnessing utter depravity.

In time the ache subsided and the sense of devastation grew dull. But as our challenge continued, the not so distant memories rooted us to the eternal. The lessons we learned in China reverberated in the core of our being, offering perspective when we needed it most.

Fifteen

I've been tired, getting no where
Waiting for a better day
Trying so hard not to fall apart
Lost on highways with no name

"HOPE FLIES"

After researching vans for over a month, Don and I sit side by side in a car dealership cubicle. Insisting I take ownership of the purchase, he hands me the check book. On my fourth attempt, I still can't control my shaky hands and mental fog. I want a cherry red SUV with a sun roof and leather heated seats. With only months before my youngest graduates from high school, I'm buying a mini-van instead—in case I need a wheelchair in the coming years.

Officially deemed *disabled,* signing the check seems to seal my fate.

The white van with a beige interior, feels bland to me. But it has electric doors. With a push of a button, I can open the side and back door with ease. My friends at the Vocational Rehabilitation Agency (Voc. Rehab) strongly encouraged my choice. Most SUV's don't accommodate power chairs and since the state is paying for my hand controls I'm required to buy a vehicle medically designed for long term use.

My insides have panicked throughout the entire process. I've wanted to run from the reality in front of me, but my legs don't move fast. Stuck in a body that plays host to a damaged appendage, I long for more freedom. Hand controls should help. As Don chuckles, I finally get it right. Then I take the keys to my new van and drive home.

I met with an intake counselor from Voc. Rehab last summer when pain limited my ability to drive. A semester of private student instruction had worn my body down. Since I struggled to drive and climb stairs, let alone survive each day, a neurologist recommended I look into getting hand controls.

Within a few weeks, I entered the Voc. Rehab office and sat at the end of a long conference table with pages of medical jargon to prove my need. I wasn't faking or being dramatic. Still my throat tightened and tears stung my eyes when the intake counselor asked, "Are you disabled?"

My right leg had never fully recovered. Weak muscles impeded normal healing. Painful nerves daily reminded me of damage done. Yet I still held onto the image of myself as "normal."

After wiping a few tears I finally looked at the counselor and replied, "I guess so."

Then I handed over the muscle biopsy report that confirms the mitochondria—or powerhouses in my cells—don't do their job well.

When she left to make copies, I laid my head down on the hard surface and listened as a war raged inside. The voice of fear said if I accepted changes to how I maneuvered on the outside, I'd lose who I was on the inside. The voice of reason insisted nothing could change my inner core if I didn't let it. But fear shouted louder and grabbed hold in a way I never should have allowed.

In time, the Voc. Rehab staff helped me gain perspective.

A few weeks later, I met with my assigned Voc. Rehab counselor. Not only did she begin the paper work trail that would lead me to hand controls, she ordered a work assessment. The test results boosted my confidence and gave me options for income should I choose not to teach music.

When the leaves began to change color a few months later, I heard from a Voc. Rehab engineer who assessed my needs from a mechanical standpoint. He visited my home, sat at my kitchen table for over an hour, and asked more pointed questions. I, in turn, described my limitations—again. Then he asked, "Have you considered getting a power scooter?"

Anxiety welled up and tears rolled down my cheeks. I apologized for the emotion but found it familiar. Every time someone mentioned a new device for me to consider, fear taunted me, "*The more contraptions you use, the more disabled you will be.*"

The lie kept me bound. Confined to my limits.

"I don't think I need a power scooter yet," I replied.

"What about a stair chair so you won't have to climb stairs to get into your home?" he countered.

"Maybe later," I confessed. "I can only handle thinking about hand controls right now."

In hind sight, I should have asked for the stair chair. I have one now. I ride up my basement stairs every day.

Besides, after turning him down, severe nerve pain shot from my hip to my foot when I stood to leave. Embarrassed, I continued to insist I was fine as he watched me hobble around, collecting my purse and music books. I'd balked at the notion that I needed more assistance, yet could only limp to my car.

I climb into my new van on a rainy day, headed to meet with a new counselor about hand controls. Nervous, I wonder if my hands can do the work. Unreliable at times, my wrists tire and nerve pain limits activity. But they're stronger than my right leg and wrist supports help.

Once called back to the small office, I answer the same round of questions again, "What's wrong with you? Are you disabled? Why do you need assistance?"

Used to the inquisition, I don't tear up. Longing to drive with less pain, calm reigns.

Soon the middle aged woman leads me to a van where my training begins. I climb in behind the wheel and she sits to my right. When I explain my concerns, she shows me several types of hand controls to choose from, including right hand controls, left hand controls, and variations of both.

Unsure of what to choose, she attaches right hand controls and encourages me to drive. Nerve pain shoots through my right hand almost immediately. Within minutes I know the appendage can't handle the load. I almost cry.

"Don't worry," she contends. "There are a lot of other choices. Pull over and we'll try another one."

Parked in a commercial lot, she attaches a different right hand gadget. I drive again and the pain continues. So I pull over again. This time, she gets out of the car, opens my car door and attaches a left hand control.

"Push the handle forward to brake," she motions, "and pull back to accelerate."

When I back out of the space and start driving, I slight smile forms on my lips. With no immediate ache or stabbing nerve pain, the left hand control shows promise. Aware that my hands may fatigue with time, my instructor decides to keep my foot pedals uncovered so I can use them if needed.

After enough practice to prove I'm road worthy, we drive back to command central where mechanics install the new controls. When they finish, I sign paperwork and head on my way—in the rain.

My left hand grips the dark plastic accelerator and breaking handle with ease. My right hand grasps a nob installed for one-hand steering. My left elbow rests on the window sill and my right elbow on an arm rest. The set up works well.

As I pull out of the mechanic's garage into a back alley, I'm sixteen again, driving for the first time. Nervous and concerned, I ease onto the main road and keep my distance from other cars. I may be disabled, but as I maneuver the roads without stressing my right leg, I sense renewed freedom.

After months of inner turmoil, the end product brings joy. My boundaries have expanded and I realize what the counselors have been saying is true. The new equipment allows me to be me. It doesn't take away from me. It helps my soul stay alive.

I still have many steps to take but this forward momentum helps.

Sixteen

Ever since I was a young girl
I've been searching for my place
In this wide open world
Never ever satisfied,
Always hoping to arrive
Where my heart can twirl

"RIGHT HERE, RIGHT NOW"
Life of Love, Track 11

Home safe after our two weeks in China, life actually stabilized. The results of a second MRI came back with no indication of tumor growth and an eye doctor prescribed prism lenses that helped Jason's vision. So while catching a Frisbee still proved a challenge, Jason could drive, draw, and savor thoughts of being a dad.

I, on the other hand, had some adjusting to do.

Used to the rigmarole of school, I grew restless. Without a job or another way to perform, insecurities surfaced. Forced to face how much of my self-worth relied on good grades and accomplishments, I struggled to find fulfillment in our daily routine.

Some of the toiling eased after Nathan was born in the wee hours of a Sunday morning in late March. Focusing on the infant's care left little time for self-reflection. Thankfully, after years of helping his sister care for her twin boys, my spouse was much more at ease with our newborn than me.

He carried Nathan with unusual confidence. He bathed him and cared for his umbilical cord with ease. When the scale indicated he'd lost weight at his two-week check-up, our doctor insisted we supplement breastfeeding with formula. No worries. Jason took charge. After I fed Nathan, my determined spouse took over, using special equipment designed to teach the baby how to suck properly. It took a lot of time—even in the middle of the night.

While we caved to bottle feeding months later, Nathan grew just fine and we enjoyed him so much that we expanded our family as soon as an insurance change allowed. Convinced the brain tumor ordeal was far behind, we welcomed Sam eighteen months later, before the sun came up on beautiful October Saturday.

We brought Sam home to a small, brick ranch located north of Atlanta, GA, much closer to family and illustration opportunities. A large fenced in yard came with the move. A third bedroom served as Jason's office so we spent most days in close proximity, even as the boys grew.

It was a simple, sweet time. We enjoyed our boys and they enjoyed each other.

We once found Sam peeking out from under a pile of cloth diapers, smiling. Nathan had tossed them in his crib, but he didn't seem to mind. On another occasion, the older sibling upped the ante by dropping several wooden blocks into Sam's playpen. Quite naïve, he could hardly wait for his squirmy baby bro to become a real live playmate. As if on cue, Sam's first belly laugh resulted from Nathan's brotherly antics.

Watching them grow made it easy for tumor fears to stay in the back ground, at least for me. Instead of worries about Jason's health, journal entries from that time expose my lack of self-confidence, heightened by the transition to full-time mom duty.

I wanted to be sold out to Jesus and a good mom and wife. But I also wanted to sing. Overweight, bored, yet totally in love with my kids, I was anxious for more.

Mommy day care proved the antithesis of smuggling Bibles into China.

Nursing a relational wound also ate at my peace. When we moved away from Nashville, I left a friendship I held dear—and not by choice. Feeling dumped by someone I idolized, left me emotionally injured. As a typical co-dependent, I didn't know how to separate the loss from the good in my life. My confidence eroded and I cried out for answers.

The break-up stung because my friend was the first to suggest that my emotions had a God-given purpose. By considering that the Holy Spirit spoke through some of what I felt, she freed me to trust those feelings as more than a bundle of overwrought nerve impulses. Gut instincts could serve as hunches worth valuing, bringing rhyme and reason to my heart.

Jason had embraced my sensitivity and my friend gave it purpose.

Valuing the inner nudges changed me. However, living through the end of our friendship undid me. The pain simmered. The hurt gnawed inside. I questioned God over and over: *If you really love me, why did you let this happen? Why must I hurt so much?*

Answers didn't come overnight. Inner healing takes time—especially when the emotional pain is rooted in family-of-origin issues. But as I cried out, God gave me a picture to hold onto in a most unusual way.

Sam's last feeding occurred when *Star Trek* reruns played on our tiny TV—the kind that required tinfoil covered rabbit ears for reception. Having never watched *Star Trek,* I began to look forward to our fuzzy, end-of-the-day, wind-down show.

As Christmas approached, one episode stood out. A man boarded the Enterprise who could sense everything around him. He heard what others thought and felt what they felt—the good and the bad; the joy and deep sorrow. His unique abilities made him a catalyst for healing and division; his strength also a veritable bone of weakness.

As he made friends—and enemies—the Enterprise encountered a large, unmanned ship. Details escape me, but in the end, the man who discerned everything beamed over to the unmanned space craft and essentially became one with the unseen, higher power that ran the gargantuan machine.

In the closing dialogue, the captain of the Enterprise expressed concern for the man's safety. As they spoke via telecom, the stranger explained that the unmanned craft had been beckoning him. Thus it was destiny for him to use his intelligence and telepathic communication abilities in conjunction with the uber-advanced technological capabilities available on the ship.

He wanted to be alone with the cyber being—away from the hum of humanity that reverberated too loud in his head.

As I sat in church on Christmas Eve, the episode replayed in my mind. Carols resonated with the wonder of the baby's birth. A holy hush filled my soul. And in the quiet moments, I sensed the whisper of the divine, *"I'm going to heal you, Susan. I'm going to make you less affected by the voices you hear."*

I wanted nothing more than to hide away with the Creator of the Universe, confident of His love, quieted by His presence—like the guy in Star Trek who ran away and became one with the machine.

It sounded crazy. Even I struggled to believe God would speak to me through a *Star Trek* episode on Christmas Eve, no less. Regardless, the image spoke to my heart and gave me courage as the New Year began. A journal entry from Dec. 30 1993 states,

> *"I tasted the birth of Christ this year as never before. The feelings were overpowering—almost too much for this sinful soul to experience. Tears fell, tears of wonder and awe that God touched us; that angels sang and filled the sky; that a woman nursed the Lord Jesus Christ; that perfect peace actually dwelled on earth.*
>
> *I want to know Jesus more. I want to get beyond myself, my fears, my desires, and see His life changing spirit touch others. And yet I'm not certain if I'll wake with joy or self-pity tomorrow.*
>
> *Tasting His wonder reveals more of my sinfulness—like I'm one of those ash, dust, and smoke covered factories in China. Not only is the building run down, but you can write your name a thousand times in the dirt covering the outside.*
>
> *Christ has made me clean. Yet I must daily choose holiness over self-indulgence and pity. It's a blessing to experience the holiness of his birth on Christmas Eve and yet it is righteousness*

to experience the holiness while cleaning laundry, dishes, or changing diapers. Perhaps for me, it's righteousness to choose to see holiness when I feel so desperately lonely and un-purposed.

God wants me to start putting these touches of His holiness to work. They aren't to be simple 'warm fuzzies' for reflection but rather new pieces of armor to use in my daily battle. If not used in the fight, the precious gift—the touch of His presence—is simply wasted."

Seventeen

If you open up your heart to love
It might just be the same
With the music of the mourning dove
May come lightning and some rain[4]

"WINDOWS OPEN WIDE"
Accepted, Track 5

Swim season has ended. Sam's new asthma medicine has calmed his
airways. And tonight, The Hodgson Singers—and Nathan—perform
in Atlanta. As I circle the block to find a parking place, anticipation
builds. Twenty years ago on this very day, I gave birth to my oldest son.
Eager to hear him perform with the elite vocal group on *our* special day,
I arrive early, with gifts.

While my oldest celebrates twenty years of living, I feel the weight
of twenty years of mothering. The tentacles of co-dependency tethered
deep in my mother psyche may be to blame. But this birthday feels
different, like we've both made it through twenty years of change.

---

[4]   Levi, Allen,"Open Windows", 1995.

His absence hurts less now that he's almost finished with his sophomore year of college. But it's taken time. Fortunately, a nurse call—only weeks after my muscle biopsy and spinal tap—punctuated his departure. Home from dropping him at band camp, the call interrupted my grief. When I learned a new medicine might help, the distraction proved invaluable.

I swallowed my first pill a few days before moving him into his dorm. When I arrived home at one in the morning, I burst into tears, paced around the living room, and then realized my legs were still moving with relative ease. The medicine was working.

My boy was gone but my legs were mysteriously stronger.

The timely change distracted from the empty seat at our table, but a Nathan size void remained. Wise beyond his years, his timely encouragements started young. Very young.

A year into my stint as widowed mom, I wrecked my car. The damage took a month to fix. When the vehicle still wasn't ready for pick up on New Year's Eve, I sank onto the floor in front of the kitchen sink, and cried.

Five-year-old Nathan found me and asked, "What's wrong, Mommy?"

"Oh, I just wish I hadn't wrecked the car," I replied between sniffles. "But you know me. I'll be all right. I'll stop crying soon."

With that he wandered off and left me feeling strangely alone. His absence fueled my pain, but not for long. When he reappeared, his little hands held a large flower-shaped pin from my jewelry box.

"Here, Mommy," he stated. "Put this on. It will make you feel better."

Crumpled on the floor I felt the Spirit's whisper, *"Put the flowers on, Susan. Celebrate the New Year. Everything's really okay. It's just a car."*

With that, I pinned the flowers on and called some friends. Dinner out cured my blues. And from that point on, Nathan often spoke as the creative voice of God. When desperation clouded my perception and I couldn't see the way, my oldest tended to speak with an innocent candor that broke through the haze.

Letting him go left me insecure. But stronger legs offered renewed balance.

And tonight I get to see him, even if from a distance.

I grab his birthday gift as I exit the car, and then search for a way into the church. A covered entrance leads to a door, but it's locked. A small garden offers a bench, so I sit. Relaxed under a canopy of green, I enjoy a slight breeze—and memories.

The evening hours steal the light of day. So I'm thankful when the door opens and singers walk out. I ask if they know Nathan.

"Oh, yes!" they reply.

My mother heart leaps in my chest, almost embarrassing me.

"Do you know where he is?" I feign control.

"Most of the choir is changing their clothes in the back," the tall one explains.

"Would you mind taking this to him?" I ask, holding out the gift bag.

"Sure," they reply, somewhat eager.

"We didn't know it was his birthday."

"I'm not surprised."

With that, I slip in the door with them and sit in the lobby. When the Sanctuary opens, the architectural masterpiece enchants me. The floor slants upward from the front to the back, allowing a clear view from any pew. Renowned stained glass windows tell the Biblical story in intricate detail and color. Dark wooden panels hold the glass in place. Jason's parents are already seated so I slide in the pew behind them and whisper a greeting in the holy place.

My sister arrives with two of her children—and our aging grandmother who doesn't know how to whisper. Hunched over, her grey, tussled hair and wrinkled face announce her ninety-plus years. A purple jacket enlivens her frame—the same one that was dressed to the hilt for my concerts.

My mom arrives from west of town. Jason's sister slips in after work. And Don even shows up before the program begins after a long day's work in the store. The party has gathered. Not to cut cake, but to simmer in harmony. Scattered among a few pews, we sit tall when the choir enters.

Small in stature, the group's conductor commands the stage with acute skill. In return, The Hodgson Singers respond to his lead with a sensitivity that defies their collegiate age. The music flows in fine-tuned colors, sparkling like the windows lining the room. The evocative sound expresses a wide berth of emotions that carry us well beyond the daily grind.

A closing spiritual brings tears to my eyes. When the music ends, Nathan heads our way. With little time to spare, we hug, take a few photos, and sing Happy Birthday. A weekend family party is only days away, so I leave comforted that I'll see him again soon.

After one last quick hug, my twenty-year-old son heads to the waiting bus and I drive home with hand controls. We're both finding our way.

Saturday dawns with blue skies. After participating in The Color Run, Nathan arrives home, lit up like a rainbow. Doused with a different color during each leg of the 5K, he bolts for a shower soon after a hug.

Sam and I try starting the grill—the ancient kind that requires charcoal and lighter fluid. Our first attempt fails. So I call Don who explains the routine once more. Pile the charcoal in the center. Pour on lighter fluid. Light. Cover and let simmer.

"I already did that," I insist. "It didn't work."

"Did you put fresh charcoal in?"

"Some. Maybe I need more."

"Yes, you need the new stuff to make it burn."

We hang up. I try again. This time, flames shoot high, straight toward the ceiling of our covered porch. Startled, I cover the coals, hoping the fire will calm. It does, but when grease runs from the burgers onto the coals, flames shoot up again. I burn an entire batch of hamburgers.

"Mom, let me do this," Sam grunts. "It's not that hard."

Happy to oblige, I head to the kitchen. Sam grills the meat to perfection, assuring me there will be plenty to eat after all.

Family arrives in small groups. We pull out tables, set out side dishes, and finally say a blessing. As everyone eats, I feel deeply satisfied.

My niece, Jessica, finds me after the meal and whispers, "Aunt Susan, do you have any eggs?"

"Eggs?"

"Yes, eggs." Cupping her hand to my ear she explains, "I want to resurrect your egg tradition. We should crack an egg on Nathan's head for his birthday. Hasn't it been a while?"

"It's been years," I retort. "But we never cracked eggs on birthdays..."

"I know," she confesses. "But it would be so much fun. Pleeeeze?"

"Oh all right," I chuckle. "I've got some eggs, but don't you dare tell him I gave you permission. You're on your own."

Years ago, when my boys were in first and third grade, I inadvertently started a tradition on our last day of school. Frazzled from all the activity, I arrived home in a rare mood. As we lingered in the kitchen, I decided to play the old crack-an-egg-on-a-head-with-your-knuckle joke.

Pretending to get an egg, I went to the fridge. Then I wadded up my fist, knocked firmly on Nathan's head and slowly spread my fingers out, immolating a runny yoke.

He didn't go for it.

"That's not a real egg, mom," he insisted and then spun toward me. "That's your fist."

To prove my point, I went to the fridge again and got a real egg. Then I held it in my hand and tapped it gently—but with some force—on his head.

It cracked. Right there in my hand, the egg cracked.

Sam took a defensive posture, "Don't do it, mom," he bellowed in his mighty-first-grade-manly-voice. "You better not do it."

Wide-eyed Nathan readied to pounce. As my personal Tigger-in-motion, I knew he would retaliate if I dared to cross the line.

Their wild looks made me chuckle and fueled inner indignation. In charge of the outcome, I wondered how to end the stand-off. Seconds later, surprising myself, I reached up and cracked the silly egg on my own head. It was amazing. Egg yolk dripped from my hair onto my beige denim skirt, and then on down to my black, platform sliders.

Sammy looked in horror, "Mommy, why did you do that?"

Nathan jumped up and down, crying, "Where's a camera? We need a camera!"

I doubled over in laughter amazed at myself. An outsider might have thought I'd lost my mind. But since I lived the moment from inside my skin, I knew better. I'd discovered a harmless way to express the madness and move on. So for many years, we celebrated the last day of school by cracking an egg on our heads.

The first year we cracked them on our own heads. Then we took turns cracking them on each other's heads. One year we orchestrated an egg fight with cousins and learned the hard way that you can't throw eggs at each other unless you want to get belted with something akin to a rock.

Sam eventually concluded he didn't like our family ritual and bowed out. Nathan and I ventured on alone for a time. And now Jessica is arranging an ambush with skill.

Cameras roll and several eggs are positioned. On the count of three, Jess and a friend smack them on the unassuming birthday boy's head, leaving a trail of slime running down his face and shirt.

Laughter erupts. Nathan takes the hit in stride, promising revenge. While trampled egg shells get carried into the house, I don't care. The memory has been made real once again. We didn't just celebrate twenty years; we resurrected a forgotten tradition—along with a part of me.

We're both growing, yet anchored by memories that forever tie our hearts. Nathan may not live at home and rock my world with his uncanny insight. But my world forever changed the day he was born. I became a mom. And no matter how far he roams, that will never change.

The ache continues to subside, the loss overshadowed with hope. And since *"hope does not disappoint"* (Romans 5: 4 NIV), I can—and will—carry on.

Eighteen

Distractions by the mile mess with my mind
They keep me always looking left and right
It's hard to walk this narrow path
When I'm slipping on gravel
Give me steady feet and a true blue heart
To keep me on this road I travel

"FREE FROM THE NEED"
Life of Love, Track 1

While I remained grounded by diapers and bottles, the New Year brought with it several divine encounters. Confined to the limits of my earthly shell, I questioned them. Grasping their meaning took time. Regardless, each touch served as a reminder that we were on a life journey, destination unknown.

They began in mid-January as I drove up a major highway, singing loud as worship music blared. There in the confines of my messy car, a holy presence wrapped around me like a cozy blanket. How it happened I don't really know, but in the sacred hush, I sensed that June would be a big month for our family—for Jason and me.

I listened with piqued interest, wanting more, and imagined we would move to another home, a house of healing. But nothing happened in the coming weeks to confirm the notion. In fact, it all seemed a little nutty.

Not long after, I attended a women's church circle event at a member's home. Agenda items discussed, a recently widowed mom shared her testimony. I knew her story. A brain aneurism had taken her husband's life six months before, on a warm summer's day.

As I listened, familiar emotions stirred again. Fear climbed out from hiding and spilled over into unwanted tears. Not wanting to make a scene, I slipped from the room with my infant son. Safe in the kitchen, I held Sammy tight and wept.

"Are you okay?" another mom asked when she found me alone.

"Probably," I shared, embarrassed, "It's just that the last time I felt weird like this, my husband was having brain tumor symptoms he hadn't told me about."

It sounded ridiculous—especially when sharing it out loud to a relative stranger. After polite reassurances, I couldn't wait to get home and drill my spouse. I left as soon as etiquette allowed.

"Are you okay?" I blurted when I walked in the door.

"What do you mean?" Jason asked.

"I had one of those crying spells like I had the night you told me about the double vision. Are you okay? Are you having more symptoms?"

"I'm fine," he offered, "But we should probably schedule another MRI."

Still quite practiced in questioning my instincts, I let it go. Surely God wouldn't reveal Jason's health issues to me twice through tears at a church gathering. My spouse promised to make an appointment for an MRI and I continued to wonder and pray about what God had planned for us in June.

A month later, we traveled to Nashville for a wedding. In close proximity to my former friend—without plans to visit—the rejection weighed heavy.

Desperate for answers, I called our pastor friend. After patiently listening, he said, "God has not rejected you, Susan. No matter what happened in that relationship, God has not rejected you."

The simple truth penetrated my wounded frame. Revolutionary, it brought a new dimension to my understanding of God. Yes, I felt deeply hurt. Yes, the wound was real. But people hurt people down here. We live in a desperately fallen world. However, the relational pain we experience is not reflective of God's acceptance, love, or character.

He is who He is. This world is what it is. He died on the cross to give us a way to rise above the hurt and live above the fray. While tons of books have been written on the subject, I had never thought to separate what happened to me here from who God is—until that day.

God had not rejected me.

I was not rejected.

My feelings didn't change right away. I didn't exactly *feel* accepted. In fact, the hurt didn't go away for months. But the cognitive shift proved vital and the phrase replayed in my mind, paving the way for God to break through at the right time.

When spring grabbed hold, Nathan woke with a cold that made me nervous. A visit to the doctor only peaked my concern. Since some cold viruses prove detrimental in newborns, he warned us to keep an eye on five-month-old Sam.

By mid-afternoon, he began making a strange clicking sound while trying to drink a bottle. Having never experienced someone in respiratory distress, I hesitated to rush back to the doctor. However, the sound finally unsettled me enough that Jason and I left Nathan with family and headed to the ER.

Within minutes of our arrival, Sam was placed on oxygen. By evening, he'd been admitted and was lying in an oxygen tent.

Jason climbed into the crib, covered with a clear plastic tarp, and cradled his son. Sam lay still, unmoving; his lifeless body unlike our typical boy.

Since antibiotics don't treat RSV (Respiratory Syntax Virus), we turned to prayer. But several days went by with little change and the doctor finally admitted that if Sam got much worse, they would have to try a treatment that could make him even worse before he got better.

After the stark warning, Jason fasted. Behind on work, he drew pictures in the waiting room while we both desperately prayed. A long night passed with little change but suddenly, mid-morning, our little boy lit up. Smiling for the first time in days, he let us know he was on the mend. Discharged by evening, we went home with a nebulizer and a lot of medicine.

His miraculous turn around—right when things looked the worse—made us feel heaven heard our cries, and answered prayers always buoy hope.

Strengthened by the divine touch, Jason scheduled an MRI appointment and we made plans to travel to Nashville again in late May. A week before the MRI, our entire family flew to Philadelphia to visit my grandparents one last time before they moved to a retirement village.

Their home of thirty years sat high on a hill, surrounded by tall, looming trees. Flowers bloomed in their front yard forest. After morning naps, we hiked down their steep driveway and turned right. About a quarter mile down the road, on the far side of a cobblestone bridge, a gated entrance opened into a state park.

There, the creek drifted beside us as we walked. Reminiscing, I recalled many long walks with family in the summer and freezing cold. If the stars aligned, snow would fall and we'd pull a wooden sled to the park so we could race down the famous big hill.

Basically, the tall oaks and lazy river bed served as an extended back yard we played in for years. Soon, the familiar paths would be a distant memory. Sharing them one last time with my family felt rich. Each step weighted with meaning.

We stopped near the river's edge to let the boys play. Leaning over, I held Sam's little hands as his toes dipped in the cool water. Distracted, at first I didn't notice when two women approached. However, when they spoke with my grandmother and headed my way, I stepped away from the river's edge.

"We're nuns and feel led to pray for you," one of them explained. "Do you mind?"

"Not at all!"

"We don't do this often," she continued as she took my hand, "but we feel led to assure you that God is with you. You're not alone."

The divine affirmation deep in the throes of the sacred state park shouldn't have surprised me, but it did.

The sacred sisters prayed for me, our family, and God's continued work in our lives. As they walked away I couldn't help wondering what was so important that God sent nuns dressed in street clothes to lift us up. But June was only weeks away. So I felt strangely excited. Something was up.

I was not rejected and God was with us.

What more could I want?

Nineteen

I'm in a crowded room
Full of friends I know
Wondering if I dare
Let my true feelings show
Superficial care keeps my spirit closed
Open wide my heart and let it flow

"ACCEPTED"
Accepted, Track 3

Sam graduates from high school in a matter of weeks. End of year events punctuate the crossing. Awash with emotion, I slog through each juncture, dreading the empty nest. Planning a porch party at our home adds to the strain. Sam promises the small invite list is fine. It feels more like a reminder of lost community to me.

As I try to not cave to the sense of loss, I sink into my favorite spot on the living room floor, open my laptop, and begin to craft a letter to my graduate. The youth group from the *other* church hosts a senior banquet every year during which parents and their teens read letters to each other. With only hours till the event, I pour mom emotion into words.

111

Finished, I scrutinize my clothes and choose a pair of light-mint, cropped pants with a favorite soft white flowing shirt to disguise my added weight. Mint and gold butterfly earrings complete the understated outfit. Though I've attended a handful of Sunday night services with Sam at the church, my nerves won't settle.

A slight panic grips my chest even before I enter the long hallway with Don and Sam. The patterned carpet throws my gait. Balanced with my teal cane, we walk toward the large foyer filled with round tables. Certain we'll see some of the people I let down the most, I feel undone. While stronger since the fall, my youngest is about to leave, throwing my inner equilibrium off kilter.

I want to go home but I sit still as Italian fare fills our plates.

Small talk keeps our table from awkward quiet and I breathe deep as chatter fills the vaulted room. Then the letter reading begins.

Embarrassment overtakes me when I realize I wrote my letter all wrong. Others crafted cute poems and described sweet childhood memories. In contrast to the lighthearted fare, mine is laden with reality and regret.

I squirm in my chair, wondering if I can do an impromptu rewrite. But no matter how far back I go, trials abound. Brain tumor drama infiltrated most of Sam's infancy and toddlerhood and my grief tainted early elementary years. As I listen to other's tales, I grieve our life. I know I shouldn't. But I do.

Another mom, also named Susan, reads a letter to her son, Sam. So I take my cue. Anxious to get it over, I stand and joke about following the Susan and Sam duo with another pair similarly named. While others laugh, the joke does little to calm my nerves.

As I start to read, my hands begin to tremble—uncontrollably— followed by tears that eventually choke my words. I struggle for breath, feeling like I'm confessing my own judgment in front of a jury as I read to my son:

> *Not long ago, Nana said, "Boy, Sam's high school years have*
> *flown by." I immediately replied, "They may have gone by*
> *fast for you—but not for me." We've both had muscle biopsies*

and spinal taps, resulting in a diagnosis neither of us wants—mitochondrial disease.

It didn't help that I fell a month after your biopsy, adding two major surgeries to the mix; surgeries that permanently damaged my right leg. So while you've been adjusting to too many meds and the idea of a lifelong energy deficiency disorder, I've been adjusting to life with a cane and unreliable legs.

It's not been easy.

Even today someone asked, "Didn't you become disabled in the last three years, Susan?" And I thought, "Yeah, all while Sam's been in high school."

She didn't know she was confirming my thoughts for tonight. But her casual remark stirred the emotion I've processed as I've reflected on the last four years.

I wanted to be strong for you. But many times, you were strong for me instead.

I wanted to make sure your faith in God stood firm. But you dug deep on your own and even helped me climb out of the darkness that overwhelmed me last summer.

I wanted to cheer you on at every turn, but a few times you had to pack your swim bag and head out on your own while I rested in bed.

In the last few days, I've grieved the loss. But when the tears dried, I saw the gain.

You kept your head on straight—a testament to the character God is forming in you. You made great grades—a sign of true diligence. You fought me enough (and kept your room dirty enough) to qualify for a teen; yet respected Don and I in many ways far beyond your years.

You kept a rigorous swim schedule as well as commitment to Bible study and fellowship. And when I needed it most, you watched the video that was taken only months before your dad died—the one where I expressed my mountain top, crazy, God is bigger than everything faith. And when we talked about it later, you asked in your very pointed way, "What happened to you, Mom?"

Good question… easy answer. But you made me look deep and challenged me to start climbing back out of the hole I'd sunk into.

We have a unique journey ahead. You may still be strong for me some days. And others I hope to be able to support you. The best part, though, is that we both know that in our weakness, the Creator of the universe is strong on our behalf. May His strength continue to make you every bit the man of God He created you to be.

With a whole lot of love, Mom

Polite applause punctuates the end. Sam walks to my side and embraces me with a warm hug. My face lights on fire as I sit back down in my chair. Tears keep falling and I can't look another in the eye. Not until several more letters are read and mine fades into the background of laughter and other parent's tears.

Admitting my struggle in the place of my despair has left me feeling utterly exposed. Emotionally naked. Yet as the evening continues, a divine presence clothes me in peace. As another sojourner in Christ, I'm simply trying to find my way. Yes, I've fallen. But God is picking me up. And right now, that's what matters most.

The letter reading ends and the seniors gather for a photo op. Sam plays the jokester while smart phones flash. A woman I don't know corners me and compliments my words. "They were so meaningful," she asserts.

"Thanks," I reply, reticent to open the wound again.

Thankfully, Sam's ready to go and we head to the car. Assured I didn't embarrass him, I head to bed, thankful the event is over.

The weather has cooperated on this bright Sunday afternoon. Tables and chairs strategically line our covered porch. Nathan's graduation party included a much longer guest list but I've lost touch with many friends. Sam swears he doesn't care since he likes smaller groups. So soon an intimate huddle of family and friends gathers around a table near our front steps, eating Moe's burritos.

With belly's full and entertainment lacking, my niece, Jessica, whispers in my ear again, "Got any eggs?"

I roll my eyes.

"We're celebrating the end of school," she asserts.

While I feign non-involvement, I'm soon a dastardly part of the plot. After eggs have been passed out in secret, we announce that it's time for a photo op. Sam sits in the middle of our elegant wide front stoop while his friends and cousins circle round. Always a ham in front of the camera, he strikes a noble pose.

I snap a photo, capturing smiling comrades around the unsuspecting victim. The next frame denotes the same but with eggs raised around the insufferable graduate. The third picture in the series catches the moment all mayhem ensues.

At least ten eggs crack on Sam's head at once. Yoke drips down his face as he leans forward in utter dismay. The smiling group disappears, anticipating retaliation. Video rolls until he regains composure, rises from the ashes, and heads straight toward me with gooey hands. After sufficiently sliming my head and shirt, he turns toward his nervous friends. And the grand chase begins.

Egg shell drippings trail from my front stoop into the kitchen. Anxious kids run in every direction, through the front door, out the back, and around the sides. The most athletic of the bunch, Sam keeps them on the run, in his bare feet, on our concrete driveway.

Micah's reaction amuses me most. The youngest in a family of girls, he cooks more than me, leads the senior Bible study, and plans to attend Bible College in the fall. Quite mature, he's not used to being chased by a friend bent on revenge. So he runs, howling like a kid let loose on a playground.

All the graduates run free, embracing their inner child. On the cusp of adventure and change, they let loose and play. As they leave, covered in egg slime, they tell me it was the best party ever. No awkward silences. No proper politeness. Just messy fun.

While I can't completely separate *what is* from what part of me argues *should be*; the distinction is getting clearer. My life is not normal. No one's ever is. But ours carries a unique set of oddness that requires embracing the moments as they come, rather than grieving what I wish they could be.

I miss community, but Sam has his own. He's ready to launch without regret. Maybe I should do the same.

Twenty

Morning will dawn changes will come
But He is faithful like the morning sun
And though we don't know what lies ahead
We know He'll always provide daily bread

"HE WILL CARRY US THROUGH"
Accepted, Track 1

A week after our encounter with the nuns, Jason and I pulled into the Vanderbilt Hospital parking lot on another perfectly blue-sky day. As we got out of the car and breathed in the crisp morning air, I said, "It sure doesn't feel like a red letter day. Everything will be fine."

"I hope so," he mumbled.

A few hours later, we sat in a stark, windowless office with a very high ceiling. There, an emotionless doctor entered, sat down, and shared, "Your MRI shows growth. We expect you have two to three years to live."

Unable to compute his words, I sat emotionless.

"We'd like for you to have a PET scan today to see how fast the tumor is growing. But since we have no treatment options available, we'll send your scans to a doctor near your home if you'd like a second opinion."

It was all so matter of fact it felt like he said, "After this test you should go home to die. There's nothing we can do."

Unable to let his diagnosis grab hold for fear I would shrivel up and whither into a nothing mom and wife, I held it together as we walked to the PET scan waiting area. When the test started, I left the hospital and drove to our old church, only minutes away. A receptionist located the pastor who had encouraged me months before—the same one who went to China with us.

When I entered his office, I blurted, "A doctor just told us Jason's tumor is growing."

His face reflected both surprise and concern.

"What I don't understand," I went on, "is that God's been speaking life to us. I've been feeling like June would be a big month since January. Just a week ago, two nuns stopped me in a park to pray with me and remind me that God is near."

Unwilling to accept the reality that June had turned into a life changing month indeed, I kept rambling, "He can't be dying. He's my best friend. It doesn't make sense."

When I wound down, my pastor took my hands and offered, "We know God is a healer, Susan. And we know we can trust him. So let's pray. Let's lift all of this up to our Father in heaven."

And so we did. When we finished praying, I drove back to the hospital. The PET scan confirmed the tumor remained a slow growing glioma. But the fact it was growing was not good.

We called home to share the news with our families and the tears finally fell. Later we met some friends at Cracker Barrel where they listened as we tried to process the diagnosis.

What did God want from us? How did this fit with our life plan? How do you live with a brain stem tumor with no discernable treatment option?

Our friends attended a charismatic church that believed in divine healing. The theology was relatively new to us but facing our fight with faith made sense. Or maybe we just didn't have any other option but to believe God for the miraculous.

Too busy talking to drink, thirst forced me to the water fountain as we left. When I lifted my head after a few sips, I saw a plaque that read: *Faith Moves Mountains.* Similar faith messages cover a lot of wall space these days—unlike back then. Unfamiliar with the timely message, the words jumped into the depths of my soul. The guidepost confirmed I should stay strong for the journey ahead.

But I needed many more signs and God lovingly obliged.

Before we left for home the next morning, our host called us to the phone. My sister, Laura, answered on the other end.

"George and I are in town for a wedding," she explained. "We want to know if you have time to stop by the farm before you head home."

"Sure," I replied, without asking Jason—since we'd just been invited to my favorite singer's home.

An avid fan of Amy Grant's music, I attended several of her concerts growing up, owned all of her recordings, and had even seen her at church on occasion when we lived in Nashville. At the peak of my infatuation, I learned my sister's fiancé had family ties to the artist—ties that might help me meet her someday. But that hope had long been forgotten the morning Laura called.

The drive through the Nashville countryside offered a respite from our internal fury. After several turns, a long driveway led to a two story, white farm house. Behind the home on the right, kids played in a swimming pool. As we parked, Laura and George greeted us and led us to the pool deck. George and Jason took off to ride four wheelers and I stood awkwardly with my sister.

Amy approached. Shorter in person than I imagined, she beamed with compassion. Our conversation went something like this:

"I hear you got bad news this week."

"Yes, it doesn't sound good," I replied.

When she asked how I was doing, I dove into my litany of confusion, "Jason can't be dying. God has big plans for our lives. He's been speaking hope to my heart all year."

Amy listened patiently as her kid's splashed in the cool, blue water.

"You know," she began when I paused, "the one thing I respect is that you're not pulling back. Some people pull back from those they love when they get bad news. But it sounds like you're pressing in."

I heard her words but didn't digest them till later.

The subject changed and she asked our opinion on what kind of roof she should put on her pool house. Having no clue, Laura and I continued our tour.

A barn stood behind the pool where kids had once gathered and a favorite record, *Songs from the Loft*, was born. To our right sat a muddy lake where Amy and her kids used to swim. George and Jason flew by on four wheelers and I stood in the open air, entranced.

The day after a doctor told me my husband was dying, I had met my childhood music hero, in person, at her home. The timing was not lost on me and I felt certain that faith could move mountains.

Not wanting to overstay our welcome, Jason and I soon began our drive home. As we descended the mountain that led to the Georgia border, scattered prose led to an epiphany.

"You know," I began, "I think I finally understand what Amy was saying."

"Continue," Jason invited, looking my way.

"She made the comment that some people withdraw from those they love when they get sick. Looking back, I think I've had some of those feelings this weekend. Like I want to pull in and protect myself. But I can't. It won't help anything."

A long silence lingered until I concluded my thoughts.

"I can either run from the battle or press into the fight. So I'm going to press in. We're going to fight this thing with faith and whatever else God brings. It's the only way."

My conflicted spouse smiled a little but had his own inner fight to contend with.

Regardless, when we crossed the state line, I was a different person than the one who had gone over the mountain days before. Ready to learn and practice my convictions, I wanted to see what difference a stronger faith could make.

Would it make the sick person well?

I didn't know. But I had to try. It wasn't just a weapon of choice; it was the only one we had.

Twenty-One

I'm finally finding me
After all this time
I'm finally finding me
Right here by your side
I'm finally finding me
Here in your arms
And it doesn't matter
What all went wrong
Love kept us strong

"FINALLY FINDING ME"

After two days at the ocean's edge, my ankles feel brittle, like they could snap. Even with braces and a brand new shiny-red walker for support, I

ate breakfast, knowing I must rest indoors while the family enjoys the outdoors. I clean a few dishes, brace myself for a quiet day, and head back to my bedroom.

I purchased the new mobility aid after my cane proved insufficient to help me through the long lines at Sam's high school graduation. Hoping to maximize energy at the beach, I ignored the inner voice of decent and bought the device the day before we left. While using it has eased physical stress on hard surfaces, it requires courage—courage to ignore stranger's looks as well as my own feelings of consternation.

Reminders of loss invade my place of refuge, so I decide to write. Hunkered down in the master suite with a view of the bay, I sit with my laptop and type.

A publishing company invited writers to submit love stories for a book compilation and I have two. The first came easy. My story of young love that began with a letter and ended in tragedy flowed effortlessly.

But since my second spouse deserves the same, I begin again. Perched on a fluffy white comforter with Florida sunlight bouncing off the wall, I sift through memories.

Don and I have been in counseling now for several months. Not every week, but enough to keep conversation flowing and relational issues in the forefront. We've made progress. But store hours still demand his attention and my health forces limits.

When I close my eyes and sink into vacation mode, I float above family stress and an internal feeling of judgment. Detached from pain, love for my husband bubbles up from the depths. As the vice grip of guilt loosens its hold, I remember why I married the football playing, farm boy from South Georgia.

On one of our first dates, we drove back roads through North Georgia and came across a rattle snake sunning itself on the pavement. A child road her bike close by, so after we passed the resting viper, Don slowed the car, put it in reverse, and parked on the side of the road. Without saying a word, he got out of the car, found a long stick, and approached the venomous serpent.

Safe in the vehicle, I screamed like a ten-year-old girl, "What are you do-ing?"

If he heard my cries, he never let on. He raised the stick in slow motion instead, and struck the beast with a fatal blow to the neck. After scouring his trunk for a knife, he cut off its head, skinned the creature, and dropped the snake skin into a plastic cup—a souvenir for my boys.

My mother was appalled.

Fervent chatter interrupts my thoughts. The five teenage cousins, Nathan, Sam, Trey, Drew, and Josh enter my unit, collapse on the living room floor, and pull out a game of risk. The game will last all week with boyish banter that's as much of the sound track of the beach as the nightly song of the frogs. I listen in on their conversation till their theological debate goes over my head. Then I drift back to the Georgia Mountains.

With the snake safe in the trunk, my blood pressure began to drop and Don started the car. As our jaunt through the country continued, I learned that he and his brothers often killed rattlers as they worked in the fields. A stranger to farm life, I was both fascinated and terrified by his unique ability. Suddenly aware that I sat next to someone who could fight for me, I wasn't sure my issues required such honed skill.

I had been alone a long time. Strong and independent, I was drawn to and unsettled by the unusual strength I saw demonstrated on that lazy summer afternoon. On the one hand, who could fight spiritual battles better than a serpent killer who fought off snakes with bare hands and a stick? On the other, his untamed brute force was unlike anything I'd encountered in the world of men.

Despite my fears, the kindness in his eyes won my heart. And true to form, after we married and blended family issues stirred angst, Don began fighting our problems with his rock solid, unbending strength. He was immune to what people thought—at least on the outside. He traversed rocky relational landscapes without losing his footing while my legs wobbled even without the odd looks and awkward glances.

He wanted to be my strength. To provide all the support I needed. But it didn't take long for my hero's unwavering stance to become my undoing. I longed for an emotional empathy he struggled to provide. I craved a break from awkward interaction, while he desired a confident bride by his side, one that trusted he would keep her from harm. When my insides couldn't meld with his outward calm around friends and family, the divide began to form.

A kitchen cabinet door slams shut, bringing me back to the present.

"You guys hungry out there?" I ask.

"Maybe a little," someone answers.

Snacks abound for the four cousins who are old enough to make their own lunch, but I want a distraction. So I start toward the kitchen.

On the other side of my bedroom door, their game of risk is sprawled on a low-lying coffee table. Having never played the game, I don't understand their intrigue. But I do know they each represent a different country and fight to control the board. In time, alliances will be made but my Sam often wins. He plays recklessly, and his gutsy moves pay off.

They moan and groan and argue at times. But their scuttlebutt is as much a part of the week as the sand and sun. The cousins don't throw punches anymore. They engage in verbal tussles on a variety of topics.

Before I've even made coffee some days, they've returned from their morning bike rides with my dad in passionate debate. A proponent of world view discussions, dad buys iced lattes half-way through the rides and they sit around a café table and respond to his pointed questions. Sometimes the discussions don't end—all day. They reverberate till dinner, on the beach, at the pool, in the unit before and after Risk.

The teen deliberators are taller than me. Robust and full of life, they've worked through their differences over the years and become good friends. I almost envy their bond but enjoy watching from the outside, a generation removed.

Once sandwiches fill their stomachs, they consider their next move, the pool or the ocean. With the sun still hot, I rub suntan lotion on a few backs and return to my perch on the fluffy white comforter on my bed. Complete silence makes it easier to capture thoughts into words. So while they head to the waves, I float back in time.

Six months after we started dating, the man who killed the rattler had a dream—a rare thing for the farm boy. He felt God spoke the word "flawless" to him, concerning me. Not long after, he purchased a cross necklace with a tiny flawless diamond in the center.

He knew my past and the insecurities I still battled. So when a mutual friend of ours cornered me at church one night and expressed her dismay at our choice to date too soon after his wife died, he responded to my tears with the reminder. Still a puddle of emotion hours later, he stopped by with the flawless cross diamond in hand. As he hung it around my neck, he explained it didn't mean I was perfect, but rather forgiven, made new, bought with a price.

Flawless.

I was to wear the cross as a reminder. And I tried hard to live up to its meaning. To face rejection with the overwhelming force of acceptance that's mine due to what Jesus did on the cross.

Don reinforced the message when he proposed months later. Driven by the image in the dream, he incorporated a small flawless diamond into my engagement ring. Knowing our marriage would have challenges, he wanted the message of flawlessness to be a part of our covenant exchange. The symbol of our unity was to also represent Christ's undying love on the cross on our behalf.

But some days it wasn't enough.

When we failed to find common ground in our day to day issues, in time I actually grew to resent the diamond and its meaning. Tangled in relational confusion, I grieved that I had failed to stay strong. And the message taunted me.

After marriage counseling, and renewed understanding, I began to realize how special the gift was. Married for twenty-five years to his former wife, he was aware of potential minefields and had purchased something of value to tangibly demonstrate his love for me. The powerful gesture held new meaning.

The heart of a warrior battles the serpent. And just like I'd finally given in to my need for a walker, I understood that God had given me a spouse to lean on—a spouse who sees God's heart for me even if we don't always connect emotionally in day to day life.

As I write, the story flows. I see it more clearly. When I hold it just right, sunlight reflects off my engagement ring and dances on the wall. My husband may not be able to spend the week with me at the beach, but tiny rainbows created from my ring remind me of our togetherness while apart.

I am flawless in Christ. Forgiven. Set free. A beloved child of God.

Waves of peace wash over me, softening hardened places in my heart. While it's never fair to compare spouses, this new perspective highlights their unique roles in my life.

As a highly insecure young teen, I needed the artist to awaken the creativity that lied dormant in my soul. His soft-spoken ways nurtured my wadded-up sensitivity until it blossomed and I understood our Creator's love in new ways. Awakened from slumber, I could stand on my own even after he died.

While stronger, I was still thrown and tossed by what other's thought of me. My colors changed in different circumstances, like a chameleon. So God brought me Don, a man who can take a stand and swim against the current, perhaps a little too easily.

Undaunted by societal norms, he pursued me. And while I knew God had spoken to my heart and said, *"This is your man,"* it took me years to understand why. I didn't need coddling anymore. I needed greater inner strength.

Don provides a framework of support I desperately need. And the tiny stone on my wedding band offers a daily reminder that everything else comes from the God of Wonders who longs for us to embrace the reality that we are flawless in Him.

There are still challenges ahead. But I'm living a second love story, building a history with a very different kind of man which requires a very different kind of me.

The afternoon sun no longer blazes. So I lather up and find the gang at the pool. As my feet dangle in the lukewarm water, I watch as the cousins race, pile onto each other's shoulders, and play Marco Polo. They hardly squabble these days, having navigated childhood tantrums to form lifelong friendships. No longer a referee, I watch from a distance as they reminisce and laugh at the ways they once picked on each other and stirred strife.

It was part of the growing process. A process they never gave up on. And if they can navigate years of growing pains and come out strong, then Don and I can as well. We just can't give up.

We're rising from the ashes, having been purified in the fire. Flawless even in the flames.

As I sit at the ocean's edge once more before we leave, years of hurt drain away, washed away with the tide. When I return home, I'll have both a walker and a spouse to lean on.

Twenty-Two

Oh breath of life breathe into me
Waken my spirit set my soul free
Till every part is brimming with hope
Right here I'll be waiting cause your touch
Your touch is all I'm thirsting for

"BRING ME ALIVE"
Accepted, Track 6

Jason and I knew a prophetic church existed across town but had never attended a service. Borderline charismatic types, we weren't sure if we believed in modern day prophecy. A terminal diagnosis made it easy to abandon theological concerns. Thus, a Friday night service in a barn held renewed intrigue.

The small space had been converted to accommodate weekly services so the inside didn't look like a backyard shed. A tall man led worship in dim light while we juggled seven-month-old Sam and two-year-old Nathan. After an hour of singing, a lengthy sermon preceded more music, meaning the boys fell asleep long before the prophetic ministry began.

Desperate to hear more from God—even if in a barn—we watched with yearning as a team of trained intercessors began choosing individuals at random and speaking into their lives.

Close to midnight they finally approached us and I burst into tears as they spoke:

> *Son and daughter I have put a vision within you and you've been wondering what direction to take. I'm going to take you one step at a time. For it's going to be a step of faith. And I'm going to show you this faith; you're going to walk this faith; and it's one that's going to be a deep faith—one that you're going to be able to share with others and show them how to walk this step of faith. So do not fear. Do not be discouraged. But know that I am with you; that I am with you every step of the way. You will make it—you will go through.*

Faith. There was that word again. Over and over.

What did it mean? We drove home wondering how to truly walk out faith; how to know faith; and even more, how to be transformed by faith.

Some might say the prophetic message could apply to anyone, and indeed, all believers in Christ are called to walk by faith. But since we'd already felt God saying faith would make a difference in our journey, the message emboldened us.

Within a few days we contacted our pastor and asked if we could lead a healing service at our church. When he agreed, I wrote a letter asking others to join our faith fight by fasting for twenty-four hours and attending the service. While I hoped for a slew of mail to arrive in response, our mailbox stayed empty. But family and friends met in a basement room on a warm Sunday night just over a week later.

I led worship and Jason preached—or rather spent time explaining why we felt led to step out in faith and pray for healing. It needed explaining.

The day before, a young father who had impacted many lives in our church, lost his life to a brain tumor. The irony wasn't lost on us. A funeral and a healing service were squeezed tight into the same weekend. The reality of loss collided with the quest for life.

Even we asked: Who are we to pray for healing with boldness? Why should we lift up our dad when another young father just died? Is it even possible to conjure up a level of faith to make an inoperable brain tumor disappear?

Questions swirled, no doubt. But buoyed by scriptures and the call to faith, we stepped out onto the unknown ledge:

> *"Believe me when I say that I am in the Father and the Father is in me; or at least believe on the evidence of the miracles themselves. I tell you the truth, anyone who has faith in me will do what I have been doing. He will do even greater things than these, because I am going to the Father. And I will do whatever you ask in my name, so that the Son may bring glory to the Father. You may ask me for anything in my name and I will do it"* (John 14: 11 -14 NIV).

> *"Jesus asked the boy's father, 'How long has he been like this?'*

> *'From childhood,' he answered, 'It (a demonic spirit) has often thrown him into fire or water to kill him. But if you can do anything, take pity on us and help us.'*

> *'If you can?' said Jesus. 'Everything is possible for him who believes.'*

> *Immediately the boy's father exclaimed, 'I do believe; help me overcome my unbelief'"* (Mark 9: 21 – 24 NIV).

> *"But he was pierced for our transgressions, he was crushed for our iniquities; the punishment that brought us peace was upon him, and by his wounds we are healed"* (Isaiah 53: 5 NIV).

We had been inundated by healing scriptures in the few weeks since the diagnosis. They jumped off the age at us. So it was easy for Jason to share why we had taken such a bold step at the healing service. When he finished his thoughts, we took communion and prayed.

Many had needs of their own. So we spent time in quiet reverence, crying out to God collectively. But before we dispersed, everyone held hands in a circle and prayed for Jason's healing.

An hour after I began this chapter, an email arrived in my inbox. Pam, a friend of Jason's from high school, found me online. Hoping to jog my memory, she mentioned she attended the healing service. Amazed at the timely connection, I asked what she remembers about the service and her answer didn't disappoint.

Not only did she recall everyone holding hands in the circle, but she remembers a distinct smile on Jason's face that spoke acceptance and longing—a longing to live juxtaposed with a surrender to God's will.

Just as he saw colors in a way few identify, Jason's artistic perception and physical struggle left him wise beyond his years. He floated above entangled emotions that bog many of us down. Receiving a death sentence at the age of eighteen only enhanced his gentle approach to life.

But I also knew the man who fought fear and didn't want to die. So as we stood together with family and friends, we declared the beginning of a journey we hoped would end soon.

But God had others plans. He knew what we didn't. That our first step of faith was one of many to come.

We would indeed walk out our faith day by day, moment by moment, and month to month. As we walked, we would grow. Stretch marks would form and we would tire. But miracles would dot the landscape and build a faith not yet our own.

Twenty-Three

I turn each corner never knowing what's ahead
I could be flying or facing what I dread
When I'm trying to make sense of it all on my own
I lose my sense of balance and feel lost and alone
So here I am, hold me close
Jesus come lead me home

"LETTING GOD LETTING GOD
Accepted, Track7

Back from the beach, the countdown begins. Sam leaves for college in six weeks. While I've found renewed balance with my walker and spouse, his departure symbolizes the end of an era. The empty nest looms and I'm not ready.

I want to wrap up our summer with a cheery red bow or herald the end with fireworks and carnival rides. But Sam's schedule is full and my body quite slow. So the countdown begins in earnest with little fanfare. Change is creeping my way and there's nothing I can do to stop it. Absolutely nothing.

From the day I became a single mom, I purposed to nurture my boys as they grew into young men. I weighed every activity against family time. A week apart unsettled their hearts, requiring focused attention once I returned. So eventually, I reduced outside activities to maintain balance and stability. After I married and my illness grabbed hold, most of my energy still remained focused on my boys. It had to. There wasn't much of it to pass around.

So when Nathan left, the change jarred me. I wept bitter tears, afraid they would never stop. Even though life went on and I adjusted in time, a similar sadness builds as I realize how little time is left with Sam. I don't want to cry that hard again. So I'm thankful Grandma needs help.

My dad's mother has lived alone in a retirement home for years. Increased dementia and an infection on her leg require added care, meaning we must move her from her apartment to the fourth floor. Not one for change, she laments our packing. The chaos only lasts a few days, but at the height of confusion, she balks. So we make jokes and keep things moving, hoping to calm her nerves.

The walker helps me traverse the long hallways but questionable looks make me want to shout, "It's mine. I own this walker. A granny walker thief, I. Am. Not."

Able to contribute to the three-day effort with less fatigue, I grow comfortable with the added support and tootle along with the other slow people. Within the halls of the retirement center, I fit in and compare my device with the assortment of models that pass by. I may not have grey hair, but I feel strangely at home with the elderly and their mobility aids.

With the furniture sorted and her new room arranged, we sort through Grandma's clothing. Having agreed to label every garment, I stop by after dinner one evening and empty her drawers one by one. She sits like a queen in her wheelchair, watching my every move. When I pile her underwear garments on the bed her interest piques.

"Do you wear all of these bras, Grandma?"

"Oh leave them alone. I may use them one day," she crackles.

"Are you sure? I don't think you need all these slips either."

I pick them up one by one, trying to weed out the nonessentials. Exacerbated, she finally blurts, "Oh just leave them all. You can have them when I *die!*"

Stunned and humored, I struggle for a respectful reply. "I don't want them when you die, Grandma. I can't wear your bras or girdles. They're not my size. I'm just trying to make everything fit in your new apartment."

"Well I want to go back to my old place," she retorts.

Unable to comply, I opt to label everything in her precious underwear drawer and let her be.

She doesn't like change either. She never has. I can't blame her though. From the day she moved into the retirement center, she knew that moving up to the top floor would indicate a downhill slide. While dementia clouds her reality, I'm convinced she still knows what the move means.

So while Grandma watches me with subtle disdain, I take it in stride. We're both adjusting to new realities, evolving from one phase of life to another. I feel her pain.

Her move complete, I savor moments with Sam before he leaves for a beach retreat for families affected by cancer. Although invited, I felt certain my red walker and I would be more of a hindrance than help. So I try to plan an outing with him, but time slips by. Busy coaching a swim team, my man-child has little time to soothe my apprehension. While I want to hold onto each moment, serendipitous, he is not.

Shortly after he leaves for the beach and my quiet house begins to taunt me, Laura takes Grandma in for a check-up. Her blood pressure registers low, so she's sent straight to the ER. When her stats fail to normalize, a doctor admits her to the hospital and we, the sisters, share the burden.

When I take a shift at Grandma's bedside the next morning, she starts showing signs of intestinal distress. A stool sample confirms C. difficile, forcing yellow infectious disease gowns to become part of our routine.

As a result of the infection in her leg, Grandma had taken strong antibiotics. The antibiotics upset the bacteria balance in her gut. The imbalance caused a highly contagious form of severe diarrhea, called C. diff, thus the yellow gowns. Upon entrance into her room, all visitors and personnel are required to cover their clothing to keep the bacteria from spreading.

Caring for Grandma distracts me from Sam's absence. Sleeping on a thin sofa in her hospital room tires me out. Hospitalized for a week, she repeatedly asks, "Where am I? When can I go home?"

As the infection subsides, Laura looks for a care facility that accepts C. diff patients. In time, the retirement home where she lives admits her as a patient to their nursing home, lockdown ward. Tile floors and stark walls limit our ability to transform her room into a cozy atmosphere. So we wean her belongings again, hoping she will be able to return to her fourth floor apartment in a few weeks. But she's disoriented, and so are we.

During meal times, nurses wheel her to a community room with several long tables surrounded by aging patients with blank stares and quirky behavior. There, nurses wrap a large bib around our style-conscious grandmother. The setting stirs deep emotion for all of us since every visit includes her litany of questions, "What happened to me? Why am I here? When can I go home?"

We write answers in a notebook since she can still read. But after ten minutes, she forgets the notebook exists and asks the questions all over again. So we answer them again. Over and over.

While we've been caring for Grandma, Sam has come and gone one more time. We managed to do some dorm room shopping while he was home. But in typical male fashion, he made the entire process low key—a gift for my tired body. The days sped by and he boarded a plane with my dad to the northwest, headed to Glacier Park by train for a graduation gift. Gone for another ten days, the eerie quiet suffocates me. So I escape again to see Grandma.

Parked near the front door, I pull out my walker and head toward the lobby. As I enter the building, my cell phone rings. Nathan's name appears on my screen so I sit on a bench and enjoy the unexpected call. We discuss his end-of-summer plans and debate when to move him from his summer dorm to his fall accommodations. The thought of seeing him lifts me from the doldrums.

Refreshed somewhat, a surprising ache grabs hold when my sister and her family walk by on their way to visit Grandma. Together, her family unit makes me long for mine. So when Nathan and I hang up, I sit like a statue, unable to move to where my sister's family is providing musical entertainment.

Fighting tears, I grab hold of my walker and head back to the parking lot.

Home. I want home. I need to sink into the quiet of my house and grieve the coming loss. There's no escaping the reality today. It's time to mourn.

A week later, we gather at my sister's home to celebrate August birthdays. Grandma seems to be on the mend, although still living on the lockdown ward. Sam and my dad are home from their train trip through Glacier Park with stories. For a moment, we enjoy the constant banter and teasing that binds us as family.

Grandma sits quiet, her dementia evident. But she's present, the matriarch of our crew, disheveled and regal all at the same time.

After dinner, cake and presents, Laura and I drive her back to her sparse room. Without aid, we search for fresh pajamas and dress her for bed. The woman, who once lifted our arms and pulled off our shirts, now lets us to do the same. Stripped of any remaining dignity, she doesn't flinch as we cover her bare chest, lay her gently in bed, and arrange pillows to her satisfaction.

There we linger, not wanting the moment to end. We sing a lullaby of sorts, read scriptures, and pray over her frail body. Now adults, we nurture our childlike grandmother like she nurtured us when our parents went on vacation and left us in her stead.

The tables have turned. The generations grown.

Within a week, the C.diff infection returns and Grandma's fight continues. A doctor prescribes more antibiotics along with an appetite stimulant and we wait and see. The aging beauty rarely eats and begs to be taken back to her room if we visit during meal time. In the confines of her own space she asks the same questions, "Where am I? Why am I here? When can I go home?"

Her questions resonate in me. I want someone to answer the same. As Sam fills our spare bedroom with boxes and his room empties, I wonder, "Where are we headed? Why am I here? When can my boys come home?"

I'm mothering my grandmother, and setting my son free.

The boxes soon fill our van and we wake early to drive to the city to move my baby into his new dorm room. When I hug him goodbye, I leave my youngest child near the heart of a metropolis, free to roam at all hours without a mom to interfere.

Just like before, the tears don't fall until I walk up the steps to my home. But once they start, I'm afraid they won't stop. Frightened by the stark quiet, I cry myself to sleep and wake to another round of tears and snot. A site to behold with nowhere to go, I call my friend, Reva.

She knows my story well—every detail. And just over a year ago, she lived her own faith challenge when her thirty-year-old son succumbed to sinus cancer. The bond runs deep every time we touch base and today is no different. While she doesn't cry on the phone with me, her grief is still evident. Connecting with one who understands eases the pain and offers a glimmer of hope.

I still cry after we hang up, but the utter darkness has lifted, the clouds are no longer quite so grey and menacing. Still, I nurse my wounds in the quiet of my home for another day.

When Don and I walk into the church lobby late for Sunday services the next morning, Sherrie walks straight toward me. As the head of our women's ministry, I know her from afar.

"I've been meaning to ask you something." she begins. "I lead a Bible study on Monday nights. We're a quirky bunch and I'm protective of those girls. But we were wondering if you'd like to join us."

Surprisingly, I don't hesitate. "Yes," I reply, "I'd like to come."

"Great," Sherrie continues, "I'll email you the information and we'll see you tomorrow night."

I haven't been a part of a women's Bible study in years, especially after being so hurt by well-intentioned believers. Surprised by my eagerness, the set up feels providential. While Grandma is on her way to glory and Sam is launching, maybe there's a new path for me.

Twenty-Four

I will lay my head and rest
A child of the King
I will lay my head and rest
Cause you are all I need
I will lay my head and rest
As your love washes over me
I will lay my head and rest

"LAY MY HEAD AND REST"

A few weeks after Jason and I led the healing service, our church readied for its annual summer youth camp. A highlight of the year, teenagers and counselors often left with transformed lives. With only days to plan, someone invited Jason to attend—to live in a cabin with youth and draw pictures for the daily updates. While I didn't like the thought of being alone all week with the boys, I helped pack his bags.

Miracles occurred at summer camp. If a week apart led to his healing, it was small price to pay. Or so it seemed.

Rain fell every day. Torrential rain. A Noah's ark, end-of-the-world type flood. Alone with the boys, fear rose. The "what if's" started talking.

What if Jason isn't healed?

What if our boys grow up without a dad?

What if I spend every night alone, without my friend and loving partner?

A few days into the week, one of my boys cried for his dad, stirring more fear.

How will I answer a similar cry if Jason dies?

How will I console my hurting children if their dad simply doesn't come home one day?

The week continued downhill from there.

Nothing went right. Friends and family struggled to provide comfort. Slowly sinking in the never ending rain, I agreed to share the cost of a hotel with my friend, Reva, so we could attend the last night of camp. My soggy soul needed an encounter with God.

At the camp, the boys and I found Jason after dinner and went on a short walk in a light mist. I longed to hear him report that a brain tumor symptom had eased. While he enjoyed the week away, praying with friends and soaking in good sermons, nothing drastic had occurred. Disappointed, our little family walked on a side street, facing the reality that a long journey lay ahead.

Nathan and Sammy fell asleep and someone offered to watch them so I could worship without distraction. Jason sat with the students from his cabin while I settled on the back row. As the speaker spoke, I struggled to pay attention to—let alone believe—his admonition.

While the animated pastor talked about God's love for us, I sat in the back, nursing the notion that if God really loved me He would have already healed Jason. It made sense to me. We needed one simple thing from the Almighty—divine healing.

We'd been told our faith would make a difference and we'd even held our own healing service. We'd waited an *entire* month for God to do something and camp seemed the perfect place for that something to happen.

I had so much to learn.

When prayer time began and we were invited forward to receive a touch from God, I sat in my seat, angry. Determined it was time for God to respond to our faith and heal my spouse, I refused to budge. Normally one to respond to alter calls with enthusiasm, I informed The Almighty that I wasn't going forward and that He needed to fill *Jason* to overflowing and heal *his* wounded body.

Hidden on the back row, the response I heard to my childish demands startled me, *"Is it not enough if I heal you, Susan?"*

The words rang clear as if someone had spoken them out loud.

While I had often obeyed inner nudges as divine guidance, I had never heard the still small voice with such clarity. Humbled by the grace filled response, I stood and walked to the front. After navigating the sea of people, I found two of our friends.

Forrest and Gary, Reva's husband, pulled up some chairs. Jason's good friends sat in a small circle with me as I rehearsed the events of the week. Every fearful moment. Every hurtful word said. In between stories, they prayed—for a long time—till I ran out of things to say. After one last time of prayer, a strange peace settled the storm, and I said, "I think I can go on now. I can face another day."

So we stood, embraced, and I left to gather my boys and drive to the hotel. It was only then that I realized the significance of the change in me. I felt a deep peace, a renewed calm, or simply put, the absence of the voice of rejection.

I woke filled with a sense of inner rest the next day and began to believe a transformation had taken place. A holy love quieted the gnawing insecurity that had plagued my days. I no longer had to say "I'm not rejected." I actually felt accepted.

As I basked in the change, Reva and I checked out of our room and drove to pick up our spouses. Excited to share my bubbling enthusiasm, I rambled on the drive home, encouraging my tired spouse. When I ran out of words, a song formed in my head:

> *His love is deeper than the ocean.*
> *His love is wider than the sea.*
> *And it's reaching down from heaven above to touch both you and me*

His love is warmer than the sunshine
His love is gentler than a breeze
And it's waiting here for everyone who will open their eyes to see

Jesus, thanks so much for loving me
Thanks for bringing your life on earth to die to set us free
Jesus, I want to the whole world to see
It's your love that brings peace and victory

Our pastor let me sing my new song at the coming home service that night. Performing my own music felt almost as significant as a symptom change in Jason's body. The comparison may seem strange. But having lived with little confidence in my words, the symbolic breakthrough was significant.

During the next three weeks, I wrote thirteen songs. The lyrics wouldn't stop. While one of those songs is recorded on a CD I made years later, most of them remain just words scribbled in a notebook. Yet every time I crafted lyrics into song, I knew I'd been changed. My creative soul had burst forth and drowned out my inner critic.

Even though I had known Jesus for a very long time, I had been at war to know the very essence of me. And while the battle would always continue, and skirmishes come and go, sacrificial love had overcome my doubt and insecurity and begun a transformation I had never even known to expect.

And that's what startled me most.

It was like an entirely different Susan had been buried for years and finally awoke. While I'd been aware that I wasn't living in the fullness apostles wrote about in the scriptures, nothing in my years in church prepared me for the dramatic change that occurred that night. A divine touch I can only call God's holy love, penetrated the place of rejection and infused me with peace.

In retrospect I understood the change began months before, when my pastor friend emphasized that I wasn't rejected. As the seasons changed from winter to spring and then to a blossoming summer, I'd mentally rehearsed the notion that God hadn't rejected me.

Then, on a warm summer night when I didn't think I could go on, I poured out my heart and prayed with my friends. While I wanted a concrete answer concerning my husband's fate, I left knowing I was loved instead. The God of the Universe had touched my soul and whispered change into the very essence of my being.

There was a stark difference between who I was—the rejected Susan—and who I became—the Susan loved by God. Scriptures took on new meaning:

> *"If from there you seek the Lord your God, you will find him if you look for him with all your heart and with all your soul"* (Deuteronomy 5: 29 NIV).

> *"If you seek him, he will be found by you…"* (1 Chronicles 28: 9 NIV).

> *"If my people, who are called by my name, will humble themselves and pray and seek my face and turn from their wicked ways, them will I hear from heaven and will forgive their sin and will heal their land"* (2 Chronicles 7: 14 NIV).

While God's word constantly refers to our need to earnestly seek the Lord so we can find Him, know Him, and walk with Him, I had underestimated his transforming power for years.

Once home, surrounded by diapers, food prep, and the daily mundane, I realized the breakthrough posed a challenge. Would I cherish the place of peace and trust, or cave to the fear and struggle we faced every day? Would I allow God's love to anchor my soul or sink as the storm raged round?

As the days went by, I understood I would have to fight for my soul. Our problems hadn't gone away. The brain tumor threat remained. But God had made the place of refuge real. It was my job "to hide in the shadow of his wings".

But how?

A simple answer emerged. When stress began to jeopardize my sense of peace, I closed my eyes and stated, *"I love you, Lord, and you love me. I love you, Lord, and you love me. I love you, Lord, and you love me..."*

I rehearsed that phrase over and over throughout Jason's illness. It served as mere stones I threw at our giant—our brain tumor giant. Emotions loomed large over us like Goliath who once threatened the Israelites. But David confronted their giant with only five smooth stones and a sling—and won.

> *"Then he [David] took his staff in his hand, chose five smooth stones from the stream, put them in the pouch of his shepherd's bag and, with his sling in his hand, approached the Philistine... As the Philistine moved closer to attack him, David ran quickly toward the battle line to meet him. Reaching into his bag and taking out a stone, he slung it and struck the Philistine on the forehead. The stone sank into his forehead and he fell face-down on the ground"* (1 Samuel 17: 40 & 48-49 NIV).

Goliath didn't go down without a fight, just like God hadn't chosen to miraculously make Jason's tumor disappear. We were at war, like the Israelites. And I wanted the courage of David; the ability to head toward our oncoming foe and attack, rather than crumble.

It sounds valiant and brave. But I really didn't have a choice. Two little boys needed a functioning mom. I could either cave into despair or sling verbal stones, fighting to bask in our Savior's love. So I ran after that love and channeled my emotions into song.

A few weeks after the breakthrough, my sister called. A pediatric neuro-oncologist from Duke University had contacted the congressional office she worked in, lobbying for brain tumor research funds. After mentioning our situation, the doctor told my sister to have us call him. He believed a new chemotherapy regimen might offer Jason seven more years.

His offer served as the answer to our prayers. Since the doctors in Nashville had offered little hope, we hadn't taken any steps toward medical intervention. We simply prayed for guidance. Now, a clear path opened and we walked forward.

After speaking with the doctor at Duke, we scheduled an appointment. Since Jason was originally diagnosed as a late teen, the pediatric physician was willing to take him on as a patient. While the idea of months of chemo felt daunting, the doctor offered so much hope that we couldn't turn down his gracious offer.

Love and hope. The two essential ingredients for joy became real in our home. Perhaps more so for me than my ailing spouse. But as his caregiver, it mattered. Romans 5 took on new meaning:

> *"We rejoice in the hope of the glory of God. Not only so, but we also rejoice in our sufferings, because we know that suffering produces perseverance; perseverance, character, and character, hope. And hope does not disappoint because God has poured out his love into our hearts by the Holy Spirit, whom he has given us"* (Romans 5: 2 – 5 NIV).

Within a month, we packed our bags, kissed Nathan and Sammy goodbye, and drove to Duke for the first of several appointments.

Twenty-Five

We're accepted, you and me
Accepted, in God's family
Accepted, though we'll fail
A thousand times
Accepted and loved
As His only child

"ACCEPTED"
Accepted, Track 3

I pull up the steep drive way, unsure. A room full of women I don't know lies just beyond the threshold. Cautious but in need, I get out of my car, lean on my cane, and walk toward the open garage. A handicap ramp leads to the entrance.

Twenty-four hours have passed since Sherrie's offer—enough time to bail if it weren't for the quiet oppression that lingers in my home.

I knock but no one answers. So I turn the handle, push the door open, and step into a small laundry room. From the laundry room I enter a kitchen that includes a cozy eating area framed by a bay window. Following the chatter, I turn a corner into a large den with a high ceiling and mirrored wall.

Friendly greetings calm me and I feel strangely at ease. Eyeing a chair across the room, I cross the grey carpet and settle into my place in the circle. Seated in a room full of relative strangers after hiding from women for the last several years, I'm surprisingly comfortable in my skin.

Sherrie, a skinny blonde with shoulder length hair, calls us to order. We start the evening with introductions and I begin to understand why I feel at home. Isabel, Sherrie's neighbor, starts us off.

After losing her vision due to a botched surgery years ago, the young mom with growing teens can't drive and remains dependent on friends for the smallest errand. Faith isn't easy for her, so she visits Sherrie every week and they work through our study together.

To her left, another skinny but tall blonde shares that her son suffered a stroke when he was five years old. While he recovered well, continued therapies, growing teens and marital stress keep her dependent on God.

Next in the circle, Lu and Bonnie sit side by side in their own living room. While it's somewhat obvious, I learn that Bonnie's arms no longer work due to the effects of ALS (Lou Gehrig's disease). While she can still walk some, the handicap ramp to the home allows easy access for her power chair. Her medical struggles trump mine, but as their story unfolds I know I've found a kindred spirit.

Bonnie married Eddie, Lu's brother, later in life but lost him to pancreatic cancer as her arms grew useless. Widowed and alone, she needed help traveling home after the funeral. Unemployed at the time, Lu offered her a ride but then never returned home. Now, she feeds her sister-in-law, takes care of her medical needs, and hosts our group every Monday night to center their faith. Sitting across from them encourages my own.

Next in the circle, Dionne shares that she's a retired teacher whose husband lost his job over a year ago. While it's evident she loves Jesus and prays with unusual boldness, dwindling financial resources stretch that faith and create conflict in her marriage. As a middle aged mom with unfulfilled retirement dreams, she comes to vent and focus on Jesus to keep her soul intact.

Next we hear from the recovering alcoholics, Somer and Shawn. Obviously close friends, Shawn explains that Somer was her sponsor in AA, thus they relate in a way few of us can. Somer shares her oldest daughter has spina bifida, reinforcing the sense that their stories run deep with redemptive scars. Their candid confessions add a rare depth to the group.

The short brunette wears a backpack that holds a feeding tube. Diagnosed with gastroparesis years before, she struggles to digest food—but not God's word. As the night progresses, it's obvious she knows His truth and lives it out despite her ailment.

My head spins as I explain mitochondrial disease, our newly emptied nest, and our blended family stress. Once overwhelming, my stuff now feels small, faded into the canvas of all of our lives. Refreshed by the array of struggles represented in the room, I thank them for inviting me and turn to the woman on my left.

Andrea, a kindergarten teacher, sits next to Sherrie. Recently divorced with two adult children, her pain shows. She doesn't explain much, so Sherrie finishes us off by sharing she's married for the second time, has one son, and battles blended family stuff like me. In fact, she's at her wits end, trying to find the God path through a maze of family drama and strife.

Introductions complete, we begin our study:

> *"I thank my God every time I remember you. In all my prayers*
> *for all of you. I always pray with joy because of your partnership*
> *in the gospel from the first day until now, being confident of*
> *this, that he who began a good work in you will carry it on*
> *to completion until the day of Christ Jesus"* (Phillippians 1:
> 3-6 NIV).

When discussion begins, I wonder if I've ever sat in a room full of Christ followers with so many physical, emotional, and spiritual needs. I soon consider that I've sat in a sanctuary full of people with serious life issues every week, just not in a place where those needs are honestly exposed. The transparency in the room strikes me.

No one ranks higher than another even though they come from all walks of life. Some have followed Christ since childhood, others for less than a decade. Some are married. Several divorced. But no one attempts to personify the perfect Christian life. The room is full of ragamuffins and they know it. Undone by their imperfections and life's complications, they gather to fill up for the remaining six days of the week.

And thankfully, I've become a member of the club. My need for them becomes all the more evident several weeks later.

It's late. I'm cooking dinner. And Don and I are trying to sort through difficult stuff. I want to feel connected, understood. He responds with rationale and object reasoning. It doesn't work and my insides tighten.

Boiling water cooks spaghetti noodles as we fight. So I move from the living room to the kitchen and he follows. When my threshold is reached, I state, "I can't do this anymore. I'm about to lose it."

But he ignores my plea.

As I pour steaming hot water and noodles through a colander, his explanation continues. Hot steam burns my face and clouds my glasses—and my judgement. Emotions peak and I lose control. Detached from rational thought, I reach into the bowl of hot pasta, fill each fist full, and fling the noodles into the kitchen. A few pieces stick on Don's glasses.

Broken, I survey the mess. Ashamed, I'm undone by my lack of control and weep.

Don announces he's heading out and I'm left alone—alone with bits of spaghetti noodles clinging to the cabinets, counter, and floor. After months of forward momentum, it seems we've hit a new low and shame runs rampant through my veins.

I clean the mess, hoping to wipe away the sense of failure that penetrates deep. My mom never threw noodles or anything else that I know of. None of my Christian friends have ever talked about having a spaghetti tantrum. And it's easy to remember I'm cleaning the same kitchen Don's first wife once cooked in; the wife that everyone remembers as a role model; the homeschool mom who poured herself into family and friends and resonated Christ in a rare, beautiful way.

I've driven my husband away and created a mess that paralyzes me. While I know it's not all my fault, crippling rejection makes me sink into my skin and burrow under the covers. In time, desperation forces me out and I head to my computer. My Bible study friends communicate via email at times and I know I need prayer. So I send an SOS through the internet and crawl back into bed.

My phone rings in the morning.

Sherrie's voice offers immediate empathy. Connected through the airways, I realize she doesn't think less of me. There's no judgement in her tone or words, only concern and the assurance that the God of Heaven still loves me. I don't know her story, but I get the feeling she knows. That she's been in my shoes even if she hasn't tossed spaghetti noodles in the air.

Her compassion soothes me. I'm not alone. Not a failure. And still welcome on Monday nights.

Later, my phone rings again. It's Somer.

"It's really no big deal," her perky voice asserts.

"No big deal?"

"Yeah, this kind of stuff happens sometimes. You just move on."

Her casual tone jars my intensity. Having been unable to move on from the vice grip of failure our marital strife has held on me, her perspective rocks my world.

"But I'll call you noodler from now on," she jests.

I laugh. For the first time since my outburst, I laugh.

Gifted with rare insight, Somer works as a rehab counselor. Her blunt, almost painful approach delivers discernment like an arrow to the heart. I've seen it in action on Monday nights. But her understanding comes from a hard life. A very hard life. And while I've never walked in the dark places Somer has, her words free me.

My new friend, who doesn't feel comfortable in big women's gatherings either, stirs the kind of life in me I've been longing to find. The recovering alcoholic speaks Christ's truth in a way that permeates my pride and perfectionist demands.

So when I show up on Monday night and take my place in the circle, I still belong. I don't shrink away in fear. Shame doesn't hold me back. I sit down as a sojourner in Christ, struggling to find the God path through the maze of crazy life.

Twenty-Six

Let me still my soul within you
Like a child with its mother
Let me still my soul within you
And cling to no other
For you are my hope, Lord
Both now and forevermore

"PSALM 131"
Accepted, Track, 10

A tall, arched window offered a view of the bright summer day as chemo dripped into Jason's veins. Nestled in a tiny room in the old part of the Duke University hospital, we were soothed by the antiquated architecture that transformed the exam room into a tiny sanctuary.

The drugs took hours to administer but after listening to doctors, nurses, and social workers map out our new normal, we valued the silence. The detailed layout provoked fear and raised questions.

How will we parent while dealing with chemotherapy? Will Jason be able to provide for us? What will our boys think if his hair falls out? How will we pay for it all?

While we hoped the chemo would serve as part of his healing, the IV drip of heavy drugs made our situation all the more real. So we did the only thing we knew to do when questions swirled. We opened our Bibles and read.

In the quiet, I remembered the word that had built in my spirit early in the week—*victory*. Shortly before we left for Duke, I'd spent some time journaling. As I wrote, the word *victory* formed in my mind and stayed.

It made sense to me. We'd fasted and prayed at the healing service. Holy love had transformed my soul at camp. Now a medical plan was in place so Jason could experience tangible healing. Even though the treatment didn't come with a guaranteed cure, we believed God partners with doctors to work miracles. So the divine could reach what chemotherapy could not.

When I connected those dots, I felt victorious and was ready for victory. Indeed, the previous twenty-four hours had worn us out.

A bedtime curveball followed our uneventful drive north. After enjoying a dinner out with a cousin who opened his home to us in Raleigh, North Carolina, we retired early, hoping for a good night's sleep. But that's when we saw them. Not just one, two, or three cats. No, *five* cats slithered out from hiding in the guest room. Unseen when we dropped off our luggage before dinner, the fuzzy creatures announced their presence. Highly allergic to cats, Jason downplayed concern and tried for sleep.

"Should we find a hotel?" I blurted, knowing cat dander could set off a bronchial spasm in a matter of hours.

"Don't worry," he replied, "I'll be alright. The ceiling is high and the room pretty big, so maybe it won't be a problem. My last reaction might have just been a fluke."

Convinced and exhausted, I fell sound asleep. When I woke the next morning, my spouse was gone. I searched the house to no avail and finally found him on the back porch. After spending the night in our car, he stretched out on the swing at day break.

I felt horrible and he sounded worse. An antihistamine helped but we worried that the doctor would postpone the chemo since he sounded so congested. With little time to worry and confident we wouldn't spend another night with the cats, we packed our bags and headed out.

A quick breakfast sufficed and after a few wrong turns we found the parking lot near the main entrance to the hospital.

Thankful that Jason would receive great care at the respected university, I didn't expect the walk from our car to the lobby to feel so ominous. But heavy strides led us to the main doors. As we navigated long hallways to the pediatric neuro-oncology department, reality supplanted my sense of gratitude.

Stepping into the office meant facing our giant head on. By signing his name at the check in counter, Jason entered us into the world where blood counts and fevers took on new meaning. With chemo running through his veins, our lives would be different—the elephant in the room quite large and on full display.

A cheery décor attempted to soothe concern, but we were soon surrounded by worried parents and sick children. Undone by their heartbreak, we eagerly stood when a nurse called Jason's name. We needed to concentrate on our battle at hand.

Led by the young professional, we entered the inner sanctum of chemo-land. Settled in a small room, she assured us they would go ahead with the chemo despite Jason's congestion. Since he didn't have a fever and we were far from home, she saw no reason to postpone treatment.

The minor victory lifted my spirit. Friendly personnel put us at ease. Then a nurse attempted to start an IV line and Jason's veins fought back. Dehydrated from the antihistamine, it took two nurses and five sticks to locate a cooperative vein. Bruised from the needle pokes, Jason trailed behind a nurse who then led us to the room with a view.

At ease in the safe haven with the cathedral like window, a team of professionals prepared us for what was to come. As the chemotherapy was administered, we were to watch for an allergic reaction. In the coming days, we could expect nausea and vomiting. Blood counts would need constant monitoring and fevers would require a trip to the ER. In time, Jason's hair might fall out, but with his type of chemo, it wasn't a sure thing.

After we signed several papers, another nurse entered with the bag of toxins and hung it on the IV pole. When it began to drip into his arm, they left us alone to process the daunting unknowns. And that's when we opened our Bibles and I remembered the word, *victory*. Feeling anything but victorious, I read:

> *"At that time the disciples came to Jesus and asked, 'Who is greatest in the kingdom of heaven?'*
>
> *He called a little child and had him stand among them. And he said, 'I tell you the truth, unless you change and become like little children, you will never enter the kingdom of heaven. Therefore, whoever humbles himself like this child is the greatest in the kingdom of heaven. And whoever welcomes a little child like this in my name welcomes me'"* (Matthew 18: 1-5 NIV).

Until that moment, I had never considered that by welcoming my children every day, I welcomed Jesus as well. While I still felt different due to the experience at summer camp, mundane tasks sometimes took their toll and I ached for purpose beyond diapers and dinner. Now blood counts and fevers piled onto the list.

Yet this simple truth held the next key. By welcoming my children, I welcomed Jesus. And by welcoming Jesus, I welcomed His Father. Since I wanted nothing more than for Jesus and His Father to fill my home with their peace that passes understanding and their wisdom that is foolishness to men, I only had to wake every day and welcome my boys.

Tending to my children took on new meaning. While simple, it felt profound. My thoughts led me to another verse:

> *"People were bringing little children to Jesus for him to place his hands on them, but the disciples rebuked them. When Jesus saw this, he was indignant. He said to them, 'Let the little children come to me, and do not hinder them, for the kingdom of God belongs to such as these. Truly I tell you, anyone who will not receive the kingdom of God like a little child will never enter it.' And he took the children in his arms, placed his hands on them and blessed them"* (Mark 10: 13 – 16 NIV).

Jesus valued child-like hearts. He even stated that the kingdom of God belonged to them. It made sense. More often than not, when my boys woke in the morning, they embraced the day with sweet, sleepy smiles. They didn't wake with worry and stress. A morning sky signaled time to play; the new day opportunity for adventure, not fear.

My children didn't question if we would have food for them. They didn't worry about how to pay the bills. They trusted their father and me implicitly.

As chemo filled Jason's system, I realized that if they trusted our ability to provide for them, then I should wake with an even greater trust in God's ability to provide for us. I needed to study and learn from their child-like hearts—hearts that woke with wonder, not worry; awe instead of angst.

Victory, indeed.

My mother heart buoyed, I turned to Jason who was wrestling with his own insecurities. Even though we sat in an office with other families in crisis, he felt utterly alone, like no one had ever gone through an experience like his. Logic argued against the irrational emotion but the feeling only dissipated after time in prayer in our tiny sanctuary.

A journal entry from that day mentions, *"God showed Jason how throughout scripture, people fought impossible situations. We are not alone."*

Noah built an ark. Abraham believed in faith for an heir until his wife had a child in their old age. Joseph was rejected by his brothers, sold into slavery, and yet used by God in his later years to save the very people who abandoned him. Years later, Esther dared to approach the king with a plan to save the Israelite's, not knowing if she would live or die. David fought Goliath, rescued his people from ruin, and then spent years on the run from jealous King Saul.

God rescued his chosen people from every dire situation with one grand conclusion in mind—Jesus. God's son hung on a cross, as the weight of the sin of world bore down on his soul and made a way for heaven—and us—to overcome every kind of impossible.

"He has sent me to bind up the brokenhearted, to proclaim freedom for the captives and release from darkness for the

prisoners, to proclaim the year of the Lord's favor and the day of vengeance of our God, to comfort all who mourn, and provide for those who grieve in Zion—to bestow on them a crown of beauty instead of ashes, the oil of joy instead of mourning, and a garment of praise instead of a spirit of despair" (Isaiah 61: 1 – 3 NIV).

The theme echoed again—we were not alone. We were part of a legacy of believers who believed in the face of doubt. Once home, we would have to partner together to keep the big picture perspective so our challenge wouldn't swallow us whole. But scripture promised beauty instead of ashes, joy instead of mourning, and a garment of praise instead of a cloak of despair. The cross provided a way for an upside down response to life's hardships, and we had a choice in the matter—a daily choice to make once home.

Living through the unknown with a child-like perspective would help. Pressing into the lineage that is ours in Christ would remind us daily to take up our cross and stand with the multitudes that have persevered in the face of suffering.

By the time a nurse pulled the IV out of Jason's arm, he felt good enough for us to begin our long commute. If we didn't hit traffic, we'd make it home shortly after midnight. So with nausea churning and meds to help, we started south.

With every mile, we left chemo-land farther behind. A sense of victory settled in again as I drove—even with a tired, drugged spouse in the co-pilot seat by my side. While he threw up once, we made it back to our small brick ranch in timely fashion and crashed till late morning. Ready for sweet hugs, we picked up our boys soon after and our new normal began.

Twenty-Seven

Now she's dancing, singing
Twirling about
She is safe in his arms
Laughing out loud
She is free from worry
Filled with delight
Everything is more than alright
She is finally home

"FINALLY HOME"

Almost a month has passed since Somer gave me my new nickname and I now sit in the Monday night circle, one of the gang. My cell phone rings, interrupting the closing prayer. So I wait to listen to the message until after I'm home and later regret the choice. Grandma's fallen—again. Watching her slow demise is hard on all of us.

Even after IV fluids and medicine to increase her appetite, she's fading day by day—the c. diff infection more than her 94-year-old body can handle. When I visit, she pines away, wanting to be moved from her bed to her chair or vice versa. Restless, she only nibbles at food and asks when she can go home. Watching her frail frame wrinkle like a prune leaves us longing for her ultimate release.

Skin, bones, and heart. That's all that's left of the woman who danced and cooked and served us well. How long must she suffer?

As my mid-October birthday closes in, Mom invites me to a performance by the Atlanta Symphony Orchestra and Chorus. When Dad mentions he's going to hear her sing with the renowned group the night before my big day, I agree to meet him downtown.

While I know the group is performing Verdi's *Defiant Requiem,* I am unaware that the piece is being performed in honor of the holocaust victims and survivors who gave it that name—until I take my seat. The program notes indicate recorded interviews with holocaust survivors and dramatic readings by local actors will accompany the composition that brought hope to a group of Nazi prisoners held at Terezin.

Fresh from a visit with Grandma, I easily imagine a chorus of hungry, tired prisoners, digging deep into a reservoir of strength only few choose to access.

Hidden in a damp cellar, they memorized Verdi's Requiem from a smuggled score and performed it over a dozen times in the course of three years—even as singers were deported to certain death. Their conductor, Rafael Schachter, told them, *"We will sing to the Nazi's what we cannot say to them."*

His leadership stirred hope, life, and defiance in the face of utter depravity and loss. I weep when the performers leave the stage.

As I drive home, three highlighted dates twirl my insides:

> The Terezin chorus performed the requiem for the visiting Red Cross on June 23, 1944. I married my first husband on June 23, 1990.
>
> Rafael Schachter was born on May 27, 1905. My first husband was deemed terminally ill on May 27, 1994.

The beloved conductor was then sent to Auschwitz
(where he died soon after) on October 16, 1944. Jason had
brain surgery on October 16, 1996 (Sam's third birthday).

While I try not to make too much of the coincidence, the
corresponding dates swim in the recesses of my mind. There I think about
the artists and singers, forced into a dank ghetto, who found nourishment
in the music, sustenance for their very soul, even as their bodies perished.

Memories surface. Jason memories I've tucked away. Though we
were never forced into hard labor and our situation pales in comparison,
we found sustenance in our faith, strength in my songs, and much
nourishment for our souls as we read scripture, discussed healing, and
refused to bow to the tyranny of illness.

For a moment I value myself anew. While I don't even sing on a
worship team now, my songs matter. If just for a moment in time, they
matter. They sustained me, and us. In the darkest times, they kept my
soul alive. And maybe, that's what matters most—simply having the
courage to face the odds and not cave in.

In recent years, I feel like I've failed. But I haven't given up. I
may not be the spouse and mother I want to be right now, but I'm
still fighting. Like those prisoners. Though weary and worn, though
forgotten and judged, I will fight to sing, love, and maybe even laugh.

Knowing the end is near, I visit Grandma almost every other day.
She continues to whither like grapes on a vine. I never want to leave
but must always say goodbye. Tonight it's especially hard.

I sing to calm her down as she reaches arthritic fingers into the air
and murmurs as if someone's there. She rolls my way and pulls at the
covers. They're too heavy for her to lift, but she tries anyway and shakes
her head when I ease her back onto her pillow.

"Dancing."

In the midst of her garbled speech, I hear the word *dancing*.

She met my grandfather at a dance and they square danced and
round danced their way through life. I wonder if she's seeing through
the thin veil and reaching for Grandpa's hand. Ready to dance, she
doesn't understand why I won't let her out of bed.

She calms down for a moment. But it doesn't last. When her movements intensify again and she fights for freedom, I call the nurse. After consulting with family, we encourage morphine.

The following afternoon, I listen to an inner nudge and cancel plans so I can visit Grandma again. She rests quietly as I enter, so I sing and hold her hand. Brushing my other hand against her cheek, I tell her how much we love her. Tired, I spread out a towel on the spongy floor mat next to her bed, and curl up. Sleep comes easy.

When I wake, her breathing seems labored. Uneasy, I'm relieved when my brother, Mark, walks in. He hasn't seen her all summer, couldn't face her decline. But his timing is good. We sit side by side next to her bed and sing.

A nurse stops by and says she'll be gone in 24 hours but I'm not convinced. Grandma seems to be fading with every breath. So Mark and I continue singing hymns and praise songs as her color turns to an ashen grey. Marked wrinkles crease her face and neck. Muscles relax with each exhale and her jaw drops awkwardly open.

Certain we're watching her die; my brother asks if we can sing The Lord's Prayer. I oblige and by the time we finish, Grandma has left her earthly shell.

Our family gathers, relieved and sad. Don even leaves the store early to join us. We tell stories, provoking tears and laughter. Mostly we reminisce about her heavenly entrance, meeting the King of Kings and embracing the dance partner she missed. Thankful they're together again, our group disperses—except for me and Don.

Determined to stay with Grandma's body till she leaves the retirement home, Don and I linger. Alone together, we wait for the driver. After dodging traffic, he arrives, and zips her form into a burgundy plastic bundle and we follow as he wheels her to the back of the medical research transport van.

The transfer complete, Don takes me to dinner.

After we order and we sit in the calm, tears begin. Only after the job is done do my emotions let down. While I loved my grandmother, the truth is, a tender place inside remains vulnerable to grief—the grief of losing a spouse so young. I live beyond it most of the time. But loss triggers the deep anguish.

Don watches with tenderness, aware that words often fail to comfort a sobbing soul. Instead, after the meal he asks if I want dessert—a chocolate dessert. Soon a three layer, icing smothered piece of chocolate cake adds the best kind of sweet to my bitter.

All is not well. But chocolate and my husband soothe the inner ache and I sleep.

It takes me several days to resurface. While I spent time with critically ill people in the years following Jason's death, in time, the task wearied me and mothering took precedence. However, living through Grandma's final hours opened closed mental files.

Walking someone to heaven's doors allows me to take part in what I consider a most hallowed, sacred task. The sacrosanct journey to the beginning of the beyond pulls me from the tyranny of the now and anchors me in the reality that is eternity's shores. Confident the afterlife exists, completely void of the darkness in this world, I once offered convincing hope to several in their last days.

Singing to Grandma as she was born into eternity roused the dormant gift I had buried with my grief. Offering hope to our matriarch worked that muscle again and in that way, her death led to my resurrection.

Grandma would like that.

When I return to Bible study a few weeks later, Sherrie hands me a gift box. Inside I find a large round ceramic candle holder. An indention in the top holds a votive candle and an inscription around the vase states, *"In memory of a Life so beautifully lived… and a heart so deeply loved."*

At home I place it on top of my piano with other unique gifts. On cold winter days, I'll light a candle—not just for Grandma, but for me. Her death stirred life and will shine on as I heal.

I write a song for her service. A song that ministers to my family. She is *Finally Home.*

Twenty-Eight

Hope Flies
Graceful as a firefly
Bringing color to our night
Letting us know
Everything is alright
Hope Flies
Grounded in a certainty
So when we just can't believe
Hope carries you and me

"HOPE FLIES"

Jason tolerated the chemotherapy quite well. He lost a small amount of hair, felt nauseous but rarely threw up, and never got an infection. His blood counts dipped low a few times, delaying his next treatment, but they always bounced back. Our income even remained steady enough that he surprised me at Christmas by booking a romantic Valentine's cruise for two.

On deck, light jackets kept us warm in the strong wind. As the ship left port, the artist narrated the view. Nuances of colors shaded the sky. A rusty, aging ship would have made a great painting. A giant sailboat stirred remembrances of his lifelong dream to sail. Amused, I listened as his childlike heart took in the world with ease.

However, no matter the thrill, the ticking time bomb in his brain left a twinge of bitter in every sweet. We longed to leave the heavy reality on shore as we drifted away, but gnawing worry lingered. Unlike other travelers who reveled in their freedom, we found a quiet place on deck to reminisce.

Six months into chemo, we recognized how much we'd grown. While our journey was far from over, our faith was indeed stronger. Numerous encouraging messages had come right when we needed them. Divine affirmations appeared when our hopes dipped low. Tumor symptoms remained, but as our understanding of God's infinite power and might grew, they intimidated us less.

The God who separated the sea and land and set the sun to twirl in the heavens could eradicate illness in a moment's time. But holding fast to that hope required concentrated time in scripture, a constant stream of worship music, and quiet time together away from worried looks.

Hearts stretched wide, we read about healing, talked about healing, and prayed for insight day in and day out. Yet when people complimented our stance, Jason often said, "Peter gets more credit. He stepped out of a sailing ship and walked on water. Our ship is sinking. We either step out or go down with the crew."

Not wanting to sink, we dug our heels into the life changing power of faith.

For instance, when my birthday grew close in mid-fall, and I still felt empowered by the new awareness of God's love for me, I invited family and a few friends over to celebrate. Instead of feeling a bit lonely on the day that marked my birth, I made corn chowder and muffins for my guests. After we ate, I shared my testimony and handed out long stem red roses as a reminder of God's love. Passing on the miraculous touch made it more real to me.

When our bank account almost emptied in mid-November, the boys and I skipped an afternoon outing and watched the movie *Chariots of Fire* instead. A friend had recently loaned it to us and while I'd seen it when it first came out as a young teen, I now viewed it from an entirely new perspective.

Worried about money and medical bills, I rewound the tape and transcribed my favorite part. Even young Nathan watched the movie several times with me, enamored by the runner's determined faith. While huddled under an umbrella in a down pour after a race, Liddle said,

> *"I want you to do more than watch a race. I want you to take part in it. I want to compare faith to running a race. It's hard, requires concentration of will and energy of soul. You experience elation when the winner breaks the tape. But how long does that last? You go home. Maybe your dinner's burned. Maybe you don't have a job. So who am I to say believe, have faith in the face of life's realities?*
>
> *I would like to give you something more permanent but I can hardly point the way. I have no formula for winning the race. Everyone runs in their own way. But where does the power come to see the race to the end? From within. Jesus said, 'Behold the kingdom of God is within you. If with all your heart you truly seek me, you shall ever surely find me.' If you commit yourselves to the love of Christ, then that is how you run a straight race"* (Chariots of Fire 1981).[5]

Overdue payments finally arrived, filling our bank account, but the pause in our norm allowed for focused attention on building our faith muscle. Opportunity came with every crisis. Would we worry or trust? Believe or cave to fear? We didn't always get it right, but with each crossing, the choice grew clear.

---

[5]   *Chariots of Fire*. 1981. DVD. United Kingdom: Hugh Hudson.

The ocean stretched far to the horizon on each side of the ship. Settled in deck chairs, enjoying the breeze, our smallness contrasted against God's bigness. There, we watched the sun set and the moon rise, and savored the rhythm of life. Moonbeams danced on calm, rippling waters. Stars dotted the night sky. Peace pressed in from the beauty around and we caved to its beckoning.

The following day we would live as tourists. As the evening hours passed on our first night at sea, however, we cherished the surrounding beauty as mere children of God.

Our ship docked in Nassau the following day. Before we set foot on land, we determined to avoid pesky merchants. But a certain young man derailed us with a bargain and soon seated us in his carriage, promising a tour of local landmarks.

Not long into the ride, I noticed a large Bible on the front seat. After he explained a few sights, I asked if he read it much. Darren, our driver, began spewing the gospel with an enthusiasm that surprised us. When we told him we were both believers, his excitement grew. When we further explained that Jason was battling a brain tumor, he pulled his buggy off the road, took our hands, and prayed for us. Right there in the Nassau Square.

As Jason and I wandered the market for gifts to take home, we valued the encounter more than sightseeing. Far from home, in another country, a buggy driver encouraged our faith. We would need the encouragement when Jason ran a fever two nights later.

It came on suddenly during dinner. Pale and clammy, he asked if we could leave early. When we reached our room, it was clear he had a fever. Chemotherapy protocol required medical intervention. So after calling the ship's doctor, we prayed—bold, loud, desperate prayers.

Within the hour, we received a call back from the clinic and met with the doctor. By then his symptoms had abated and his temperature was normal. One could argue we only thought he had a fever and overreacted. But having lived through the ordeal, we felt a divine rescue allowed us to enjoy the rest our trip instead.

We spent our last day on a private island, enjoying sand and surf. Jason still wasn't quite himself but his childlike nature had taught me to enjoy the sun and water. So I tried to lure him from worry into the light of the brilliant day.

As the afternoon waned, we walked hand in hand far down the beach from the crowds. Soon we would be back home and head off to another appointment with the doctor at Duke. The six-month check-up was part of the routine but the sobering reality weighed heavy even in tropical paradise. So we walked, wanting the moments to last forever.

After dinner, we took our place at the stern of the ship to watch the sunset. Colors stretched across the never-ending sky in a display of creativity man can only mimic. As the brilliant hues faded, we walked to the other end of the ship and watched a full moon rise. The extra-large globe filled the darkened sky as it peered over the horizon. Cooled by the slight breeze and enthralled by shimmering waves, we stood wrapped in God's glory.

We took our time disembarking the next morning, not wanting the magic to end. Once back home, we found some cheap tickets, allowing us to fly to Raleigh. Safe in the cathedral like chemo room, the poisonous drip entered Jason's veins again. Encouraged by how well he tolerated the treatment, our doctor continued his rhetoric of hope. Repeat scans were scheduled a few months out, but for a moment, all was well.

And we certainly didn't mind.

Twenty-Nine

Your laugh, your smile
Your grace
Like sunshine on a rainy day
The way you stood in faith
Kept us strong
When the storm clouds raged

"DEBI'S SONG"

Don and I linger till an almost empty sanctuary indicates we should leave. Relatively new to the church, we reach out, trying to meet new people. Little by little our lives have connected with others, enriching our own. Building community anchors us as we mold our hearts as one.

We joined the new church last summer due to my jangled nerves. When pastors we knew and admired opened the church five minutes from our home, I asked if we could visit. Reluctant to change venues again, Don hesitated, and rightfully so. In time, the close proximity and a warm welcome won him over. Sheltered in the walls of Sanctuary Church, we are finding a new groove.

The new church meets in a building that was home to a Baptist congregation for years. The aging community prayed that God would awaken a purpose for the building and property—even marched around the walls in fervent prayer. In time, Craig and Sonny—our pastors— stopped by, in need of a place to plant their new church. The duo met with the Baptist minister and a rare bond formed.

The traditional sanctuary has now been remodeled so we worship in the round. A circular stage sits in the center and on Sunday mornings, the worship band and singers set up on the floor around the stage. The pews lie in an octagon type pattern around the band. Thick, lace covered spherical tubes hang from the center ceiling to help with sound, and create a throne like atmosphere.

It's unusual but classy. By not focusing on individual performers, the leaders purpose to worship God in spirit and truth. It works for me. A traditional exterior hosts a contemporary interior. The old embraces the new and the blend feels apropos. For even before the fancy remodel, the first time I entered the building, I felt relief; God-centered in a new way. Eight months later, I'm still enjoying my new stride.

Wanting to serve, I taught fifth grade Sunday school over the summer. A cute girl with long blonde hair, named Olivia, stood out. Always well behaved, her innocent countenance drew me in. When she asked us to pray for her mom as fall approached, I suddenly knew why.

A recent list of church-wide prayer requests mentioned a young mom who was battling colon cancer that had metastasized to her liver. My heart went out to the family, but all the more so when I realized that the young mom belonged to Olivia.

On our last Sunday together, Olivia and I talked as we waited for her parents. When her mom walked in—the sick one with terrible cancer— her radiant demeanor floored me. Sparkling blue eyes complimented her shoulder-length, curly blonde hair. Too bouncy to be sick, I struck up a conversation with Debi and got her phone number before we left.

Within a week, she called me, "I'm going to a healing service tonight and wondered if you want to come with me."

Speechless, I froze in my seat. God had pulled a fast one on me.

"The church isn't that far from here," she continued, "and it's a really special time."

"I know the church you're talking about," I finally replied, "Don and I used to go there."

Someone had invited me to the healing service that takes place at the *other* church months before, but I turned them down. After trembling in front of the senior night crowd, I had no desire to go back. Besides, Sam had graduated and moved on from the youth group, giving me every reason to leave that chapter behind.

But the bubbling blonde wanted a friend to go to a prayer service. While fighting her own physical battle, she cared about mine. She didn't know about my past and the lingering hurt. She simply wanted me to trust God, step out in faith, and let others pray for our healing.

Her innocent request broke through my protective wall and I agreed to go. Days later, we meet in the lobby with the swirling carpet and sign in for prayer. A small crowd of Debi's friends have gathered. Olivia and her sister, Makayla, stick close to their mom. Both homeschooled, they long for a miracle with an earnestness I remember well.

As worship music quietly plays, we sit in the dimly lit, large auditorium, waiting for our numbers to be called. Snuggled close on a row of chairs, I feel like part of the family, soothed by their warm embrace. Apprehension fades into the bonds of acceptance. So when they call us forward to cross to the side where fervent prayers lift high, I walk with peace. Prayers offered, we take communion and leave.

Pride kept me away, now a friend has taken me in.

Don and I greet Debi and her family almost every week after church. Her constant glow amazes everyone. Independent and strong, she considers holistic options before agreeing to an aggressive chemotherapy regimen. Knowing tough decisions linger, weeks after my birthday I ask if I can stop by their home.

I held my own birthday luncheon for years—the one where I cooked corn chowder and muffins, shared my testimony, and gave out red roses. As time went by, they shrunk in size, and after I remarried they faded into the background of times gone by. Displeased with having let them go, I eventually decided to share my story and give out roses at least once a year—even without a party. Passing on His love needs to be part of my routine.

This year, I want to share my story with Debi and her girls—the story about how God's love changed me at youth camp and gave me what I needed to survive beyond my husband's illness. As much as the story means to me, it leads to treacherous ground since they're where I once was, believing God can do the impossible and eradicate terminal cancer.

I don't want to discourage their quest. But I long to honor the day God started a deep work in me by quieting the negative and making loud the voice of love. So I stop by. I share my story surrounded by soft yellow walls in a homespun kitchen, and our friendship deepens.

We talk several times a week, comparing doctor visits and kid updates. I enjoy our chitchat not only because she laughs a lot and offers down-home wisdom, but because she's managing a bad hand with amazing grace. Not only does Debi have cancer, her husband lost his job in the economic down turn—along with their health insurance.

Recently employed, their income stream has improved, but the job doesn't provide health benefits. They live on a tight budget and plan to sell a cherished tiny, farm home nestled in the North Georgia Mountains. Though grieving, she still smiles, laughs often, and rarely complains.

I want to believe Debi will be healed. But either way, I have a new church friend. One I will journey with, grow with, and enjoy. Walking close with another whose battle trumps mine minimizes the trial I face. Her fight to believe strengthens my own.

Thirty

Help me dream in color
Bout' what lies ahead
Help me dream in color
Like my Bible says
I want to see it clearly
Even on a cloudy day
So help me dream in color
Chasing all my blues away

"DREAM IN COLOR"
Accepted, Track 8

Our small brick ranch more than tripled in size when warmer temps welcomed us into our large fenced-in backyard. Jason hung a swing from a high oak tree branch so the boys could soar through the air. A small play set added additional swings with a slide that descended from a small fort. As we lingered outdoors, relishing the end to winter's hold, God continued to surprise us with divine encounters that let us know He was near. The most memorable began in a produce aisle.

Shortly after I pushed a buggy into my favorite grocery store one day, I saw a woman with dark, curly hair and two small boys at her side. For a split second, she stood out as if highlighted with an invisible glow.

And I had no idea why. Thinking my eyes were playing tricks, I went on with my shopping without offering even a simple hello.

For some reason, I stopped by the same grocery store the next day. When the sliding doors parted, I stepped into a scene from my own version of the movie *Groundhog Day*. The same woman and her children perused the same produce section as the day before. While the unusual encounter puzzled me, I was on a time crunch. So I offered a pithy greeting as I hurried by.

The same week, Suzette called, insisting I visit a popular Bible study. Mutual friends had introduced us since the young mother was battling aggressive breast cancer with chemo—and healing prayers. Standing in the trenches with a like-minded soul nourished us both. While we enjoyed phone time, she'd been insisting I try out the community-wide Bible study. Her persistence paid off and I finally agreed to attend—just once.

We sat on the left side of a rectangular shaped balcony, peering into a large sanctuary below. When the large group teaching concluded, a fifteen-minute break ensued and everyone headed to their small groups. Suzette motioned for me to follow her as she snaked her way through the front pew near the balcony edge to the other side. As we rounded the second corner, I came face to face with the woman from the grocery store and could hold back no more.

"I have to know who you are!" I blurted. "I saw you in a grocery store near my home twice last week. I'm supposed to know you for some reason."

She laughed shyly and introduced herself, "I'm Susan."

"Wait a minute," Suzette interrupted, "I know you. We go to the same church. You're in my Sunday School class—aren't you?"

"We sure are," Susan realized.

We didn't have much time to talk before the small groups began, so we exchanged phone numbers and agreed to be in touch. When the trio dispersed, I knew more than mere coincidence was at work.

A few days later, Suzette called, inviting us to attend Easter services at her church with Susan's family. Intrigued, I contacted Susan and learned she had news of her own.

"I told my husband about meeting you," she began, "and he thinks he taught your husband at a small Christian school in Jonesboro. Could that be true? Is your husband an artist?"

"Yes!" I exclaimed, "He draws pictures for a living. Hold on. Let me ask him."

With my hand over the receiver, I called back to my spouse who was busy at his drawing table, "Jason," I started, "Didn't you go to a small Christian school in Jonesboro for a few years during high school?"

"Yes," He yelled back.

"Do you remember a teacher named, Mr. Nolan?"

He hesitated for a minute and then offered a drawn out, "Yes... he taught science. In fact, he's the teacher who encouraged my art the most at the school. They didn't have an art program so he came up with creative things for me to do, like making caricatures of all my teachers for the high school year book."

I pulled my hand from the receiver, "Susan," I exclaimed, "He definitely remembers your husband. A science teacher, right?"

"Yes, my husband taught high school science," she returned. "And he's fairly certain he has some artwork that Jason did in a box in the attic somewhere. He's determined to find it tonight."

In awe, we finalized details of our upcoming get together and hung up the phone. My faith soared as if God had given me a big push on our backyard swing. My husband's art work sat in a box in the grocery store stranger's attic.

The divine intervention held meaning beyond what I could ask or imagine. Jason often struggled to feel his work held significance— like most artistic souls. So God sent a man, who not only lived down the street but remembered and valued his talent. It could be said his opinion mattered little since Mr. Nolan wasn't a famous art critic. But it mattered enough through heaven's eyes that a woman I'd never met became a woman I couldn't stop running into.

Our families gathered on Palm Sunday for fellowship and food. Suzette and her husband understood our journey well. And the older guy—the man who knew my husband before the tumor—added a comforting touch. Most of our young friends struggled to relate. Who could blame them? Hanging with likeminded believers unafraid to make a stand fed our hope, and it always needed nourishing.

Not long after, Jason and I drove home in separate cars. Strapped in car seats in our four door sedan, the boys rode with the artist while I followed behind in his blue truck. Half way home, Nathan wiggled out of his seat and turned to face me. Horrified, I laid on my horn, multiple times, trying to get Jason's attention. But he never heard the blaring sound.

Roughly ten minutes from our destination, I prayed—out loud. Once we were all safe in our drive way, I explained what happened and Jason realized that his hearing was going. The incident scared us both and made the upcoming check-up more poignant.

A repeat MRI and PET scan would soon reveal the tumor's status.

Within the month, we sat in a stark exam room at Duke University Hospital, waiting for test results. The doctor's report surprised us, "We don't see any change on the MRI and quite frankly we're not sure why you have hearing loss. It could be due to slight changes in the tumor our imaging isn't picking up or radiation damage from the treatment you received years ago. It could also be a side effect of the chemo."

Though we were at a top medical institution with amazing doctors and radiologists, no one knew the exact cause.

"My recommendation is that you stop the chemo for now," he continued. "The tumor isn't growing and we don't want you to lose more hearing."

Thankful there was no evidence of tumor growth, we still ached to hear someone say, "It's shrinking."

While stopping chemotherapy would ease our load, going forward without a treatment option felt unsettling. Left alone, I stated, "Well, I guess this is where God takes over for good. He knows why you have hearing loss and He also knows how to get rid of that tumor without the help of doctors."

With those words, I stepped off a ledge into a different realm of faith. Doctors had reached the end of their medical know how, which meant diving head first in the arms of the One who knit Jason together in His mother's womb. When I pondered it all with my child's heart wide open, I felt strangely encouraged.

Man had offered his best. But Jason's healing was—and always had been—firmly in God's hands.

Floating free from the constraints of man's logic and understanding, I felt buoyed by the One who died to set me free. It didn't make sense. But faith doesn't make sense and that's the point. Faith requires a leap from rationale, a child-like interpretation of events, and a steadfast belief that despite the hardships we face, a God of love reigns and desperately longs to hold us close even when we've reached our end.

Our ship was sinking. For the sake of my boys, I wanted to walk on water. New friends and a growing faith made that possible.

Thirty-One

But the sleep you lose
Is a small, small price
For the love that comes inside
There is joy for those
Who face the fear
With windows open wide[6]

"WINDOWS OPEN WIDE"
Accepted, Track 5

Nerve pain ricochets through my left ankle, wakening me. I limp gingerly to the coffee pot to allow caffeine to do its work. When the haze lifts, I know I need help. Surgical help. Stronger, I face it sans emotion and hope positive change awaits.

Before Grandma died, I saw the orthopedic surgeon who performed my first ankle surgery ten years ago. Needing help with knee pain, I was surprised when he pulled on my left ankle and stated, "You need an ankle reconstruction."

---

[6]   Levi, Allen "Open Windows", 1995.

Before I could detest, he drew a picture to explain the procedure. Aware that my health insurance company no longer outsourced ankle surgery, he couldn't perform the operation. Busy caring for Grandma and determined to try more physical therapy, I ignored the warning and pressed on. Days of denial over, the reality hits me head on.

I call, requesting a podiatry appointment in network. Much to my surprise, a doctor calls me back within the hour. After hearing my concerns, he connects me to a nurse who schedules an afternoon appointment.

As I sit on an exam table, he cups his hand around the back of my ankle, pulls lightly, and agrees with the other doctor. A reconstruction is unavoidable. He doesn't draw a picture, he explains that he will drill several holes and thread a cadaver tendon to replace my stretched out ligament, stabilizing the joint. Reality sets in.

The holidays are only weeks away and my third ankle surgery will take place in the midst of the chaos and celebration—like the other two. With surgical openings at a minimum, I drive home in a haze.

When the office finally calls, I refuse to schedule the surgery on Christmas Eve or to wait till late January when my mom will be out of town, unable to help. However, the only option left conflicts with family plans that have been arranged for months. After much debate I convince Don to go on the road trip with his kids and let my family handle the surgery.

Ideal, it is not. But since he'll only be gone a few days, I plan to ring in the New Year with a brand new cadaver tendon while he soaks in time with his crew. While a brace somewhat stabilizes my joint, I go into planning mode.

Since I spent months sleeping on the floor after the last two surgeries, I ask Don if we can purchase a new bed. A fancy sleep number bed. He agrees. So we pull out my walker and head to the mall one afternoon to try them out. We agree on the sale model with the allergy free, cushy top. Relieved, I thank my spouse profusely, excited that my days of sleeping on the floor may come to an end.

Next, I search for a knee scooter. With six weeks of no-weight-bearing required post-surgery, my upper body needs help. Crutches won't do. When I find one listed an hour south of the city, I ask Nathan to drive. Home for semester break, he agrees.

A Cracker Barrel breakfast keeps him going when holiday traffic snarls. Close to home after purchasing the medical device, we run a few errands. Excited to try out my new wheels, Nathan drops me at a department store before returning an item across the street. After making my purchase, I ride outside where long sidewalks tempt me.

Unable to sit still, I ride up and down the cement walk ways as a cool breeze blows on my face and tangles my hair. A setting sun provides the perfect backdrop for my evening ride. I haven't moved beyond a snail's pace in years; gave up bike riding at the beach long ago. So as I cruise back and forth, free from restraint, a forgotten sense of freedom envelopes me.

Like a kid excited to see Santa, my heart bursts with possibilities. Maybe I can do more. Go to a museum. Enjoy the aquarium. Race the cousins at the beach.

After Nathan picks me up, we stop at the grocery store, together. The wheeled device slides across the smooth floor, like ice skates on a frozen pond. One push of my foot provides the necessary momentum to roll from one end of a long aisle to the other. Feeling quite spunky, I pick up speed.

At the cash register Nathan comments, "Mom I haven't had to work this hard to keep up with you in years!"

"I know," I retort, "Isn't it great!"

Debi calls soon after, "My friend has a stair chair you can buy if you want. She'll sell it to you under cost."

"What a great idea," I exclaim. "Let me check with Don."

Steps lead to the front and back of our wrap around porch. Another staircase leads up from the basement garage. All quite steep and hard for me to manage, a ride-up chair would ease my joint load—before and after surgery.

My husband agrees and I'm relieved. Soon a metal chair will carry me from the bottom to the top of our basement stairs and right back down again.

Excited, I survey the dismal staircase that leads into the darkness below. Used to entering the house from the outside porch, I decide to transform the narrow, dingy pathway. After considering traditional options, a color combination grabs my attention—Bay Side and Moon Dance—a sea foam green for the stairs and a soft yellow for the walls.

Amused with myself, I waste no time. I scrub the stairs before Don comes home and balks at my choice, and paint them from the top down. As I near the bottom, our kitty, named Killer, shows interest. Staring defiantly from the top, she saunters down the freshly painted steps.

"No, Killer, no!" I exclaim.

Half way down, she freezes.

"Stay, Killer. Don't move," I continue, as if she'll respond to dog commands.

The gray feline, with the mismatched name, bolts up the stairs while I envision Bay Side cat prints all over my kitchen and living room floor. When panic gives way to action, I hop up every other step—on dry paint.

No prints. No mess. Deep sigh.

Olivia and Makayla, Debi's girls, come over for dinner a few nights later. While Debi and Carl go Christmas shopping, we hang out in my stairwell and paint the walls, transforming the cavernous hallway into my very own "Sunshine Alley".

Good with a paint brush, their help proves invaluable. Together in the tight space, we laugh and carry on. I'm facing a surgery, but their mom has started hard-core chemo. Terrible mouth sores inhibit eating and the cold hurts her nerve damaged hands. Wracked with side effects, her bright-blue eyes still sparkle and she strives to maintain traditions and keep life normal.

Makayla opens up, "You believe Mom will be healed, don't you?"

Dressed in paint-covered old, clothes, my thoughts collide. Diving deeper than the stair well, I can't pause for long. I don't want my doubts to fuel her own.

"You remember my story, right?" I ask.

Makayla keeps painting, so I go on, "I'm the one whose husband died and now I'm married to a man whose wife died."

Nervous, I look her way. She just listens, so I weigh every word, struggling to speak truth that won't snuff out hope.

"The thing I'm totally sure of is that God's love is bigger than all the hard stuff we face. He certainly can heal your mom. I don't doubt that. But after praying a lot for my first husband's healing and then living through life without him, I'm a little gun shy when it comes to saying someone will or won't be healed for sure."

Deep down, I feel like a traitor. Having stood in her shoes, I want to believe for a miracle with her and trust God to do the impossible. I want to be her friend in the fight, not a force to contend with. I don't want my future expectations of God to only be defined by my experiences of the past, but it's hard to step out from what I know. So I try another tactic.

"Put your paint brushes down for a minute," I insist. "Come sit in the living room. I'm going to do a dramatic interpretation for you."

I feel strangely vulnerable as I lead the way. "You might think I'm crazy," I begin, "but I want to share a passage of scripture that my boys and I memorized years ago. It's one of my favorites. Sometimes we yelled it at bedtime. Together. And it helped."

They look my way with blank stares, unfamiliar with someone yelling scriptures out loud for therapy—especially Old Testament passages with highbrow verbiage. Aware that passionate outbursts were normal for me, my boys understood, But Makayla and Olivia don't know me that well.

As I shuffle around, working up the courage to do what I haven't done in years, the sisters just wait.

"Okay. Are you ready?"

"Sure," they contend.

Standing up straight, I strike a theatrical pose and begin as if quoting a dramatic Shakespeare monologue:

> *"Do-you-not-know? Have-you-not-heard? Has it not been told you from the beginning? Have you not understood since the earth was founded?"*

I continue with unusual authority and hand motions, *"He sits enthroned above the circle of the earth, and its people are like grasshoppers. He stretches out the heavens like a canopy, and spreads them out like a tent to live in. He brings princes to naught and reduces the rulers of this world to nothing. No sooner are they planted, no sooner are they sown, no sooner do they take root in the ground, than he blows on them and they wither, and a whirlwind sweeps them away like chaff."*

Beckoning my young audience, I bellow, *"'To whom will you compare me? Or who is my equal?' says the Holy One. Lift up your eyes and look to the heavens: Who created all these? He who brings out the starry host one by one and calls forth each of them by name. Because of his great power and mighty strength, not-one-of-them-is-missing.*

Memories surface and I slip into family mode, *"So why do you complain, [oh Nathan]? Why do you say, [oh Sammy], 'My way is hidden from the LORD; my cause is disregarded by my God'?"*

And then as if sharing the best news one could hear, I thunder, *"Do-you-not-know? Have-you-not-heard? The LORD is the <u>everlasting</u> God, the Creator of the ends of the earth. He will <u>not</u> grow tired or weary, and his understanding <u>no one</u> can fathom. He gives <u>strength</u> to the weary and <u>increases</u> the power of the weak."*

On the home stretch, I relax, remembering the favorite adage, *"Even youths grow tired and weary, and young men stumble and fall; but those who hope in the LORD will-renew-their-strength. They will <u>soar</u> on wings like eagles; they will <u>run</u> and not grow weary, they will <u>walk</u> and not be faint"* (Isaiah 40: 21 – 31 NIV).

As my recitation comes to the end, I picture a determined Sammy on a top bunk and an emboldened Nathan on the bottom, yelling the same words with all their might. Makayla and Olivia look a little startled, but humored. Our family tradition may not mean as much to them as it means to me, but yelling words of hope with dramatic flair empowers my faith.

Debi and Carl arrive and our evening comes to an end. The stairwell almost complete, I forget thoughts of surgery and focus on the busy holiday week. Presents need to be wrapped and meals planned. Like Debi, I fight to squeeze as much life as I can into the moments we're all together.

A few days after the grand holiday, our new bed arrives. After one night of enhanced rest, Don leaves with his family and I head to my pre-op appointment. On the way home, I pull out my scooter and glide through a few stores, hoping to find reasonably priced bedding.

After several stops, I almost give up. A short rest refuels me at home, so I try one last store. Post-holiday stock limits my choices so I consider something different. Surprisingly, I come face to face with my dream quilt.

A few years earlier, Don booked a weekend stay at a fancy resort for my fortieth birthday. In the bedroom, a beige and red quilt contrasted nicely with light-blue walls. A bit radical for me, the color scheme stirred emotion. I felt happy, alive, and free—like I feel riding my scooter.

Now I hold a similar pattern in my hands. Burgundy red flowers accent a beige background. I stare at it with longing and run my hands over the packaged quilt. Turning it over, I gasp at the name—Cassie—my grandmother's name.

Don and I inherited Grandma's bedroom furniture, complete with glass table top coverings that protect crocheted doilies. The deep cherry dressers add a richness to our room. Unable to walk away from the find, I find pillow shams to match the king size set and head straight to the check-out counter. The attendant gives me an additional 25% discount and I drive home triumphant—with the Cassie quilt.

Before I leave for surgery, I transform our bedroom walls from beige to blue. The fresh, light color blends nicely with our white trim. The dark furniture looks stately against the light hue. And the freshly washed Cassie quilt completes the change.

While a tad feminine for his manly ways, Don affirms the quilt's deeper meaning. Married for 61 years, my grandparents left a legacy. Filling our bedroom with remembrances of them awakens longing. When I return home to Don's care, we'll continue building our legacy, standing on their shoulders.

By the time I'm wheeled into the operating room, the vital transformation allows me to relax into the process and embrace another round of brokenness that should lead to wholeness. With the help of family and friends, color has entered my world in the places I needed it most.

Thirty-Two

It's as if a million butterflies
Have gathered at my door
Each a blessing to me
And all the joys and all the sorrows
I have brought to each tomorrow
Flutter soft on their wings
All my worries fade
In colors bright as sunshine
Oh my life is sweet
Why should I be pressing time

"RIGHT HERE RIGHT NOW"
Life of Love, Track 11

As the weather warmed, we enjoyed more time outdoors. With a hefty push, the boys swung high on our tree swing. Delighted squeals turned to calls for more when the pace slowed. And I could relate.

In early June we acknowledged the one-year anniversary of our faith journey. Both slowed by the heavy reality, Jason and I decided to take advantage of time away when he was invited to youth camp again. In need of forward spiritual momentum, we went our separate ways.

With the boys too young to participate in camp, I accepted an invitation to visit friends in North Carolina. As Jason drove east, I headed north. After visiting for a few days, though, an unexpected restlessness seeped into my soul. I ignored the inner yearning at first, but when it grew stronger, I followed its lead.

"Are the mountains far from here?" I asked.

"It's a little drive but not bad—a few hours at least," Ruth, my hostess, replied.

"This may seem odd," I explained, "but I feel like I need to drive to the mountains."

Knowing better than to question my resolve, Ruth waved goodbye as we pulled out of the driveway. While I didn't always understand God's work in my life, by that point, I knew better than to resist a Holy Spirit nudge. Destination unknown, I followed the inner urging and drove to the mountains.

Hours later, I saw a sign for a familiar place, Montreat, North Carolina. I hadn't visited in years so I pulled off I-40 and drove to the college campus and retreat center. Ready for action, the boys and I walked familiar paths and eventually rented a canoe for a ride on Lake Susan. Centered in the heart of the campus, we rode across the calm waters, enjoying their rare vantage point.

Memories flooded in.

When my family attended the Christian Life Conference in Montreat, my sister and I enjoyed a rare type of freedom. Within the confines of campus, my parents let us roam, unchaperoned. Youth activities kept us busy. So while we met up at meal time, we spent much of our day traipsing around campus, with an occasional mountain climb thrown in.

In time, my dad coordinated the conference, making me feel like a minor celebrity.

"Yes, I'm Bob Snelling's daughter," I would answer with pride.

By the time he took the reins, we knew most of the attendees from Lay Renewal events. So not only was the environment family friendly, it felt like old home week among those who participated in renewals throughout the year. Gathered with our faith family, we grew close to

God, watched the Wimbledon Finals after Sunday lunch, and celebrated the Fourth of July.

On the far side of the lake, to the left of the dam, Jason had slid the light-blue, sapphire ring on my left hand. A year later, we arrived at the conference the day after he proposed. Excited to announce our engagement, we showed off my ring countless times.

As the boys and I drifted on the water, I was overcome with thankfulness for the spiritual truths that grounded me at a young age. The relationships and experiences molded me into a dedicated Christ follower. While my recent dive into faith healing theology felt like a far cry from my Calvinistic roots, I recognized anew how much I valued the people who made hope in Christ real to me. Without that hope I wouldn't have been able to endure our year of waiting.

Our rental time elapsed. So we left our canoe and climbed a steep set of stairs to the lobby of Assembly Inn. There, I found a pay phone and on a hunch looked up the number of one of my favorite renewal couples. Soon after I dialed, they invited us to stay for the night.

Retired in Hendersonville, NC, not far away, they attended most of the Lay Renewal teams my dad coordinated. Even though I hadn't seen them in years, they greeted us with warmth—and dinner.

Conversation turned to Jason's tumor and my enthusiasm concerning faith and healing made them somewhat uncomfortable. Terminal illness talk stilted most discussions, but when I prattled on about expecting a miracle, I sounded more like a delusional mom ensconced in denial than a faith filled believer overcoming great odds.

While I loved being with them, I felt uneasy when we went to bed. Nestled in the foothills, I felt thankful for my past in a new way, but sensed there was more. So when I woke the following day, I asked if we could stay one more night. The aging couple agreed to my whim and gave me directions to the entrance of the Blue Ridge Parkway. Noted for its scenic mountain beauty, it seemed the perfect day trip. We'd drive an hour or so into the mountains, eat lunch at an inn, and head back, hopefully satisfying what stirred inside.

As morning nap time approached, I strapped the boys in the car and headed out. Asleep within minutes, I didn't want to disturb them by asking for directions when I couldn't find the parkway entrance.

Hoping for a road sign, I drove on and found a major highway instead. Following that inner nudge, I got on.

With no cell phone, GPS, or even an old fashioned map, I simply drove. At times I argued the sanity of my choice. But alone with sleeping boys, I felt buoyed by a presence I'd learned to trust. Since the worst case scenario involved turning around and driving back the way I came, I stayed the course for well over an hour.

About the time I considered turning around, advertisements appeared indicating The Great Smoky Mountains lay only a few miles ahead. Excited, I took what looked like the main road and headed further in. Our options expanded. The Cherokee Indian Reservation and a place called Santa's Land appeared to be close by. So I followed the signs, opting for Santa's Land—an amusement park for small children.

As we wound through the thick forests, I saw another sign for the Blue Ridge Parkway. Making a mental note, I determined to drive back to Hendersonville via the alternate route. But before we left for home, we spent hours eating hot dogs, riding mini-roller coasters, and enjoying the feel of Christmas in the midst of a hot July.

Nestled in the heart of The Smokey Mountains, I felt secret success. I didn't know why God had sent me there, but as my boys played and ran free, it didn't matter. Away from stress and our normal routine, we enjoyed the afternoon outing.

When the park closed, we buckled up for our two-hour drive. I filled my tank at a nearby station and drove to the Blue Ridge Parkway entrance. As we ascended into the hills, the late summer sun began to set. We continued skyward till mountain top scenes came into view.

When we passed a mile marker that stated, "The highest point on the Blue Ridge Parkway", I pulled over. At 6047 ft. elevation, I stood in wonder. For days I'd heard the holy whisper of God call me to the mountains. Now, without even following a plan, I stood at the highest point on the parkway. Looking out to the horizon, the moment felt surreal.

I'd questioned my motives and the sanity of my choice to keep driving after missing the original turn that would have led me only part way into the foothills. But by following my heart, without a map of any kind, I stood on the high place, more certain of God's work in my life than ever before.

We couldn't linger due to the long drive ahead. So we buckled again and drove toward the setting sun. Spectacular views greeted us around every corner. Colors lit up the sky, enhancing each panoramic scene. Lost in wonder, I felt Him speak:

> *"Stepping out in radical faith, expecting a miracle, stretches what you learned growing up—perhaps even seems too risky. But by following the path I have for you, I will carry you to higher places in me. Like today. If you had followed the directions given to you, you would never have made it to the highest point on the parkway. But you listened to me and the view is yours to enjoy."*

The only thing missing was my spouse. Without cell phones, several hours lay ahead before I could share the wonder and glory that buoyed me as I drove. Close to the clouds, the brain stem tumor seemed small, doable, far from the impossible. God's bigness spoke possibility and stretched my heart wide, offering a big faith push forward. As His love surrounded me in colors and spoke peace to my soul, I grew confident that the God of Wonders could heal my husband at any moment, at any time.

Hope swelled, busting the confines of fear.

An hour later, we passed Mt. Pisgah, the place we had originally planned to visit. While still high in the mountains, it wasn't nearly as high as the mile marker we'd already passed. Our descent continued as surrounding colors faded into the night sky and we arrived at my friend's home a little after dark.

They expressed worry while I overflowed with joy. My day in the mountains affirmed my need to follow the Holy Spirit's leading. My sea legs had found a stronger rhythm. And I was ready to go home.

Thirty-Three

What have I to dread
What have I to fear
Leaning on the everlasting arms
I have blessed peace
With my Lord so near
Leaning on the everlasting arms

"LEANING ON THE EVERLASTING ARMS"
Life of Love, Track 4[7]

I wake from anesthesia to concerned looks. Not only did my ankle need reconstructing, the doctor sewed up an inch-and-a-half split in a tendon. Photographic evidence taken during the surgery explains why I've battled pain since spring. Recovering from both procedures will take patience and time, and more help from friends.

I exit the hospital with my mom after a two-night stay. She drives me to her house. With Don busy at the store, my dad gives up his side of the bed so I can nestle in my parent's first floor bedroom. There,

---

[7]   Showalter, Anthony J., and Hoffman, Elisha, "Leaning on the Everlasting Arms", 1887.

I begin to heal with free entertainment from Lily, my mom's King Charles Cavalier, who offers her version of comfort that often includes a persistent need for play.

As I grow more comfortable on the scooter, I chase her down the hall till she cowers under my dad's desk. Feeling triumphant, my momentary thrill fades when she begs to go outside. Stationed in front of my parent's back door, she gazes earnestly with big, round eyes. When I cave and open the door, she shrieks with a piercing bark reserved only for her back-porch-freedom-run. After flying across the planks, she tears off down a steep flight of stairs. Safe in her backyard domain, she runs with abandon. Trumped, I watch from the sunroom as she traipses around, declaring herself queen of the green grass.

Envious, I long to run free, to chase the birds and squirrels before splashing in a lazy creek. So I live vicariously through my sister dog and chase her on my scooter into Dad's office again when a mischievous bent won't fade. Amused, I eventually coax her from hiding and we cuddle on the couch.

Debi calls, "Are you up for a visit?"

"You don't need to drive this far, Debi," I protest. "We can talk on the phone."

"Nonsense," she contends, "The girls and I want to come see you."

Still on chemo, Debi's hair has started falling out, and the side effects make everything hard. With school and daily chores, I hate for her to drive the distance to see me. But she insists.

Propped up on pillows, although not enough to convince Debi I'm comfortable, we sit in my parent's room and chat. Her blue eyes still sparkle, and her girl's innocent demeanor allows us to talk without interruption. She's hunting for a wig and filling out forms. Lots of forms.

A local hospital offers aid to those without insurance, but their help requires a ton of paperwork. Overloaded, Debi still needs to encourage others. Focused outward, she stays positive. Her presence in the room reminds me to do the same.

In need of a testimony to write for a local paper, I call Somer. Propped up on the same pillows, I listen as she shares her life story. Something about her draws me in. Though extremely different, we passionately love the same Jesus. While one could say I've walked a more virtuous path, I feel one with her. Not better. Not above. But rather the same.

Debi reminds me to live beyond myself. Somer reminds me my righteousness is filthy rags, leaving me desperately in need of Jesus like every other human walking the earth. I don't like my circumstances. But neither does Debi—or Somer for that matter. So we seek to overcome, together.

As my two-week check-up approaches, Bonnie and Lu offer to help. Mom drops me off at my sister's home for the night, and the spunky duo picks me up mid-morning. Since Bonnie can still walk short distances, I settle in the back of their mobility van while she rides in the co-pilot seat. Short in stature, Lu navigates the interstate with focus and calm—despite Bonnie, the backseat driver.

When we arrive, they walk in, sit in the lobby and wait patiently as my stitches are pulled. Then we ride through a fast-food joint and picnic in the car. My friend with ALS and her caregiver spend the afternoon listening to my concerns and frustrations—barely mentioning their own.

Warmed by the love of friends, I later crawl up my front porch steps to spend one night in my own home. Christmas lights still shine from the front porch railing since Don never unplugged them and the holiday glow feels apropos.

Sam calls and asks if he can stop by with his new friend, Courtney. Anxious to visit with his female comrade, I encourage the social call. The following afternoon, we sit in my newly painted bedroom, complete with the Cassie Quilt. The cute red-head makes conversation easy, so I tell embarrassing family stories like a typical mom. Sam obliges with unusual calm, and I grow suspicious.

Young love has lassoed my son.

As evening approaches Sam and Courtney make their leave, and Don drives me back to my mom and dad's home for a few more days. But I don't stay too long. I'm ready to get back to my routine.

The hand controls in my van make driving possible, but getting up and down the entry stairs in my house remains virtually impossible. So once home, I stay put and watch too much TV until Don carves out time to install the stair chair. When I ride my Princess Chair up and down Sunshine Alley, I value the change and yet grieve the need. Each new mobility device still helps and hurts.

As week four post-surgery nears, my days end in exhaustion, and I grow tired of the scooter. But a decrease in pain assures me the ankle is healing. Longing for distraction, I'm thankful when Sam calls, "Would it be okay if I come by and practice making a heart-shaped pizza?"

I stifle a giggle, "A heart-shaped pizza?"

"Yes, it's a surprise for Courtney."

Ah, Courtney. My suspicion was right.

"Sure," I reply, "Feel free. You know I love having you here."

I watch as he molds pizza dough into a heart and layers it with toppings. Satisfied with the results, he packs up the ingredients and necessary dishes and drives back to campus. The heart-shaped pizza must have proved a success because within a few weeks he calls again.

"Mom," he starts, "do you have time to talk?"

"Sure. What's up?"

"I want to marry Courtney... before the end of the year."

Mother alarms blare, echoing loud in my heart. Defenses engage.

"Are you kidding?" I wail. "You haven't even been dating for three months!!"

"Can we at least talk about it?" he insists.

When I accept he's totally serious, I agree to a Sunday afternoon sit down and then call his, older, reasonable sibling.

"Have you talked to Sam?" I ask, hopeful.

"No, why?"

"He wants to marry Courtney—before Christmas," I blurt, anxious for him to jump on my worry train and talk sense into his brother.

"Really?" he replies with genuine surprise, "By Christmas?"

"Yes. I told him to wait at least until next summer, but he's quite persistent. Will you talk to him?"

"Sure, but I doubt there's much I can do." And he's right. Even level-headed Nathan can't talk Sam down from the marital ledge.

I like Courtney, but hardly know her. The thought of them marrying in the middle of their sophomore year stresses my entire system. I married young, so I'm not completely against lovebirds marrying in college. But Sam has hardly dated before now and certainly never gave me any impression that he would commit this soon.

Within days, Courtney and Sam arrive for our Sunday afternoon get together, essentially asking for our blessing. I don't have one to give. So I voice questions, concerns, fears, and doubts while the strength of their young love remains undaunted. Together, they face our dismay without flinching.

My youngest wants to leave the nest for good.

Safe in my Bible study circle the next day, I share the news during prayer request time. My new friends listen with appropriate concern and promise to pray. Debi and I chat on the phone soon after and she expresses more excitement than worry. She married young too and asks, "What's the big deal?"

When I meet with my parent's a few days later, they just smile and remind me that choosing a mate in a promiscuous culture is a respectable choice. Feeling out-numbered, I inch towards understanding.

As my initial fears abate, I start physical therapy and begin walking on the stiff joint. The workouts tire me more than I expect. So when Sam and I go at it again via a phone call one afternoon, an epiphany bridges the divide.

While recovering from a hurtful encounter with a distant family member years ago, a young Nathan fell through a fire pole exit high on a playground and broke his elbow in several places. A long cast stretched almost to his shoulder. Ironically, his fall occurred only two days before we were to attend a gathering that included the individual that caused him pain. When I asked what he wanted to do, he thought for a moment, plopped his big cast on the table and stated, "Mom, my broken arm is this big."

Then, while holding his hands the same distance apart, he continued, "Seeing (that person) is this big."

Then, after stretching his arms wide open, he stated, "When you put them together, it's just-too-big."

His wisdom surprised me then and made it easy to honor his heart.

As I struggle to explain my emotions to Sam now, I remind my younger son of the story we all know well and conclude, "Learning to walk on my ankle is a big task right now. Trying to wrap my brain around the fact you want to get married in a matter of months is even bigger. Together, they're just-too-big. And I can't handle both at the same time."

When he doesn't balk, I plead, "So give me some space. I'm not saying, 'No.' I just need time to think and pray while learning to walk again."

It works. He agrees to wait on my answer and I'm able to focus on the matter at hand. Thankful for the reprieve, especially when a stress fracture forms causing more pain, I limp forward with the help of my friends.

Bonnie and Lu drive me to more follow-up appointments. Dionne, another Bible study friend, fills in when Bonnie and Lu have a conflict. Ann even takes a shift one day, now that her husband is much stronger.

When I learn that Nathan will perform in *The Magic Flute* as a last minute substitute, Mom not only agrees to drive the distance, she plans to share a hotel room to make it easier on me. Comfortable in a handicap seat with my foot propped on my scooter, I watch him sing, certain I've lassoed the moon.

The road to healing still stretches out long and wide. But in between activities, when life slows and my ankle throbs, Debi calls to chat. My boys may have launched, but God is actively filling the void.

Thirty-Four

Lord send me a touch of you
I long for so much more
The fullness of your spirit
Bringing riches to the poor
I want to know and love you
Every moment
As the days go by
Oh Lord have mercy
And hear this sinner cry

"TOUCH OF YOU"
Life of Love, Track 6

I arrived home from my mountain top experience, hoping Jason felt revived as well. Fresh from youth camp, he had stories to tell. Traces of the divine remained evident, but we both longed to see our faith made real—or a mere hint of his miraculous healing manifested. In the coming months, we wavered through the ups and downs, craving stability in the storm.

Journal entries from that time illustrate the struggle well. Some days I wrote, triumphant:

"Today I begin my second journal and believe it will be a very different book than the last. The last book is a constant cry for change, for understanding, for Jesus—All I need! I believe those cries have been heard and that God has graciously taken me to a new place. The double-mindedness has been replaced with a much steadier focus on Him and His promises.

As we lived through the Holy Week, leading to Easter, I was struck with the wide range of emotions the disciples must have experienced during those days: joy, grief, shame, guilt, sorrow, amazement, wonder, salvation. When Christ rose and revealed Himself to them, their faith was cemented forever.

Jason and I have experienced many of the same emotions during the past eleven months. One day, I believe, we'll live our 'Easter Sunday' and witness a tangible victory that can never be taken from us. I don't know how long we have to walk. But I know there's victory at the end of this path."

While Easter proved a high point, at other times, my confidence crumbled:

"I'm always amazed at how mundane tasks weigh me down. Dishes. Laundry. Supper. Finances. Potty training. All these realities make me approach Your word with heaviness and a lack of expectation. Forgive me for allowing these petty trials to take my joy—but our medical debt is overwhelming. Please touch our finances and release the burden. I can hardly keep the house going and kids happy, let alone balance a check book and budget."

Breakthrough would come and my heart would overflow:

"Yet again, another victory. I got through the afternoon wonderfully! My house is relatively neat. We ate a decent meal. The lawn is almost mowed. And mostly, the still small voice reminded me that the key to victory lies in a constant *surrender of myself to Him. He doesn't need my praise—it's my offensive weapon."*

Then the roller coaster ride resumed:

"The same struggle continues. It's like I'm running a twenty-mile race and losing stamina at mile seventeen. It feels like we're close—very close. Yet the emotional burden is almost unbearable right now. Silly things affect my stability and today I was sobbing again. I feel like there's a wall between Jason and me. How I long for Him to feel God's peace and to know it's there to stay. Just tonight he said some men prayed for him and he was disappointed that nothing happened—that God didn't do enough. I almost felt angry with him, but why should I? Look at my attitude!"

A movie escape lightened my tone:

"Sometimes it's awfully hard to wait. But my heart feels light and secure after watching, 'The Sound of Music' today. If I can stay anchored in positive thoughts, I'll be fine. But now and then I want to hop into the movie and run free into the mountains."

At times, we truly felt alone in our battle. As time wore on and we continued to trumpet healing, conversations grew awkward. As a young, idealistic couple, others concluded we were facing a terminal diagnosis with utter denial. Behind closed doors we fought the reality every day.

When the boys were sick, in need of inhalers, we prayed late into the night. Time spent on our knees ushered in breakthroughs with their health. So when someone stopped me in a fast food joint one day and asked how we were doing, I said, "We're getting good at casting out colds. We just haven't conquered the brain tumor yet."

And I was totally serious.

At my yearly GYN appointment, unexpected, excruciating pain left me curled in a ball. Sent to the ER, I waited alone, quite scared.

When Jason arrived, we cried out to the God of Heaven for healing and after a short time, something flipped in my lower abdomen, releasing the pain. Having endured a few kidney stone attacks since that day, I'm fairly certain that was my first. But when my doctor later shared that she had planned to do exploratory surgery on me, I left convinced God saved me from an unnecessary operation.

Expecting friends for dinner that night, I saw no reason to cancel. As I cooked, I felt like Peter's mother-in-law,

> *"When Jesus came into Peter's house, he saw Peter's mother-in-law lying in bed with a fever. He touched her and the fever left her, and she got up and began to wait on him"* (Matthew 8: 14-15 NIV).

I attended a song writing seminar and left quite disappointed that my songs didn't meet industry standards. Scheduled to sing The National Anthem at a ceremony the following day, I longed to hide rather than step into the spotlight. However, when I showed up, my sister explained the occasion had escalated into the weekend press event for the Speaker of the House, Newt Gingrich.

As my sister, the Speaker, and I discussed the order of events, a crowd of reporters circled tight around us. When I stood to sing, I faced a host of TV cameras. The day before, I'd felt like a big musical nothing. While I wasn't on the news or touted for my rendition of The Star-Spangled Banner, as I walked to my car, I heard, *"At the right time, my child, I can do anything I want with you. Trust me. Trust my timing. Trust my plan for your life—for Jason's life."*

In mid-September, we received a call from a woman who was praying for Jason's healing. She encouraged us to attend a faith healing conference scheduled not far from our home in a few months. While we didn't believe a person's level of faith was the only basis for healing, we did believe that standing in faith allows God to do abundantly more than all we can ask or imagine. So when I had a vision of lightning as our friend talked about the weekend away, we decided to go.

196

Combining the conference with a couple getaway made it an easy choice. Two months later, we packed out bags and drove south.

The weekend away without thoughts of chemo or worries about kids gave us rest on several fronts. But when we entered the auditorium the last day with no miracle to claim, we felt letdown. Inspired teaching and abandoned worship with enthusiastic believers encouraged our radical stand. But we ached for healing, for the assurance that Jason wouldn't die, but live and declare the goodness of God.

As we sit in a large, civic auditorium under a gamut of speakers and wires, the teaching began.

> *"Listen, my son, to a father's instruction; pay attention and gain understanding. I give you sound learning, so do not forsake my teaching. When I was a boy in my father's house, still tender, and an only child of my mother, he taught me and said, 'Lay hold of my words with all your heart; keep my commands and you will live'"* (Proverbs 4: 1-4 NIV).

Enthralled, I scribbled in my journal:

> *"Give The Word attention. Keep it in front of your eyes. The Word is life unto us and health to all our flesh. Store up the Word of God so it will overflow. As long as living water pours out, trashy thoughts can't come in. So operate out of the overflow… Divine health requires living day by day, hour by hour, staying in touch with God. God has always healed his people. He wants his people well."*

A roar of thunder interrupted the speaker and shook the building. Rain began to pour.

I looked to Jason and said, "That's my lightning!! It's like my vision. Something must be about to happen."

A second rumble reverberated across the ceiling, but sounded more like a train. The force grew strong, then abated, and then raged toward us again. A large swath of the ceiling tore away at about the same time

I realized a tornado was overhead. Frozen in place, we looked up and saw wires and speakers dangling against the dark sky.

Our speaker began to pray, and led the group to rebuke the tornado and command it to be still. As rain poured into the building and participants put up their umbrellas, she then preceded to teach.

No one ran. No one screamed. An army of believers put their hands in the air, prayed bold prayers, and stood their ground.

It was epic. Totally epic.

In time, building personal requested that we leave the auditorium and ushered the large group into another area with cement floors and concrete walls. Again, no one ran. No one pushed. The crowd left in peace.

The teaching ended, but the speaker insisted on praying for everyone who asked for prayer. We waited in line, received prayer, and left with little fanfare. The following day, the local newspaper reported that the tornado left a path of destruction that ended at the civic center. Our prayers had conquered the spiraling foe.

> *"They were terrified and asked each other, 'Who is this? Even the winds and the waves obey him'"* (Mark 4: 41 NIV).

Sometime later we were sitting at a Wednesday night church supper when a tornado alarm sounded. Everyone emptied into a long, windowless corridor. Some battled fear as the storm raged, others waited it out. I hovered against the wall, remembering the crowd of people who stood boldly against the storm, demanding the winds calm. Crouched on the floor, I wondered why the group didn't think to pray.

The contrast saddened and emboldened me. I may have sounded like a lunatic, believing for my husband's healing, but so did Jesus. He claimed to be the Son of God. The divine come to earth, born to save the world. He healed bodies and broken hearts. He raised dead people to life and often stated that faith allowed for the miraculous. Those who exhibited rare trust in the divine benefited from their faith.

While I didn't know what miracle we would or wouldn't experience, I grew quite confident that God died and rose again for us to live with a far more active faith than our over-churched society has grown accustomed to.

We valued our church family. Their love and support helped. But we grieved that few could comfortably stand with us as we prayed for Jason to live and father the boys he greatly loved.

When yet another member of our church died of a brain tumor shortly after Christmas, we visited a more charismatic congregation, planning only to avoid the sadness for a time. But Jason liked the faith driven teaching, so we stayed. We left those we loved and joined those who—right or wrong—fought the fight in a more overt way.

Shortly after we visited I wrote in my journal again, *"Jason quoted something not long ago that fits us both: 'We are fighting to see ourselves as God sees us—not how everyone else sees us.'"*

And maybe, that was the biggest challenge of all. Could it be that seeing ourselves as God sees us would prove the biggest miracle of all? To know the love that surpasses knowledge? To feel accepted in our failures and uniquely crafted souls? To wake with a sense of approval from heaven just because we're His creation? To weave through all doubts and insecurities with the assurance that Jesus is on our side, working all things for our good?

Could that be the greatest miracle of all?

Only time would tell.

Thirty-Five

When we walk through that door
We're never turning back
Traveling down a different road
Another winding path
Saying goodbye
Holding memories so dear
Life can seem so funny
Without our daddy near

"EXTRAORDINARY GIFT"
Life of Love, Track 12

Luggage and coolers cover the kitchen floor, but my boys don't seem to notice. Sam sits behind his computer at the table, finalizing an engagement ring order. Fresh from Europe with a host of memories, Nathan is unpacking and repacking in a jet lag haze. If we can get ready, we'll leave for our last nuclear-family Florida trip. But distractions abound.

A day after we return from the beach, Nathan leaves to work at a summer music camp for six weeks. Two days later, a neuro-surgeon will fuse two disks in my lower back. While I'm healing, Courtney will return from ten weeks abroad and Sam will propose. With the summer dispersion at hand, I just want get out the door so we can connect for a few days in the sun and sand.

Precious family time is slipping away.

Shortly after demanding time to process Sam's desire to marry, my good ankle grew weak. It was then that I realized life wasn't going to serve up stress-free time for me to ponder Sam's fate. It didn't matter. A barrage of information came my way in the form of three Christian magazine articles on the benefits of marrying young. Recent research confirmed the advantages of committing to another early in life with real life stories supporting the evidence.

The stories rang true. So as my thoughts swirled after my ankle surgeon refused to reconstruct my right ankle until someone dealt with my back, my vulnerable heart strings fell prey to Sam's explanation, "Mom, I may not be able to walk when I'm forty. So I want to marry young, have kids, and raise a family."

With my history and our similar diagnosis, I couldn't argue. It helped to learn Courtney's mom had grilled her too. As a nurse at the famed Shepherd Spinal Center in Atlanta, Gloria had firsthand experience with mitochondrial disease. Knowing she'd specifically asked her daughter if she was ready to raise a child with the potentially life-threatening disorder put me more at ease.

While I wasn't certain Courtney and Sam knew what they getting into, I married a man with a brain tumor and wouldn't trade the heartache for a simpler life. So as I drove to several doctor's appointments, and heard three specialists encourage me to go forward with back surgery, heaven seemed to whisper, *"Let go, Susan,"*—like the night my strong-willed, second-born child, dove into the pool with breathing issues and purple hands. Nervous even then, God assured me I could let Sam go and trust him to the one who put the stars in place. Banking on that promise, I gave my blessing on their marriage and focused on my health—and now our trip to the beach.

The pile in our kitchen grows as I add grocery bags full of food. Sam finalizes his order. Bent on creating something his sweet heart will treasure, he studied designs with intrigue. Today his efforts pay off.

With a final click of a button, the order is complete. My son will soon propose and begin plans for a Christmas wedding.

Today, I would simply like to see and hear the ocean.

As the boys lug stuff to the van, the skies open. A deluge pours and a bolt of lightning hits so close I scream, and they laugh. If we'd gotten our act together earlier, we would have beaten the rain. But not this year. We drive south under a line of storms.

Soaking in the moments, I long for them to last. Our last threesome family trip has begun much too quick. It's not that I don't like Courtney, I just wanted to make more memories before my boys took off. But my body betrayed me, and they can't wait for me to stabilize. Adventures must be lived—with or without mom.

I manage well in their absence. In fact, Don and I have found a new rhythm with the lighter schedule. But when they come home, memories surface. Lots of sweet memories. As I drive through the pouring rain, facing the unavoidable juncture ahead, I pass the miles, remembering how far we've come.

We forged a rare bond when their dad died. Determined to personify the best of their dad in my parenting, I sought to model the heart of a child. Yet from very young ages, my boys had an uncanny ability to offer grown-up insight at the right time—especially Nathan. As I stooped to their level, they often spoke to mine.

"What happened to daddy's body when he died?" Nathan's four-year-old self asked only a few weeks after his dad left earth.

Not wanting to explain cremation, I didn't answer right away. So Nathan continued.

"I know," he started confidently, "I bet angels have big pockets and an angel came down to earth from heaven and put Daddy in his pocket, and carried him away."

Relieved I exclaimed, "That's right, Nathan. An angel did come down from heaven. I felt him in the room that day."

Thankful to avoid the truth for a few more years, our conversation turned to thoughts about heaven. In true form, Nathan and Sam offered unique insight.

"I bet rainbows are big slides in heaven," Nathan stated. "And when you slide down them, Jesus catches you at the bottom."

"I bet you can play the music real loud and no one will ask you to turn it down," Sammy contended.

Days later one of them explained, "I bet nobody gets angry in heaven. Everyone's happy all the time because there are so many toys you never have to share."

"I think stars are windows to heaven," I decided, "And at night, your daddy can watch over us so he's never far away."

Creative theology soothed our inner ache. As we relished our mere glimpse of what heaven was like, we grew confident that Jason was happy, healthy, and safe with Jesus.

Still, one night, I cried bitter tears. Alone in the wee hours, I feared they would hear my sobs. So when we drove to school the next morning, I reminded my boys that rainbows grow from the perfect combination of sun and rain. Then I added that if mommy cried sometimes—like last night—it was okay because Jesus would make a rainbow from her tears.

That very afternoon, as I talked on the phone in the kitchen, Nathan came running from the backyard, "Mommy, come look! It's your rainbow!"

Hovering right above our yard, a tiny cloud reflected the perfect array of colors on a blue sky, sunny day. Nathan had not only learned the lesson, he recognized God's promise floating right above our home.

And that's how our life together continued. It was never easy. I lost patience with my boys on many occasions. But I apologized a lot, and we stayed a team.

"Want me to drive?" Nathan asks, interrupting my thoughts.

"Sure," I reply, aware of my limitations.

After lunch at an Arby's in Eufaula, Alabama, he takes the keys and slips in behind the wheel. The metal bar that attaches my hand controls to the accelerator limits knee space for the tall men in my life. So Nathan adjusts the seat and squeezes his knees in between the levers. A few miles down the road, rain pours again.

"Do you remember the time we ran through the parking lot in the rain and the car door wouldn't open?" I ask.

"Yes," he moans, not fond of the memory.

On the eighth anniversary of Jason's death, I tried to fix dinner but gave up. Hungry and foggy-headed, I drove in circles way too long before choosing to eat at a Chinese restaurant close to home. Relieved our bellies were full; my fun mom persona surfaced. When a downpour stood between us and our car I said, "Let's run in the rain. It's not that far and we'll make a memory. And I need us to make a fun memory today."

Moans emanated from my growing teens. But they quickly resigned themselves to my antics, "Okay, I'll do it," Nathan replied. "But only if I get to hold the keys."

"That works for me!" I replied.

After handing over my keys, we counted to three and took off for the car. Ironically, when Nathan reached the vehicle and pressed the unlock button, the locks didn't respond. As rain soaked through our fall clothing, he pushed the button several more times. Realizing the remote device must have shorted out in the rain; he thrust the controls at me and ran around the car with his brother. Soaked to the skin, I waited a moment and then unlocked the door with the key—setting off the car alarm.

Since I had no idea how to turn it off, we sat safe from the storm in waterlogged clothes, as the alarm wailed into the night. Desperate, I called my dad, the former owner, hoping he remembered what button to push. He didn't. Stuck in the howling vehicle, I felt like my hair was on fire.

As time passed and misery set in, I decided to drive our screeching machine to the concrete overhang in front of a near-by Home Depot. There, a group of men came running and set out to fix my problem. Unable to find another way, they cut some wires, disarming the sound.

Amused by the adventure, I chuckled. The boys moaned. But I didn't mind. A memory was made. A new year begun with an anniversary alarm.

A similar deluge slows our progress today. A detour diverts us around a bad wreck. Water fills the highway and the windshield wipers barely do their job. But we are together, in the storm, like so many times before.

A year-and-a-half after the car alarm fiasco, I arrived home from a salon with my hair dolled up like a Disney princess. Having naively trusted a hairdresser to create an up do for my wedding without a trial run, I walked in the door overwhelmed. With no time for a shower and redo, I called my sister, considered my choices, and went into action.

Hunched over my bathroom sink, with my boys flanked on either side, we pulled out the numerous bobby pins that held my sticky hair in place. Frantically working together, we brushed out the plastered strands. In time a natural curl evolved that looked perfect with my understated tiara, and I looked like me instead of a cartoon caricature of myself.

I couldn't have done it without them. In fact, there are countless moments where their presence saved me.

Now Sam wants to marry, and I'm grasping for more, wanting to know that our family has arrived at this juncture intact. I'm finally finding my way out of the darkness and they're ready to fly. It hurts. I feel robbed. I want more memories, more fun, and more connectedness.

But Sam can't even stay the entire week at the beach. He'll fly home early to coach a summer swim team. Together for only a few days, I soak in their presence as the rain pours down.

We arrive long after dark, slowed by the storms, but the boys know the routine. Bags pile high on a cart, and soon our belongings spread across the unit we'll call home for a week. There, cousin camp begins.

Over dinner the next night, the family grills Nathan about his recent European trip. Not only did he plan the trip with two friends, he booked their hostel stays and served as a tour guide during their almost three-week stay.

As I listen to him detail their journey I hear the voice of a young man who took on the world with confidence. My son doesn't need more time with mom. He just navigated through seven European countries with few mishaps. The painful reality frees me.

While I've scrambled to piece myself back together, he's been emerging into adulthood just fine. While I've been longing for us to make memories, he's been out in the world, making his own. And maybe that's how it should be.

Settled, I perk up when conversation turns to Sam's upcoming engagement and my brother, Mark, jerks to attention, "What? Sam's getting married?"

Laughter erupts. Mark often claims he's the last to know, and tonight it's quite obvious. His stunned look captures everyone's emotion—especially the cousins.

"When did this happen?" he demands. And the story unfolds.

Even with the best explanation, Mark's demeanor doesn't calm. Watching him come to grips with the unexpected news amuses me. His surprise speaks for us all. While we delicately danced around what we feel, Mark stumbled in full force, calling out the elephant in the room.

My son is getting married. The idea fits like a shrunken garment. Given time, the idea will stretch to a comfortable size. It's his life. We'll adjust. My boys are ready to grow up, and it matters little whether I'm ready to face the change or not.

A few days after Sam flies home, an idea is born. Nathan and the cousins, Trey, Drew, and Josh, decide to make a music video. On the beach. Buried up to their necks in sand.

I join with my sister's family, digging the hole and burying the crew. Trey stands well over six feet, so achieving the task is no small feat. When only their heads show, we find colorful buckets to serve as hats. Their eyes squint in the afternoon sun, but they sing their barbershop song as camera's roll.

Filming requires several takes. The song is pitched too low. Hats slide off in the slight breeze. A three-year-old boy approaches with fists full of sand. The weight of the sand leaves them short of breath.

But soon another memory is made. The Bucket Head Singers have video proof of their antics and later serenade tourists under the stars on the streets of Baytowne.

The days pass too quickly, and we start packing to leave. Life will separate us soon. So it's time I let go of the 'what ifs' and the things I wish I'd done. There's no going back, only forward. As I survey the ocean one last time, I know they're ready—and so am I.

Thirty-Six

Why does this pain wash over me
Feelings so strong I can hardly breathe
When his blood was shed to set me free
Well, I don't know, I don't know
I don't know why I fall so low
But God's own mercy and his grace
Will carry me to a better place

"RUNNING THROUGH THE HURT"
Life of Love, Track 7

I turned to wait for Jason on the far side of the library and felt my knees buckle. After voting in the primary election, I looked on in dismay as he struggled to cross the room. Wide steps combined with awkward arm motions, and I knew.

"Your balance is going, isn't it?" I whispered in disbelief.

"Yes," he confirmed.

Balance and vision. The nerves that controlled both lay on either side of the tumor. If the mass grew, doctors warned those symptoms would announce the change.

We walked to the car in silence. His arm wrapped around my shoulder to ease the cumbersome strides. Minutes that felt like years ticked by before we found words to fill the screaming void between us.

At home, our small ranch made it easy for him to hide the change. By running his fingers lightly across a wall, he hid the distress, even from himself. But out in the wide-open world, there was no hiding the struggle. Our date night turned somber.

Taking refuge in his favorite Mexican restaurant, we took time to adjust. An MRI would follow soon enough but after months of stability, the tumor suddenly announced it was winning. As we tried to eat, we decided to investigate the Brownsville Revival—a God movement that was changing Pensacola, Florida.

My aerobics instructor originally told us about the revival. Aware of Jason's tumor, she gave us a recording of a service from what had become known as The Father's Day Out-Pouring. After praying for months, God's presence had enveloped the Assembly of God church on Father's Day, the summer before. Nine months later, thousands of people attended services that lasted from seven to almost midnight, six days of the week. Many experienced a "miraculous" touch of God, which drew worldwide attention.

With nothing to lose, we soon left our boys with Grandparents, booked a hotel, and drove south. By four in the afternoon, we stood in a long line that stretched from the front door through the parking lot. After chatting with people from all walks of life for hours, we entered the large sanctuary, filed into a pew and waited with expectation.

We were not disappointed.

Over an hour of worship felt momentary. Enthusiastic believers engaged in worship with unusual fervor. Hands raised as voices sang strong. We didn't simply watch a performance; we joined together as one voice, honoring the God of Heaven.

Five hours passed. Personal ministry followed a sermon, and we watched as people fell to the floor and shook all over the building. The same thing happened the next night. While we were both touched, before the service started our last night, I wrote,

"We've experienced two nights at Brownsville and something really fun is going on here. But I don't want to write about the manifestations of the Holy Spirit we've seen, I want to write about total surrender to God. As much as we've 'lived by faith', I've been challenged by the notion of God's sovereignty. I want to go home with a healed husband. But if God chooses to wait on his physical manifestation of healing, I want to go home trusting the all-powerful, all-knowing God who sees and knows our faith. I'm not surrendering my fight for healing, but rather letting go of the how and why, like floating in an atmosphere with no gravity, trusting His care, His love, His ability to take care of my children; His ability to carry us through whatever comes. It's a humbling of self. That's what's happening here, within the walls of this church, there's a humbling of self. The goal isn't healing or prophecy. The goal is abandoned obedience that allows the supernatural to flow in whatever way the Lord desires."

Jason left the church the same as he'd come. But we'd seen God move in crazy ways. We didn't understand it all, the shaking, the falling, or the intense presence that flowed. But we were desperate for His touch no matter how He wanted to show up.

Soon after we returned home, we visited the prophetic church we'd been to before, seeking direction and encouragement. Before the Friday night service ended, the prophetic team prayed over us. While they spoke many beautiful prayers over us that night, this part stood out a few weeks later:

"I see that God is actually going to send you on a trip and I see that there's going to be a very powerful testimony that is going to even usher in the presence of God in that situation."

When Jason's parents gave us money for his April birthday, we decided to take a family trip back to Pensacola with plans to hang out at the beach during the day and attend services at night. It seemed like a great idea until Jason stepped onto the sand. Unprepared for the effort it took for him reach the ocean's edge, once seated on a towel, he didn't move. His former place of respite now mocked him. He didn't dare enter the water or carve castles in the sand.

Evening services helped, but on the last day I wrote,

> *"Oh Lord, I feel so lost here today. Jason is so down. Every time I want all of this to end I remember that if the Lord hasn't chosen to release us yet, there must be more for me to learn. But Dear God, what have I not understood yet? I guess I need to learn to let you carry the load."*

Later, after a frustrating attempt to play with Nathan and Sam, Jason lay back on the towel, defeated. While he rested, I took the boys for a short walk. As they ran ahead, I talked out loud. In fact, I rehearsed our testimony. I remembered that despite my fear-filled childhood, I was the wife of a terminally ill husband, experiencing far more peace than she ever imagined possible under such dire circumstances. My faith made real, I knew the peace and hope I felt when despair hovered at every corner were only due to my Savior's sacrifice.

Ironically, when the evening service started, Pastor Kilpatrick asked for three people to share their testimonies. Having rehearsed mine on the beach, I tentatively raised my hand—and he walked straight toward me. As he grew close, my arms started moving back and forth uncontrollably. When I stood to speak into his mic, a thick, warm presence enveloped me. Though my arms were flailing, my heart and mind felt strangely focused above the distracting movements. With Pastor Kilpatrick at my side, holding the mic to my mouth, I shared about the peace I felt in the midst of my husband's terminal illness.

The peace didn't make any more sense than the odd movements in my body. So I was all the more amazed when I finished and the pastor said, "Folks, this is like Alison."

A video of Alison Ward had been circulating as an example of how God moved in people's lives at the revival. I'd watched the clip and seen her entire body shake, jerk, and move uncontrollably as she explained the radical touch of God. Intrigued, I had even prayed, "Lord, if that's you, I want to know you like that!"

According to Pastor Kilpatrick, God had answered my prayer. The pastor's validation meant a lot. When asked to explain what I was feeling, I said, "It's like the presence of God is so strong inside me right now that my body can't handle it."

In time I remembered the prophetic prayer, *"There's going to be a very powerful testimony that is going to even usher in the presence of God in that situation."*

The experience was sweet and strange all at the same time. No matter what others concluded, I knew I wasn't forcing my body to shake. I knew a touch of God had intensified in my being to the point my flesh couldn't hold still. Like a spaceship entering the atmosphere, an intense tremor overtook me as His divine presence crossed the human divide.

When I sat down, it continued—for most of the night. I basked in the experience for hours, but sometimes wondered why God was showing up so strong in my body without healing the man I loved sitting next to me. I knew it wasn't because I was more deserving or special. Jason was one of a kind. Of the two of us, he seemed far more prepared to parent and grow the hearts of our boys. I battled insecurities on many levels and over-analyzed life on a regular basis. He was an artist with a deep soul who saw what few did and simply longed to know God. But I shook under the power of God; and he sat stock still.

When the service ended, the real world beckoned. As I transitioned back to mom mode, the shaking subsided. Back at the hotel, I realized Sam had a fever and minutes later, he threw up all over my favorite dress, bathing me in vomit.

As I hovered over the bathtub, washing my dress and Sam's favorite blanket, worship continued to swell in my soul. While great theologians and even the Bible Answer Man still debate the authenticity of what happened at the Brownsville Revival, I was stooped over a bathtub, scrubbing wretched puke, assured that the God of Heaven was more real than I ever imagined.

And that hope carried me far.

Back in Raleigh, the MRI report stymied our doctor. While there was definite change, he explained that radiation damage now mixed with tumor activity. When the PET scan still indicated a slow tumor growth rate, the doctor prescribed steroids instead of chemotherapy. We walked long airport corridors arm in arm on the way home, determined to live as normal as possible for as long as we could.

However, since we'd crossed well beyond the threshold called normal, others easily recognized Jason's mobility struggle. When friends and family gathered to celebrate Nathan's fourth birthday, they witnessed the change first-hand. The stark reality confronted them head on and a friend later confessed, "I have to apologize to you because I've had no idea what you were going through."

Since others didn't experience the double vision or notice the myokymia that fluttered in his neck, Jason had appeared normal. Now balance issues stood out front and center. Set against the backdrop of my son's fourth birthday, the marked change challenged our faith stance. Memories of Brownsville helped, but the juxtaposition of decline and glory pulled me in two.

When a woman prayed over Nathan, I held to the promise:

> *"Nathan, the Lord watches over you and He has His angels around you and He is showing things to you even now."*

Looking at me, she continued, *"And the Lord would have you to know you're not to worry about Him. God is taking care of Him."*

Not long after, Jason and I sat on our bed one afternoon, talking. As we fought through our daily issues, little boy giggles interrupted our flow. Surprised, we waited for more. When the giggles turned to full on abandoned laughter, we got up to investigate.

On the other side of the house, we found Nathan, laid back on our sofa, watching a *Winnie the Pooh* video. The on-screen antics hit his funny bone and the child could hardly contain himself. Intuitive, I'm certain he knew things weren't normal in our home. But that day, his contagious laughter lifted our heaviness, offering daily manna for our hungry souls.

"I tell you the truth, unless you change and become like little children, you will never enter the kingdom of heaven. Therefore, whoever humbles himself like this child is the greatest in the kingdom of heaven" (Matthew 18: 3-4 NIV).

Determined and afraid, we plowed on, seeking doubt-crushing faith.

Thirty-Seven

Shout for joy
Till your praises reach the heaven
Shout for joy
Fill the earth with song
Shout for joy
As this crazy world keeps spinning
With his love that's never ending
Come on and shout for joy

"SHOUT FOR JOY"
Accepted, Track 2

Home from the beach, the summer of change begins in earnest. Not only will I be healing from surgery and Sam proposing to his woman, Don is closing our sunshine store. The landscape of our lives grows disheveled, even more so when Nathan leaves. But the outcome surprises us all.

I recover from the back fusion much easier than the ankle reconstruction. Able to walk on two legs, the pain is doable. Sam proposes—and Courtney says, "Yes"—in the Atlanta airport shortly after she lands. Sweet photos of the event melt any remaining mom-worry.

Within weeks, my sister takes me to our store, without telling our mom, who would worry about an outing so soon after the procedure. With Laura's help, I grab sale items off the shelves to decorate our home. Lots of them.

"You'll never have this chance again," she reminds me.

And she's right. So I pile favorite wall hangings and trinkets onto the cart. Besides, our contract stipulates all the furniture pieces belong to me and Don. And when he measured, Don realized four of the matching shelf displays fit perfectly on either side of our living room fire hearth. A wall of shelves will soon be in need of colorful memoirs.

Though thankful that store hours will no longer rule our life, the creative works from all over the world will evoke fond memories. The store's soft yellow walls and bright pieces of art created a fun atmosphere in which to shop. A variety of music blared from well hung speakers and Don's uncanny wit charmed many shoppers.

He grew fond of—and rather good at—catching shop lifters, who then had the choice to face prosecution or attend a four-week Bible study. While the added time away from home came with a cost, my respect for Don grew when I sat through an evening session and listened to him present the gospel with clarity and conviction. Local police grew to appreciate his efforts since arrests often did little to rehabilitate offenders.

On good days, we danced together—even on the check-out counter, after hours, when songs from *Mama Mia* blasted through the speakers. Don often told people I taught him to dance and it's true. A few months into dating, a live performer played while we ate Mexican food.

"We should get up and dance," I encouraged, "There's hardly anyone here!"

"I don't dance," he replied.

"What?" I countered "You don't dance?"

"No," he insisted.

In time, that changed. And we have video proof. While I can no longer dance like I used to, Don struts his stuff on a regular basis now. So even though the early years at the store felt more like marital boot camp than fun, dancing after hours left an imprint of joy that lingers.

I won't miss the stress or the long weekend hours. But I'll enjoy the teak shelves, the happy knick-knacks, the tall wooden giraffes, the ornate mirrors, and even the colorful, metal butterfly that will soon fill our home. The reminders will reflect the best of the store and Don's unrelenting service to our King.

As the great furniture exchange continues, I sneak into my closet, step onto a stool, and unbury a long forgotten pair of heels. The dated black shoes slip on with ease, and I strut to my living room where I parade back and forth like a runway model.

Earlier in the day, I noticed my feet no longer slap to the floor, uncontrolled. What I called "foot drop" is no longer inhibiting my stride. A doctor later explains that I never had "foot drop" but rather "foot slap" which results from nerve entrapment.

Either way, I haven't worn dressy shoes in years. Overflowing, I call my sister.

"Guess what?"

"What?" she obliges.

"I'm wearing high heels and walking across my living room," I exclaim.

A long silence ensues.

"Are you sure you should be doing that?" she questions.

"No… but my feet are working better than they have in years. It's like a miracle, and I can't help myself."

"How long have you been wearing them?" she asks, using her big-sister tone.

"Not that long. About ten minutes."

"Susan," she begins in a slow, daunting voice, "That's long enough. Why don't you take a break?"

My bubble burst, reality hits home, and I consider her concern. Momentarily. But then my Ms. America façade returns, and I stretch tall, embrace the cheering throng in my mind, and walk forward with refined grace—in high heels.

I feel my sister's eyes roll as we hang up, and know she's right. But I want to prance around in the outdated fancy, fine shoes a little bit longer. So I call my mom, who fortunately doesn't express the same level of concern. But my ankles tire, forcing me to wave goodbye to my admirers. Satisfied, I slip the heels from my feet and store them in the basket that sits high on a shelf.

There's a chance I'll wear them again. But only a chance.

When my legs and ankles became unreliable eight years ago, I dropped Nathan at his tap dance studio one night and entered a specialty shoe store. Determined, I tried on several types of shoes, including a pair of rocking bottom, *Star Wars* looking, very ugly sandals. The stark black shoes rolled my ankles forward, easing my stride.

The profound difference surprised me. I studied it. Took the shoes on and off. Weighed the cost—and decline in fashion—and finally purchased the expensive, armor intensive foot coverings.

They clashed with cute outfits, but disguised my problem until I fell several years later. After the ankle surgery, the rolling motion proved too much. So my weakened joints found comfort in *Earth Shoes*, which angle the balls of your feet slightly higher than the heel.

Now, all of a sudden, I can wear heels—if only for ten minutes before my sister freaks out. As I try on other options, an old pair of tennis shoes works well too.

For a moment, I feel normal. And very thankful.

In my early days of recovery, my friend, Rosemary stopped by with a copy of the book *One Thousand Gifts,* by Ann Voskamp. As we sat on my sofa catching up, Rosemary explained that the author struggled to overcome depression until she started noticing and listing the small miracle moments that occur every day.

While far from the person I was two years ago, pressing into thankfulness unlocks another entry that takes me deeper into the land of joy. I begin my list with friends from an online group filled with others who suffer mitochondrial disease. Determined to reach a thousand in a matter of weeks, together we focus on the moments that matter and lift us above the confines of illness.

I'm thankful for a house full of new stuff. I'm thankful for the coming change that may ease our schedules. I'm thankful for the difference my husband made in so many lives; for feet that move forward with greater ease; for leaves that shimmy in the wind and announce each season change.

Aware of the deep work our Heavenly Father is doing in my life, I begin to thank Him for loss that leads to life; for painful surgeries that duct tape my weak joints; for the limits I don't like but that force me to value what I can do more than what I can't; for music that moves me; for the mundane that molds me; and for my children who reflect the heart of their father.

The online list from other struggling souls grows long. As our deadline looms, we work hard to reach a thousand. Turning our gaze from loss to life allows us to face The Son with heads held high and hearts full of abandon. Warmed by His love, we turn to the unknowns with greater ease.

I know the lesson well. I lived it years ago, when trusting God's transforming love was worth the daily fight. The inner muscle I grew back then now fires with renewed faith. I may not be able to walk far. But I can believe big and trust God to work all things for my good.

My marriage. My health. Our financial concerns.

My reputation. My fears. My insecurities.

God can work through all my junk and create a life of beauty that honors Him.

After closing the sunshine store for the last time, we crank up the music and dance. A back brace stabilizes my core, but my legs and feet move with greater ease—for now. So we celebrate the crossing, new beginnings, and an upcoming marriage with pizza, cake, and music from *Mama Mia*.

Wedding plans are underway. Nathan will be home soon. Don and I will begin life anew sans the retail store. And maybe, just maybe, I can wear fancy shoes again.

Life is good.

Thirty-Eight

Angels in the morning
I'm talking angels in the night
Angels all around us
Even when they're hidden from sight

"ANGELS"

Encouraged by our time at Brownsville and hopeful steroids would help Jason, six weeks of constant calamity blind-sided us. It all began with a simple mountain get away that I hoped would allow us to relive my recent trip. But it wasn't time—not yet.

Laura and George not only planned Jason's thirtieth surprise party in early April, they gave us a gift certificate for a two-night stay at a bed and breakfast in North Carolina. With balance issues a concern, we booked it as soon as possible—in early May. Thoughts of receiving a miracle at the highest-point mile marker I'd passed the summer before made my imagination swirl. So we drove north with expectations high.

Unfortunately, upon arrival, we found out that even though Santa's Land was close by, it wasn't open for the season yet. Undaunted, we went for an after dinner stroll down a path in the nearby woods—until our sojourn almost turned tragic.

While I held little boy hands, Jason lost his balance and rolled down the ravine. Feeling helpless and small, I watched him climb back up on unsteady legs. Remarkably unhurt, Jason held my arm as we headed back. Dismissing the near mishap, we went to bed, clinging to high hopes.

Avid lovers of all things trains, we bought tickets to ride the Smokey Mountain Railroad the next day. The excursion included lunch but when we stopped at the half way point, we learned our food waited at the top of a long, steep staircase. As we approached the climb, I asked Jason to wrap his arm around me instead of balancing on my shoulder an arm's length away. Annoyed, he took off on his own.

Looking back, I understand that by keeping an arm's length between us, he probably felt somewhat independent. Thus my request at the bottom of the hill jarred his reality. Both hurt by the exchange, I let him go when he started to climb on his own. When he almost tripped on a stair, we were both quite grateful when we were seated safe inside, together.

Forgiveness came easy—from both sides. Things were changing, the decline more obvious outside the confines of our home. So when we headed back to the train, we walked arm in arm, a huddled family held close.

Certain we could still resurrect our fledgling trip; we drove up the Blue Ridge Parkway the next day. After winding through thick green woods and watching the earth disappear below, we turned a corner— only to enter a construction zone. The mile markers that confirmed my arrival before were no longer in place. Disheartened, we drove the stretch several times, trying to find the highest lookout point. But the disarray made it impossible.

So we picked one. We pulled into an overlook with plans to celebrate communion and pray. Our time with God started well enough, but

Jason choked on the juice and coughed it up through his nose. Life seemed to mock us at every turn.

Before we left the next day, we lingered on the front porch after breakfast and met an older couple also staying at the inn. They listened to our discouragement without offering platitudes. Wise souls, their understanding helped. Though we left encouraged, we had no way of knowing that the conversation would prove life-changing in the coming months.

Without air conditioning in our car, we drove home with the windows rolled down. Once home, Jason's red, irritated eye demanded attention. In time we learned that the force of the wind had caused a corneal abrasion due to his weakened right eye muscles. Unable to blink, the brisk air had dried out and scratched his cornea. In comparison to his balance difficulties, the eye issue seemed small, but it served as a tipping point in the never ending battle.

Within days, Sammy woke from a nap, crying. A visit to the ER confirmed that he also had a corneal abrasion. While my two-and-a-half-year-old proudly wore an eye patch—like his daddy—the timing made me cringe.

Soon after we learned that a growth on the back of Nathan's neck had to be surgically removed. Stunned, we scheduled the operation. As I pulled Nathan in a red wagon through the hospital halls, Jason leaned heavy on my free arm. Thankfully, the growth was benign and Nathan asked to ride his bike soon after we got home. Relieved, we agreed to attend a friend's wedding rehearsal dinner that weekend. Dressed in our best, we headed out—hoping for a fun evening together.

Our tire went flat on the side of a busy interstate highway instead. Squeezed under an umbrella during rush hour in the rain, I sang while my ailing husband pulled out the spare. We hit the highway again, but the spare went flat—even after we tried an emergency pump. After limping into a gas station, we called AAA.

Suffice it to say, we never made it to the dinner. A tow truck driver drove us home where we sank onto the sofa in disbelief. But the adventure wasn't over.

When Jason and his dad left to get new tires the following morning, his mother looked out the window and yelled, "Susan, I think there's a problem."

I joined her at our large, living room picture window and saw an enormous puddle of oil in our driveway. We could only assume the tow truck driver punctured the oil filter when he hooked up our car to his truck. With no cell phones, we waited and prayed.

When the wall phone rang, Jason sputtered, "Guess what?"

"I know," I cringed. "The oil's in the driveway. Is the car okay?"

"Yes, it's okay," he replied, his speech slowed and slurred. "The engine locked up in the parking lot. But the mechanic said if we just leave it for the weekend, it might recover in a few days."

And they were right. Since the car hadn't completely run out of oil until it entered the parking lot, it started two days later and we avoided a major repair. The small miracle kept the potential mishap from crippling us, but the constant calamity wore us down.

Not long after, an encounter with an old friend went awry, spiraling me further. When I arrived home after the unexpected oddness, I felt paralyzed, like I couldn't go on if God didn't do something. It wasn't just the one incident. The unrelenting series caused an internal melt down that left me grappling with how to go on.

As I lay in bed in complete darkness, I cried out to God and He answered in a most dramatic way. A light shone in our bedroom; a floor-to-ceiling, intensely-bright, half-circle light appeared from our boy's room across the hall. It didn't stay long, perhaps only seconds, then faded gently into the night.

I tried to explain it away. Had there been an explosion? No. I hadn't heard the slightest sound. Was it the head lights of a passing car? No. I'd heard no sound, and car lights didn't shine with such a brilliant white. Initial fears faded into wonder and I fell asleep in peace.

When morning dawned, and Jason and I lay side by side, I asked if he'd seen anything unusual the night before. His answer surprised me, "Yes, but I didn't trust my eyes since my vision is so bad."

He went on to describe the light—as I had seen it—brilliant, from floor to ceiling. When our descriptions matched, we laid quiet and calm. For a long time.

Buoyed by the divine presence, I marched into the backyard days later, determined to break down some spiritual walls. Armed with sticks, my boys followed close, like armor bearers in the battle. I prayed bold prayers. Out loud even. Contending for breakthrough.

When I finished and walked into my home, the chorus of a song flowed completely from beginning to end, like I'd known it all my life:

> *I love you, my child; I love you, my child;*
> *For I formed you in the womb,*
> *I love you, my child; I love you, my child;*
> *And I will take care of you,*
> *No weapon that's fashioned against you shall stand,*
> *As you hold tightly to my nail scarred hands,*
> *I'll carry you on to your Promised Land,*
> *For I love you, I love you, my child.*

Oh how I ached for one of Jason's symptoms to fade—for our faith to usher in his physical healing. Yet over and over God tenderly assured us His love was more than enough to get us through every minute of every day.

Believing divine love hovered over us as the tumor tightened its grip required persistent faith. Questions lingered. But every time the darkness threatened to suffocate our hope, His light broke through, and we could face another day.

Thirty-Nine

And oh it changes everything
The way I see
My sense of peace
And oh it changes how I feel
Resting in a love
A love so real

"LETTING GO, LETTING GOD"
Accepted, Track 7

After a few weeks of normal walking, my lower, right leg feels wooden and unhinged. Our living room has transformed into a veritable showcase of creative art, but my ankle is shot. So I pull out my walking boot and strap on the heavy, cloth covering. The added support calms my lower extremity and nixes thoughts of fancy shoes for a while—even for the upcoming wedding. I want to gripe and grumble, but another's challenge trumps my own.

A few weeks earlier, when signs of ankle deterioration began to concern me, I learned that our former marriage counselor was in the hospital after collapsing at home. A CAT scan of the beloved church elder's heart indicated his aorta had torn. Doctors contemplated surgery—for the third time.

When he was six years old, the country's premier heart doctors diagnosed Ken with coarctation of the aorta. Caught early, the life-threatening defect that causes a narrowing of the aorta was surgically repaired. When he struggled to run again at twenty-six years of age, a failed stress test indicated a 75% blockage and a similar surgery soon followed.

Twenty plus years later, a CAT scan of his heart prompted minor concern since the sutures in his aorta seemed to have loosened. But the doctor simply told Ken to come back if he started having problems. And everything was fine for almost a year—until his legs gave way and went numb while he was vacuuming. Feeling returned during the ambulance ride, and Ken felt fine in the ER. As a precaution, he was transferred to another hospital where specialists ordered a second CAT scan that indicated the aorta had fixed itself.

His heart doctor explained that while the blood flow had been blocked to the lower part of his body due to the aorta malfunction, surrounding arteries rerouted the blood, alleviating the paralysis. They discussed a surgical option, but chose the conservative route instead. After a week in the hospital, Ken went home. The scare seemingly averted, his life returned to normal.

But three weeks later, he fell again. While surgery successfully fixed the aorta, a spinal cord stroke caused paralysis from the waist down. Since part of his spine died, his doctor assessed there's a 95% chance he'll never walk again.

The parade of those with hardships has been joined by another.

As our church adjusts to the reality that the spunky therapist—who often wore cowboy boots and tropical shirts—is now confined to a wheelchair, my podiatrist agrees that my right ankle ligaments are too loose. Hoping to have me walking by the wedding, he schedules a reconstruction for a Saturday in early October. Eager to start the healing process, I count down the weeks, wondering how Ken is adapting to his new life.

When an orderly wheels me into a hospital room after the operation, Don, Debi, Carl, and their girls greet me. Her tumors are growing again and she'll soon start another round of aggressive chemo. But today, her family kept Don occupied during my third surgery in ten months.

Sam and Courtney stop by with a stuffed, blue animal. Don's daughter, Nikki, and her new boyfriend, Jeffrey, join the crowd. We joke. We sing. And I enjoy my friends through a drug-induced euphoria. When darkness falls and my room empties, post-surgical pain makes for a long night. But I know the routine. In forty-eight hours it will calm.

Mom and Dad welcome me into their home once again where I celebrate my forty-third birthday only days after the procedure. The lackluster, make-up-free day ends with bar-b-que in a cool breeze on their back porch. Lily keeps me company and runs fast when I chase her on my scooter. And without the added stress of the tendon tear repair, the reconstruction heals much faster. So I ready for home.

In the confines of my home, I obsess about what to wear at the wedding, although the color choice comes easy. Courtney's mom is wearing navy. Beige and black are too dull for my tastes, and red a bit gaudy for this mother-of-the-groom. With Courtney not fond of green, eggplant remains the only reasonable choice. As the holidays near, Don and I go shopping.

Racks of sparkling holiday wear overwhelm my scooter-inhibited self. A limited number of choices fit my parameters. So Don carries them to the back of a dressing room where he sneaks in to help me change. Hidden in the back, we narrow it down to one option: a sleeveless, pleated, a-lined, knee-length, eggplant colored dress.

At home I question the find while Don assures me it's perfect. Knowing heels aren't an option for my feet, I decide to live large and search for embroidered, colorful, cowboy boots. Encouraged to try a comfortable brand, I stop by a local store. There I realize my ankles can't bend into traditional styles. So I pull a pair of dark-grey-riding-boots with beige stitching and a zip-up side off the shelf. They work. Not only can I squeeze my ankle into their frame, there's space for my smaller braces as well. More expensive than the dress, I hope to use them often.

Our church staff shares that Ken has returned home from weeks in a rehab facility. Famed for helping victims of paralysis, the specialized center offered intense therapies that prepared Ken for life at home in a wheelchair. Curious about how he's doing, I ask if I can stop by. Ken and Cathy, his wife, welcome me warmly.

We sit around a polished dining room table as he explains what happened in detail. But what speaks to me most is the shock and awe he exudes as he rehearses God's presence in the fire.

"God must have something going on here because I'm just grateful to be alive," he shared, "I should've died when I was six, twenty-six, and now again at age fifty-four. But I'm here, in a wheelchair, dependent on God in a way I've never been before. And I'm not sure I want to walk again if it would mean losing what I've learned about God in the last two months."

His exuberance reminds me of what I felt after Jason died. I'd learned so much about faith and heaven through the trial that I wouldn't have traded the staunch awareness of the divine to have my husband back. Few understand. But Ken does. Now that he can't use his legs, he understands the exchange.

"When I was in Ethiopia on a mission trip once," he recalls, "I learned that if a lamb strays repeatedly, a shepherd will break one of its legs so it can't run off. The shepherd then carries the lamb on his shoulders until the leg heals. When the lamb is set free again it never leaves the Shepherd's side. It has bonded with the Shepherd."

"As a Christ follower I had turned to Him on my time—when it was convenient," the elder admits, "When life was hard, I ran to Him. But when things calmed down I basically said, 'Thanks God, I've got it now.' I went back and forth all these years and now am forced to trust Him; to stay close enough to His side that I can truly lean on Him."

His diatribe continues, "Friends are praying for a miracle and that's a good thing. But the biggest miracle of all is that I'm in this chair and my faith is intact and I still believe God is good and loves us more than we know. I understand that love in a whole new way because of this wheelchair. And I don't want to go back. I want to move forward with more of Him."

Memories reawakened, I leave Ken's house with another piece of myself back in place. Life is hard. The trials breathtaking till the end. But there's a presence that longs to be real in the brokenness and a beauty that only comes from breaking. If years of heartache force a greater dependency on God, then I'll bow my knee to the discipline, knowing love divine finds us there.

With the dress and boots in place, I obsess over jewelry and the fine details. After much input from my children and spouse, I pull together random pieces from my closet including a black belt with a fancy silver buckle and a black, lace jacket my mom handed down to me. I special order a large pair of faux diamond earrings with a purplish tint. But knowing my neighbor's daughter makes jewelry, I purchase a few pieces from a craft store and ask her to create a handmade piece.

When she completes the project, I try on the entire outfit for her, complete with boots. She looks me over, stares quietly for a minute, and then states "It's perfect for you. You look like Ms. Frizzle, *The Magic School Bus* lady."

"Seriously?" I gasp.

"Yeah," her confident middle-school-self continues, "But don't worry. That's a good thing. You often dress like her. It works for you."

While colorful batik clothing from our store fill my closet, the only other time someone equated my attire with Ms. Frizzle was my son, years ago, when I tried on an outfit Don brought home from India. The baggy, bright orange pants contrasted with a colorful, long striped red top. Blue and Green sequins and stitching softened the glow somewhat, but not much. I understood why he referenced *The Magic School Bus* lady that day.

But today? In the outfit I've put together to wear to my son's wedding?

Stressed, my husband and boys talk me down from the ledge, and I show up on the big day with every school-bus-lady piece in place. The boots stabilize my ankles well, and Sam surprises me at the last minute by taking my arm to walk me down the aisle. There, in my place on the front row, Don and I watch my son join his life to another.

The sweet service exemplifies everything it should. As we enter the downstairs fellowship hall for a simple reception, I'm amazed by our year of growth. We've all come quite far.

Though her body is wracked with the effects of chemo, Debi and her family embrace every moment of our celebration. Her presence speaks volumes. She could have easily thrown the towel in and said, "Not today." But she didn't. She showed up smiling, encouraging, and loving me as friends do.

My old neighbors, Ron and Diana, drove the distance as did the Yeager family, dear friends from my boy's high school days. Forrest and Linda came, as clear representatives of my Jason life. Though our invite list was small, those who attended enriched our time together. The core group supported me like my eccentric boots. I certainly wasn't dressed in typical wedding attire, but our life hasn't been typical of late.

Not at all typical.

But my atypical status is becoming my norm. Like Ken in his wheelchair. Sometimes drastic changes occur and altar everything. His dramatic, momentary change punctuated the end of one life and the beginning of another. My slow decline has messed with my head, leaving me caught between worlds, not knowing quite who I am.

A formerly widowed mom, now married, I still parent on my own at times. Accepting the blend, like my good and bad physical days, eases confusion. My change isn't as black and white or as dire as Kens. But embracing it with equal resolve will allow for brighter days and riding the wave of acceptance will ease forward momentum. There, the love of God reaches the deepest crevices of my soul and anchors me again to the miraculous divine.

Forty

He will carry us through
To the journey's end
He will carry us through
As on Him we depend.
He will carry us through the dark of night
Empowered with His strength and might
He will carry us through

"HE WILL CARRY US THROUGH"
Accepted, Track 1

Even after the miraculous, divine confirmations of God's presence in our home, Jason continued to decline. Creative distractions helped and came at opportune times but every juncture stirred hope and fear. So we did what we knew to do. We prayed, shouted scriptures, sang loud, and cried. In the midst of our waffling emotions, God continued to speak.

After lunch out, the boys and I drove a familiar route home. Half-way there, a garage sale sign caught my eye. I drove past it at first, but felt a Holy Spirit nudge I couldn't ignore. So I pulled into a parking lot, turned around, and headed back toward the neighborhood hosting the event.

Once there, I followed signs through winding streets. As I drove, someone in the car in front of me pulled up the notices one by one.

Quite curious, I reached the sale just in the nick of time. Usually uninterested in other people's riffraff, I parked on a side street and crossed to the cluttered driveway.

The home owner approached me, "Can I help you?"

"I'm not sure," I replied.

"Are you looking for anything in particular?" she asked.

"Not really, but do you have any children's bedding sets?"

Days earlier, Jason and I had discussed redecorating the boy's bedroom. Originally painted mint-green in case Sam had been a girl, the boys wanted a train themed room. Longing for a diversion as Jason's body failed, we had little money to pull it off. Companies owed him payments on several large jobs, but they hadn't arrived and our account was low.

As we pondered our options, Nathan stated the comforter set needed to have "blue, green, red, yellow, and *pink* choo-choos on it."

"I'm not sure I can find one like that," I explained to my eager son—especially since I wasn't sure I could afford one at all.

But then the friendly garage sale lady said, "Actually, I do have a set. Come in here."

So I followed her to the garage where a children's train comforter set lay spread on a table—a white comforter covered with blue, green, red, yellow, and *pink* choo-choos. The set included a large decorative train wall-hanging, matching pillow shams, throw pillows, wall paper border, and *two* comforters. Her only son hadn't liked the texture of the first one she bought so she'd purchased a second one. While the first was quilted and the other smooth cotton, the patterns matched and would cover my boy's twin top and double bottom bunk beds with ease.

Stunned, I told her about Jason and how Nathan almost requested her specific spread. Embarrassed by my rambling, I wrote a check for $35, grabbed our stash, and drove home with a happy crew—God's fingerprint evident in our lives once again.

Blue paint covered their bedroom walls before long and the tangible change lifted our spirits. With the crib packed away, Nathan and Sam climbed onto their new bunk bed transformed from toddlers to little men. Money arrived before the room was complete, but a new symptom interrupted our triumph.

As I watched Jason endorse the checks, his hand shook, making his writing illegible. He had known his fine motor skills were fading, meaning he wouldn't be able to draw much longer. But he hadn't told me. A four-thousand-dollar job from the Farmer's Almanac sat on his desk. So he figured a way around the handicap.

The full color, scratchboard piece centered on a tree covered with animals and figures of all shapes and sizes. Unable to carve the caricatures at the normal size, Jason drew them much larger than needed, in a way that his hand could control the movements. Then he used a copier to shrink them down to size and cut and paste them onto the branches. Satisfied, he made one last final copy onto paper suitable for watercolor.

Then the hard part began.

"I don't think I can finish it," he told me one night. "My hands are shaking too much."

"Let's take it to church," I encouraged. "Let's ask everyone to pray over it, because I don't think God would have brought you this far for you to not be able to finish it."

And so we did. We took it to church on a Wednesday night and asked our pastor and friends to pray. As Jason went to work the next morning, I prayed from a distance. Stooped over his desk, I left him alone until evening. When I walked close, I saw him hunched over with a paint brush in hand, trying hard to control the trembling movements.

Startled I said, "That looks so hard. Are you getting tired?"

"No," he gently replied. "It's been this way the whole time. God hasn't stopped the shaking but the miracle is that I'm almost done. Will you paint that chicken's beak for me?"

"What if I mess it up?" I replied in fear.

"You won't mess it up any more than I will."

With his assurance, I painted the beak and dabbed a few more small spots with color. Before he packaged the final product, I asked to take a picture. When he agreed, he held the painting in front of the stained glass piece he made me for Mother's Day. His father had helped finish the piece that hung over my kitchen window. Both symbolized continued perseverance in the worst of situations and I wanted the moment captured for the boys to see one day.

There was no disguising his goopy right eye and disheveled hair, but I didn't care. While the camera captured his overt decline, I saw a gentleman who worked to provide for his family when it would have been much easier to give up. I loved his broken frame more than ever that day.

So when we arrived home after shipping the project, I climbed into the attic and pulled down unfinished paintings he'd never allowed me to hang on the walls of our home. Overly picky and judgmental about his work, incomplete canvases showcased places we'd lived and landscapes he'd visited long ago.

While he still devalued their worth, their impressionistic style offered a completeness that felt finished to me. So I stayed up half the night, sorting through his portfolio and hanging what I liked. Before morning, his artwork covered the walls of our home. Some pieces were framed. Others hung bare. It didn't matter. The artist's work was on display for all to see and it was way past time.

Within weeks he agreed to do what would be his last job—a group of marker comps for an advertising campaign that required less precise skill. Again, he drew the pictures very large and then shrunk them down while I copied logos he could cut and paste in place. Normally able to draw every detail himself, the necessary short cut saved time and heartache. But I enjoyed the team approach more than he did.

Depending on me underscored the painful reality that his artistic career was drawing to an end. As much as I fought to stay focused and build our faith together, our journeys were very different. He was the patient and I, the caregiver, the endless cheerleader, the voice of hope when his ran out.

Both carried a responsibility that made us lean into the other. But there were times, no matter how I tried, that I couldn't relate to his endless physical decline. I could only offer my undying love to soothe his inner ache. Sometimes it helped. Sometimes he still felt sad.

As his last job came to an end, that sadness lingered until a medical option offered distraction. With travel growing difficult and Duke far away, we got a second opinion at a hospital nearby. Doctors there proposed two treatment plans. One involved treating the symptom changes as radiation damage, the other, going back on chemotherapy.

After considering his options, Jason chose to battle the tumor head on with chemotherapy from a local doctor. When we met with the recommended physician he sat us down in his office and asked about Jason's medical history. Before explaining it all, I stated, "First, we want you to know that we're praying for a miracle, actually expecting a miracle. That said, he was diagnosed with a brain stem glioma in 1984."

"You mean 1994," he interrupted; convinced it had only been two years since the diagnosis instead of twelve.

"No," I insisted. "He was diagnosed in 1984, his freshman year in college."

"Then what you're telling me," he simply stated from across the wide desk, "is that you're expecting your *second* miracle."

Barely able to absorb his comment, we listened as he encouraged us to go forward with a biopsy of the tumor. It had grown into the cerebellum portion of the brain, making it accessible to a surgeon. Since it had never been biopsied, it was a reasonable request, but risky.

"At this point," he explained to Jason, "it doesn't make sense to start chemotherapy without knowing what type of tumor you have, especially since a biopsy is doable. I'll schedule an appointment for you with a surgeon and we'll go from there."

Back home we could only wait. Wait for the doctor's call while waiting for a miracle—a badly needed miracle. As we waited, the boys played with trains in their new room that spoke change despite our predicament. And Jason sometimes sat on the sofa and looked at his paintings on the wall, paintings he didn't consider complete, but paintings that displayed his talent during a time we all needed the reminder.

Life was moving on. In good ways and bad.

One day I woke, not knowing how to live through another day of endless waiting. I still valued the angelic light that had shone in our room and the song that promised He was near. I still remembered God's unusual presence at Brownsville and the hope that stirred faith to keep us walking on water. But the reality of Jason's decline served as an undertow, a constant pull from the shores of satisfaction.

Thoughts of laundry and dishes bored me. So I went to my room, set my laundry basket down, and perched on the side of my bed. There

I simply prayed, "Lord, I need help. I don't know how to get through this day?"

The inaudible, voice whispered, "Open my Word."

So I picked up my Bible from my night stand and randomly opened it to the book of Ruth. As I began to read, I heard the voice speak again, "Write a musical."

"A musical?" I questioned.

But as I read the story, lessons emerged I hadn't noticed before. Ignoring the fact that the three main female characters became widowed, I spent two days on a script that included five songs. As I wrote, a theme emerged. God carried the women through famine, loss, wrong choices, change, and grief. And if God carried them, he would carry me and my family through the same.

Jason particularly liked the words to this song. I sang them often. As the days cooled, our bank account dwindled, and my ailing spouse struggled to find purpose in each day, these words served as another reminder of change, hope, and the steadfast promises of God:

Challenges come we don't understand,
But we must walk on, holding His hand.
Through perils of doubt and nights full of fear,
We must remember He's always near.
And though we may stray from His perfect plan
Atonement is made with the Sacrificial Lamb.

And He will carry us through to the journey's end.
He will carry us through as on Him we depend.
He will carry us through the dark of night,
Empowered with His strength and might
He will carry us through.

Forty-One

I get lost in my mind
On a mountain of thought
And I slip down paths of worry
Then I cling to the truth
Set my face to the sun
And climb without the hurry

"LAY MY HEAD AND REST"

Memories of Sam and Courtney's sweet wedding linger, and photos prove my attire sufficed. Stabilized ankle still hurt on occasion, but not much. The winter months pass without a major medical crisis, allowing me to hope for a calmer year. But those hopes fade in mid-March

In a hurry to get out the door for church, I forget to swallow my morning medicines. When words on the screen and my pastors form splits in two off and on throughout the service, I chalk it up to fatigue exacerbated by forgotten meds. But even after I swallow my pills, the double vision remains. Not eager to share the new symptom with my neurologist, I wait a month, hoping it will go away.

It doesn't.

Now, six weeks later I accept my fate. More tests. More costs. More unknowns.

I make an appointment, finding it surreal that I have double vision, like Jason. Sobered by the symptom change, I accept what I pondered a year ago—my life may never normalize. Instead of resisting and asking why, I lay back into the river of His grace, wanting to flow where the plan leads.

When I mention the upcoming neurology appointment to my Monday night Bible study group, Bonnie and Lu offer to drive. Even though it lengthens their trip, they pick me up at my home. Now that ALS is taking its toll, and Bonnie's legs don't carry her far, I climb into the front seat while she sits in her power chair, locked into place in the back of the van.

I don't like double vision. But Bonnie's determined attitude speaks. Time after time she's sat in waiting rooms while I visit with doctors. Today is no different.

While my neurologist explains the plan of action, Bonnie and Lu read in dull surroundings. When I emerge from behind locked doors, they listen as I verbally process what lies ahead. My doctor has ordered an MRI of my brain. As expected, she has to rule out a brain tumor. The irony weighs heavy. Next, I'm to see an ophthalmologist and go from there.

The bumpy path thrills me not. But I'm in good company. For over a year, I've watched as Bonnie continually declined. Unable to move her arms, her legs now tire carrying her to and from the bathroom. Totally dependent, the former computer technician who thrived in her profession now requires someone else for mere sustenance. I'm far from alone in my daily battle.

Once home, Debi calls. She wants to know what the doctor said even though she can barely walk some days due to pain as a result of her cancer. While I see double, she grows winded with small tasks and endures excruciating episodes I hope to never face. Still radiant and determined, she presses on, seeking holistic treatments along with chemotherapy. We talk regularly and attend the healing services at the *other* church on occasion. As I explain what the doctor said, she listens, encourages, and empathizes, despite her discomfort.

My ragamuffin collection of friends keeps me honest and real. Together we laugh—and cry—at our ailments and constant stream of roving doctor appointments. I haven't known them long. Our history is short. But the connection runs deep due to the severity of our diseases. Together we cling to this truth:

> *"Therefore, we do not lose heart. Though outwardly we are wasting away, yet inwardly we are being renewed day by day. For our light and momentary troubles are achieving for us an eternal glory that far outweighs them all. So we fix our eyes not on what is seen, but on what is unseen. For what is seen is temporary, but what is unseen is eternal"* (2 Corinthians 4: 16-18 NIV).

An increase in white matter spots concerns my neurologist some. Since the location of the new spots doesn't coincide with vision issues, we agree to ignore them—at first. A week later, she calls again with a change in plans.

Due to the fact the spots could indicate a demyelination disease, like Multiple Sclerosis, further discussion with her colleagues leads her to suggest a spinal tap. My third in ten years. While her change in opinion means more needles for me, I trust her. If MS is taking over my brain, medicines might help.

I ask for drugs to stay calm during the procedure. She offers Valium. I don't want to be completely knocked out so the tiny pill works. In need of a distraction, I sing as they prepare my back for the needle stick. Curled on my side, facing bare, beige walls, I sing whatever comes to mind, mostly hymns. Music carries me above the stress more than the

Valium. If the technicians mind, they don't complain. They do their job with skill. So when I see Don again, I can honestly say I experienced little discomfort.

At home, I lay flat for forty-eight hours before gingerly moving around. A spinal bleed required a blood patch a few days after my first tap. Not wanting to repeat the excruciating headache, I move slowly for a few more days, making sure my body has healed.

One by one the results return normal. I don't have MS or anything else that explains the white matter spots. The ambiguity doesn't surprise me, but is certainly disheartening—especially when the left side of my throat tightens when I sing in worship a few weeks later.

> *"Consider it pure joy my brothers, whenever you face trials of many kinds, because you know that the testing of your faith develops perseverance. Perseverance must finish its work so that you may be mature and complete, not lacking anything"* (James 1: 2 - 4 NIV).

The new symptom requires another round of doctors. But this time an oral surgeon finds a bona fide reason. My left jaw joint is missing a sizable piece of cartilage, causing my jaw to jut forward when I sing and talk. Physical therapy will help, he insists. So I set up an appointment with a recommended therapist thirty minutes away.

> *"Because of the Lord's great love we are not consumed, for his compassions never fail. They are new every morning; great is your faithfulness. I say to myself, 'The Lord is my portion; therefore I will wait for him.' The Lord is good to those whose hope is in him, to the one who seeks him; it is good to wait quietly for the salvation of the Lord"* (Lamentations 3: 22 – 24 NIV).

While I begin therapy, Debi's health continues to decline. Her coughing spells intensify and her liver pain increases. After much resistance, she agrees to sign up for hospice since they have tools to help ease her discomfort. Lu orders a specialized lift for Bonnie, who can barely stand long enough to make it to the bathroom, and they slow their pace.

My discomforts pale in comparison.

> *"Fear not for I have redeemed you; I have called you by name; you are mine. When you pass through the waters, I will be with you and when you pass through the rivers, they will not sweep over you. When you walk through the fire, you will not be burned; the flames will not set you ablaze. For I am the Lord your God, the Holy One of Israel, your Savior..."*
> (Isaiah 43: 1 – 3; NIV).

My ragamuffin crew represents a mere sampling of the suffering on earth. I don't claim to understand why such pain exists; why loss must be part of life. I just know there's a battle raging for our hearts. And I don't want mine to cave to despair. Not again.

There will be days of grief, painful days of grief. But I have a choice to trust or deny, an opportunity to dig deep or give up. Fear may nag at my heels and worry whisper in the night. But my God has declared:

> *"I took you from the ends of the earth, from its farthest corners I called you. I said, 'You are my servant; I have chosen you and have not rejected you; do not be dismayed, for I am your God. I will strengthen you and help you; I will uphold you with my righteous right hand'"* (Isaiah 41: 9 – 10 NIV).

So I won't give up. I don't want to give up. I want to reach heaven's doors with my heart wide open, ready to embrace the onslaught of Christ's sacrificial love.

Jaw therapy helps, and I schedule an appointment with a neuro-ophthalmologist for an eye assessment. But all too soon, Debi and I share what will be our last phone conversation. She asks me to sing. So I croon a hymn, an evening lullaby, *"My hope is built on nothing less than Jesus blood and righteousness. I dare not trust the sweetest frame. But wholly lean on Jesus name. On Christ the solid rock I stand, all other ground is sinking sand, all other ground is sinking sand."*[8]

In a slightly drug-induced state, she sings a childhood song back to me. The Itsy Bitsy Spider.

Tears fall. I know the end is near.

---

[8]   Mote, Edward, "The Solid Rock", 1834.

Forty-Two

From the morning
Till the sun sets down in the night
My love flows freely
And you can try with all your might
But you only gotta' believe

"I LOVE YOU MY CHILD"
<u>Life of Love</u>, Track 10

In the midst of making major medical decisions, Jason and I received an unexpected call. The couple we met on the last day of our disastrous spring mountain trip purchased a log cabin and wanted to offer us a week's stay in October, free of charge. Close to where we stayed before, the location offered a redo of sorts. When we discussed our plans with the oncologist, he encouraged us to enjoy the family getaway before the biopsy. So we did.

Fall leaves had begun to appear when Jason and I drove north. We headed up a few days before my mom brought the boys, choosing some alone time. Arriving after dark, an eerie silence surrounded the secluded cabin. With no TV, we were alone with only our thoughts, which collapsed into the reality of his decline.

Practically wheelchair bound, I maneuvered his feet up each step to get him inside. Once there we discovered the bedroom was high in a loft. So I helped him into a hammock on the porch and unloaded the car. Sunk deep into the cotton swing, he felt useless.

As I searched for something to do, I found a puzzle in a cabinet. Jason shuffled into the small kitchen where we hovered over a tiny table, trying to match pieces. Hand tremors made it almost impossible for him to connect a piece without tearing others apart. Under dim light, he confessed what I already knew. His symptoms were getting worse.

When we gave up on the puzzle, I helped him climb the steep flight of stairs to a bed in the loft. There, a suffocating heaviness blanketed us through the night. Pounding rain on the tin roof woke us in the morning but we stayed in bed for hours, feeling hopeless and trapped by our weekend away.

Was our faith making a difference? Was God really looking out for us? Was there something more we needed to do to precipitate a miracle?

We'd fought the best we'd known how. We believed time and again when confronted with the terminal nature of his disease. Others thought we were in denial or plain naïve, perhaps even demanding children trying to manipulate God into following our plan. To us, we were simply walking in obedience, trying to practice faith against all odds.

> *"Now faith is being sure of what we hope for and certain of what we do not see"* (Hebrews 11: 1 NIV).

We'd known the risk. We knew of people who had stood in faith and believed for a miracle, only to end up mad at God for not healing their loved one. In fact, a neighbor visited us early on in the journey to encourage me to read the book by Catherine Marshall that detailed her despair when her grandchild died. *If a respected and well-known Christian like Catherine Marshall got angry with God in her grief who was I to think that I could do any better?*

When we didn't change our stance, our neighbors stopped hanging out with us. Our choice to believe caused a friend divide. So it hadn't been an easy choice. We knew we weren't God. We were just two young people in love trying to believe that living with faith could transform the impossible.

But as the morning hours passed and rain bounced off the tin roof, we questioned our resolve. Jason wasn't getting better. He was getting worse. The reality wasn't lost on us. It was quite real and scary. And as we lay there feeling helpless, I wondered if I would end up angry, mad at God, unable to go on alone.

With no answers, we slogged through the day, forced from the loft by hunger.

My twenty-seventh birthday dawned the next morning and I had a plan. After purchasing sandwiches, we drove up the Blue Ridge Parkway in hopes of finding the highest mile marker post again. This time, we were not disappointed.

Now complete, the construction work that impeded our last attempt led to a brand new rest stop and a large road sign pointed the way. After turning left off the Parkway, we drove up a steep, long parking lot surrounded by panoramic views that included Mount Mitchell, the highest peak east of the Mississippi.

The highest vantage point was now even higher and the scenes more spectacular than what I'd experienced on my former drive. My heart rejoiced—in fact it almost burst wide open in my chest. The push forward on the faith swing made me soar.

Jason valued the moment, but not like me. The scenic views didn't change the fact that his wife had to feed him his sandwich. But as we sat side by side on that ridge—on my birthday, no less—I felt held by God, empowered by the Almighty.

He was still with us, taking us to higher heights, despite the physical battle that raged. On the eve of Jason's major biopsy, He had led me back to the place of assurance, promising my faith would be made sight. The journey was not in vain. Our faith mattered. Walking with God and trusting His love would make a difference, somehow. It didn't matter if others understood. The views from the precipice of faith can only be experienced first-hand. We could try to explain, but only those who step out on the water float on the changing tides.

My mom arrived with the boys well before dinner. Poison ivy covered Nathan's face but the red rash and sores didn't thwart his excitement about the days ahead. The Santa's Land amusement park was open and the Smokey Mountain Railroad still operating. So over the next two days, we made memories with his daddy.

Santa's Land was first. The small park included several rides designed with young children in mind. Thrilled with the small roller coaster, Nathan and Sam rode it several times before heading off to feed animals and to climb onto a Ferris wheel. At one point, mom helped Jason climb onto a small train with us and we rode as a family. The team effort made the day a success—albeit a bitter sweet one.

When we left Santa's Land, we drove to the Mt. Mitchell overlook one more time because I wanted my mom and especially the boys to see the vantage point. Looking out over the endless mountain range, I rested in knowing the God of the vast blue sky watched over us and had a plan. Surrounded by the Creator's handiwork, I reminded my boys that our Heavenly Father loved us more than we would ever understand.

The next morning, we boarded the train last, since we had to wait for someone to set up a ramp for Jason's wheelchair. By the time we settled in, Jason felt certain observant eyes had judged him wrong. Still mentally sound, he looked like a young stroke victim and garnered unwanted attention.

On our return trip after lunch, Sammy's touch soothed his pain. The almost three-year-old boy climbed into his daddy's lap, oblivious to his ailments, and fell fast asleep. Exhausted from two long days of activity, Sam rested in the comfort of his father's arms. Jason later told me that as he held his son, even with an awkward grip, he tried to imagine his Heavenly Father holding him.

The sacred nap lasted till the train slowed. After days of ignoring awkward glances, Sammy's abandoned acceptance of his father, his wheelchair, and all his physical changes mattered most. Jason was still our daddy, loved, valued, and adored. No illness would ever take that away.

The day after we drove home, we headed to the hospital for Jason's pre-op appointment. By four the next morning—on Sam's third birthday—we were awake, dressed, and preparing to drive across town.

Aware that Sammy had been born around 3:30 am, readying for the day took a toll on us both. Jason lay on our bed as I scurried around, trying to stifle emotion. When I stopped for a moment he looked at me and asked, "Why?"

For the first time in our journey, I had no answer, no sunshiny thoughts to share. But as I stared at him in silence, he started quoting the words to my song:

> *"Challenges come we don't understand.*
> *But we must walk on holding His hand.*
> *Through perils of doubt and nights full of fear,*
> *We must remember He's always near."*[9]

The one time I stood at a loss for words, my dear spouse quoted my own.

So as we settled on the highway, tears fell free—deep, guttural, sobbing tears. Struggling to drive, I pulled out the only weapon I had against the flood of despair—worship. It was ugly. Off tune. A meager attempt at song to stifle heartfelt cries. But in time, Jason joined in with slurred pronunciation and we declared scripture set to melody's we could hardly sing.

In time, our sacred act of worship settled my heart. Fears calmed and bitter tears dried, allowing us to enter the surgical wing ready to face the day.

The biopsy procedure was akin to brain surgery. Instead of using a stereotactic procedure to procure the specimen, the surgeon felt it necessary to remove a three-inch diameter section of Jason's skull. After removing the bone, he cut open his brain to reach where the tumor grew deep in the cerebellum. We would have preferred the stereotactic option—where a small hole is drilled through the skull and a needle inserted to protract the tissue—but it wasn't our choice.

Thankfully, Jason survived with little fanfare. But the news wasn't good. Radiation damage mixed with new tumor growth, causing his decline. With chemotherapy no longer considered a viable option, his oncologist suggested immunotherapy treatment once Jason left rehab.

---

[9]   Schreer Davis, Susan, "He Will Carry Us Through", 1996.

There was still hope.

The artist woke briefly in ICU, told me he loved me, and then drifted into a deep post-surgical slumber. Assured he was stable, I drove home to see the boys and to grab a few more items for the hospital stay. As I pulled out of my drive way, I stopped to check the mail. Parked in the driveway, I read a card that highlighted a favorite verse:

> *"And we rejoice in the hope of the glory of God. Not only so, but we also rejoice in our sufferings, because we know that suffering produces perseverance; perseverance, character; and character, hope. And hope does not disappoint us, because God has poured out his love into our hearts by the Holy Spirit, whom he has given us"* (Romans 5: 2 – 5 NIV).

As I drove through traffic on my way back to the hospital, I savored the words—*Hope does not disappoint.* Since I was clinging to hope, the timely affirmation gave me courage to stay the course. Uplifted, I arrived at the hospital prepped for a lengthy stay.

When I entered Jason's room, he was wide awake and hungry. Very hungry. The night nurse commented that he rarely interacted with alert patients, underscoring that the surgery had gone well. Regardless, he didn't agree to deliver food to the salivating patient. When he left, my normally low key spouse begged me to find food until guilt drove me to the cafeteria.

The dining hall closed, I returned with only an assortment of crackers. But as I stood by his bed, nourishing his hunger, we relished an odd sense of normalcy. For the moment, all that mattered was that he'd survived the surgery. Relieved, I interacted with the old Jason and hoped to enjoy more of him in the morning.

Sadly, as I stood by his bed the next morning, he told me his legs felt numb. Unusually anxious, he was fully aware the tumor was still there and the renewed worry altered his easy-going demeanor, pulling him further from us.

He spent five days in the hospital followed by five more in a rehabilitation facility. My sister watched the boys the entire time to give them stability. So I stopped by her house one afternoon and took them on a walk. The air was crisp and the sky very blue as colored leaves glistened in the sun.

"*Your boys will mirror you,*" the still small voice whispered.

"They'll mirror me?" I questioned.

"*Yes, they'll respond as you respond.*"

The responsibility scared me and I questioned if I would be able to handle everything in a way they should mirror. Far from perfect, I didn't know what I would do without their dad. So I did what came natural. I took their hands, reminded them of how much God loves us—even though their daddy was very sick—and walked down the path, singing worship songs. Out loud. Together. Among strangers.

The answer was clear. We would find our way just as we had been all along—one praise song at a time.

Forty-Three

There may be thunder
Maybe lightning
Maybe times of howling wind
When you sleep with open windows
And you let the night come in
Maybe voices will disturb your rest
Maybe pleasant maybe mean
Maybe nightingales or siren wail
Will interrupt your dreams[10]

"WINDOWS OPEN WIDE"
Accepted, Track 5

An impromptu dinner serves up the perfect opportunity for my speech. After the waiter brings our check, I take a deep breath, brace myself, and present my case. Nathan, Sam, and Courtney listen from the other side of a very large booth.

"When we talked about going sky-diving this summer, I was feeling better than I am right now," I explain. "But I've fought serious pain the

---

[10]   Levi, Allen, "Open Windows", 1995.

last few weeks, and I think I should bow out. You guys can go ahead, but not me."

Without hesitation, my boys respond in surprising unity.

"You have to, Mom," one starts.

"You'll be fine," the other insists.

Complete with hand motions they passionately explain why. The tandem guide will strap me in tight and stabilize my frame. When the parachute ejects, the force will pull me straight up, not sideways, protecting my back. The guide will then buffer my landing, gliding us safely to the ground.

As their fervent explanation continues, I flashback to the day their eight and ten-year-old selves desperately pleaded with me to ride down a daredevil water park ride. Their earnest entreaty worked since my single parent role often included activities I knew their dad would have done—like climbing to a platform high above the tree tops only to slide straight down in record time. I tackled the high place then since it seemed to matter so much. And after listening to their reasoning, I cave again.

"I have to do this," I tell Don as we drive home. "I have to jump out of that plane with them. I don't know if it's more for me or for them, but we need to make this memory."

My husband offers no argument, so the next day I pay for and reserve a jump time on Labor Day Weekend.

The morning dawns bright and clear, so Nathan, Sam, Courtney, and I head out, expectant. Favorite music plays, and I sing annoyingly loud. Out in the country, we turn onto a long drive that leads to a large field. Avoiding the mud, we park, find the office, and watch a video presentation that requires our signatures to assure we won't sue the company if injured in the jump.

Aware of every detail that could go wrong; we head to a large hangar to wait our turn. Parachutes stretch the length of the building. Employees carefully fold them while oversized fans blow. A young child is reminded not to play near the equipment. And Don arrives and finds me sitting in front of a fan to keep cool. As we wait, I overhear a phone call.

"He's probably fine," a female assures the caller. "He knows how to handle himself. I'm sure he'll be okay."

A tense calm permeates the building and I begin to suspect something has gone wrong. After twenty minutes or so, an intercom announcement blares, "Due to weather concerns, we will not be making any more jumps today."

While only non-threatening puffy clouds loom overhead, I trust their call. However, before leaving, I walk back to the office to reschedule, knowing that if we don't jump during the holiday weekend we'll struggle to coordinate it another time. Hesitant, the office personnel oblige. Unaware of their trauma, we trudge back to our cars and head home.

Before I reach the end of the long driveway, Don calls, "Did you realize that two people collided in the air just now?"

"No," I stammer, "But I got the feeling something wasn't right."

"I saw them fall right after I got here," he continues. "I was watching with the owner. It could be bad. They were instructors, trying a specialized jump."

Not long after we hang up, we drive past several emergency vehicles near the main drag. A blue parachute lays on the ground near-by. Someone is injured. So I spend the evening searching the internet for information but find none.

The sun shines bright again as we make the same drive twenty-four hours later. The fire trucks and ambulances are gone and the muddy field is still filled with cars. When I enter the office to let them know of our arrival, I blurt, "Are those people okay? The ones who fell yesterday?"

Hesitant, one of the women states, "One of them broke his back but will be okay. He had surgery and should be able to walk."

"And the other?" I insist. A momentary silence proves I've hit a nerve.

"He didn't make it," she finally admits. "He most likely died in the air after the collision."

"Did you all know him well?" I press.

"Yes," she replies. "He was a regular here. A really good guy."

"So how are you guys holding it together?"

"We barely are," she admitted.

251

"Oh. I'll stop asking questions. I'm just so sorry for your loss."

Tight smiles acknowledge my condolence before I head out to tell the boys and Courtney what transpired. Then I call Don.

"One of those guys died yesterday," I begin. "They think he died on impact in the air and was unable to pull his parachute."

On his way to a meeting at his family farm in South Georgia, he simply listens.

"Should I still do this?" I wonder aloud.

"You'll be fine," he says with confidence. His reassurance calms my fears. The irony isn't lost on me, though. Loss has invaded our fun family memory. It lingers everywhere. Surrounded by grieving people who lost a friend, their pain is fresh and raw.

And so is mine.

Debi's life ebbed away just over a month ago, on the last day of July. I called on a Sunday afternoon and learned that Carl had been up all night, trying to keep her comfortable and safe. The dedicated spouse exhausted all efforts to keep her at home, but end-of-life delirium made her restless and in need of nursing care.

He agreed to have her transferred to an inpatient hospice care facility only after many long discussions to help calm his girls. Still praying for a miracle, they recognized God's divine fingerprint when she was placed in room number eleven. All throughout her illness, Hebrews 11:1 had been her mantra, *"Now faith is being sure of what we hope for and certain of what we do not see."* So the number eleven held special meaning and always appeared when they needed hope to stay afloat.

I spent hours with Carl and the girls as Debi battled to breathe in the hospice facility. Makayla and Olivia rubbed lotion on her arms and legs, and painted her fingernails and toenails a colorful hue. Carl stayed close, regulating care while consoling the women he cared for most. Debi's mom joined in, rubbing her fingers through her daughter's hair while recalling fond memories. We all talked and sang to her and worked to keep her comfortable, though most efforts seemed futile.

Participating in the sacred event—the ultimate crossing over—took me to the edge of this life again; to the place where holy ground awaits.

There, on the precipice of eternity, nothing here matters. Absolutely nothing.

At Monday night Bible study last night, Somer commented, "One day this week, I was driving down the road—and I have horrible road rage—and I thought, 'I'm going to really live forever. This life is nothing. What's to come is forever.'"

Safe on the other side, Somer will leave her battle with road rage—and the fears that twist inside as she raises a child with spina bifida. Debi has already left the agony of cancer—and her ravaged shell. Clothed in a beauty that defies logic, she now lives as an heir of the promise, a child of the King.

I don't know what happened to the man who fell from the clouds when he breathed his last. But the fact he left his earthly body the day before I jump from a plane makes my choice all the more poignant.

Yes, people die every day and grieving hearts cover the earth. But people still jump from airplanes, defying the laws of gravity, daring the sky to make them feel utterly alive. And maybe that's the point. No matter the loss, no matter the pain, we have to keep jumping. Even me. After everything that's happened, I have to keep jumping.

The list of reasons I shouldn't jump remains long. But God is daring me to trust Him with reckless abandon. The moments I've felt most alive have required a stepping out, a departure from the norm, a certain wildness of heart. Why should this be any different?

Nathan and Sam are called and begin to suit up. After stepping into harnesses laid out on the floor, they pull them up and buckle them into place. As I watch, somewhat uneasy, my name echoes over the loud speaker.

A guy about my age approaches and introduces himself, "Hi, I'm Charlie[11]."

As he helps me into my harness, I ask, "Did you know the young man who died yesterday?"

Veiled emotion confirms my suspicion—the entire staff is masking their pain.

"We all knew him," he replies, "and we all liked him."

---

[11]   Name changed.

"But the show goes on," I surmise.

"Yeah," he continues. "We all hung out last night, drank a little too much, and jump again today. It's what we do."

Another announcement stirs action. Our guides lead us onto a bus that takes us to a landing strip where a small plane waits. Since Charlie always chooses to board the plane last, I sit with him till the bus empties and then follow him to the plane where we climb up a small ladder.

When I step through the wide opening, I see that our group of about ten jumpers straddles two benches that run from behind the pilot and co-pilot seats along the windows. Seated at the end of the bench, I face the oversized and very open door. The motor roars and the plane starts to taxi, but to my surprise, no one shuts the entry.

As we accelerate across the sparkling pavement, I steady myself. My stomach tightens when we take off and the ground fades into the distant landscape. Peering through the large opening, I take in a view unlike any other. Feeling uneasy, I try to grab onto the side of the plane, wanting to feel anchored. Charlie redirects my effort.

"Are you nervous?" he yells into my ear above the roar of the plane.

"A little," I holler back.

"Don't grab the side of the plane," he encourages. "Lean back against me."

Strapped together in a full body choke hold, I already feel like I'm leaning on him. But he can tell I'm not relaxed. With the door still open and the ground thousands of feet below, I long to feel secure. So I relax into a stranger's embrace to keep from losing my grip.

There I picture the Holy Spirit wrapped even tighter around my being, and the divine peace I know well melts my fears. Whether walking on earth or diving out of a plane at 14,000 feet, the Creator of the Universe holds my life in His hands. Risks abound. Like marrying a newly widowed man or living with a chronic illness or loving a man with a brain tumor. But taking those risks are part of the journey.

So I sit back, breathe deep, and prepare to jump.

When we reach 14,000 feet, I shimmy to the edge of the opening. Squatted down, my instructor rocks us back and forth three times before plunging us out into the open sky. The force of the air is so strong; I can't make a sound. We're falling at a rapid pace, facedown, yet the wind resistance buffers the sensation. Loose strands of hair stick straight up. My cheeks pull tight. Goggles protect my eyes and the world stretches out wide.

We pass through a cloud, an assembly of mist, and soon the parachute deploys. Pulled tight against my mentor's frame, I feel the jolt that slows our descent—but without pain. Upright, I catch my breath and take in the view. Like Mary Poppins floating into London, I drift above farm land, trees, highways, and small homes as we effortlessly descend.

Charlie yells in my ear, asking me to practice our landing procedure. Lifting my legs in front of me, I try to straighten them out. Exerting the extra effort tires my mitochondrial disease challenged body. When he asks me to practice three more times before we hit the ground, I sense he's concerned by my lack of ability. Since he can't hear me, I'm unable to explain that I'll use everything in me to lift them when we land, but if we keep practicing, I'll run out of power before we hit ground.

In the end, it doesn't matter. The ground grows closer and closer till we pass under tree tops and glide toward a pond. Without even a bump, we touch down safely on a soft bed of grass near the hangar. As I adjust to gravity's pull, back on earth, I feel transformed by the experience.

I can't walk right away, my legs tired from the effort. But I don't care. We stand in the field for a few moments and then move forward slowly to where Courtney waits. My daughter-by-love sees me and walks my way.

"Are you okay?"

"Yes, I'm fine. My legs are little tired but it was worth it!"

Courtney didn't jump due to her own medical concerns, but she supported our adventure—like she normally does. Grateful for the young woman who loves my son and makes him a better person, I realize how much their jump into marriage was like the one I just did—crazy, risky, but God-ordained in so many ways.

All my worry was for naught.

Nathan approaches, looking a little weary, and explains that his guide chose to spiral them down several times on their descent. The one spiral I endured made me nauseous, so I understand why he looks a little sideways.

Sam advances with long strides, a big smile, and no sign of wear and tear. Confident he had the best photographer of the bunch, we swap stories, walk to the hanger, take off our gear, and wait for video proof. Disks in hand, we head back to the car to return to normal life. But it won't feel normal to me. Not for a while.

I just jumped out of an airplane. With my boys. From 14, 000 feet. Life can begin again.

Forty-Four

On that cross
You bore our guilt and shame alone
Redeemed by grace
We now can dance at heaven's throne

"BY YOUR STRIPES"
Accepted, Track 9

The end came swift, like a fast-moving cold front. Jason entered heaven a week after he left the rehab hospital. I now recognize end-of-life signs from afar, but even the day before he died, I held out hope. Vast hope. Because I couldn't imagine how the story would unfold.

Jason and I arrived home from the hospital to an empty house. After buckling a therapy safety-belt around his waist to help him out of the car, we shuffled through the garage into the kitchen. Succeeding without the wheelchair felt like a hard-fought victory. So he settled on a kitchen counter stool while I warmed a slice of pepperoni pizza.

The thick crust stuck in his throat and he almost choked. Smaller bites helped, enabling him to finish a piece. But the episode curtailed our short-lived triumph. With therapists scheduled to come throughout the week, I focused on in-home rehab potentials.

Our families gathered the next day to celebrate Sam's third birthday. For a few hours, our little boy's life mattered more than his daddy's illness. Candles were lit and birthday cake served before wooden train engines and tracks covered our living room floor.

But night came. Hours ticked by. And Monday morning dawned.

While therapists came to work with him, Jason often balked when they left, insisting his body was weakening. But I didn't want to hear the truth. No one did. We wanted him to get better. Stuck deep in the skin that housed failing muscles and nerves, he sensed the continual decline.

His lead oncologist called on Thursday, a crisp Halloween. After reviewing scans and hospital reports, he concluded that immunotherapy would not help Jason. With no treatment options left, he suggested we think it over and sign-up for hospice on Monday. Faced with the hard truth, I got out the wheelchair and asked Jason to go on a walk with me. On the far side of the neighborhood, I stooped down near his chair.

"The doctor called," I started. "He said there are no more treatment options and that we should sign up for hospice."

Silence.

"We both know God can still do this thing," I continued. "But is there anything I should know? Anything you want me to do if God takes you home?"

Battle weary as the end neared, he spoke less, but what he said held great meaning, "No chemicals."

"That's all?" I asked, knowing he wanted to be cremated.

A simple nod sufficed.

"Well, I want you to know something," I offered. "Remember that story we read last year? The one where the man died and his wife prayed and he came back to life?"

Jason nodded again.

"Well, if that happens to us," I assured him, "I'm giving you thirty minutes to go to heaven and come back. I won't let anyone declare you dead until thirty minutes have passed and you have time to consider your options."

And I was dead serious.

Friends invited us to dinner the following day. Before we left, he laid on the bed, tired and short of breath.

"Maybe we shouldn't go," he suggested.

"What will we do if we stay here?" I asked.

With no cable TV, distraction helped. So he agreed to go and we drove to our friend's home. The menu included fish—with too many small bones. So Jason ate a bowl of his favorite ice cream, mint chocolate chip.

After dinner, we talked before turning to prayer. Comfortable with our friends, I prayed a very bold, loud prayer. In response, a quiet, meek entreaty followed that felt somewhat like a correction to mine. Uncomfortable, I was surprised when Jason blurted his thoughts after the final amen.

"They don't get who you are," he forced. "No one does. Stop explaining yourself and Just—be—you."

For a moment, it felt like nobody else was in the room. I had prayed boldly for my husband's healing, giving my all in earnest supplication to heaven. He, in return, reminded me to stay the Susan he loved—a girl full of passion and sensitivity that even she didn't always understand.

After an outing with his family the next day, Jason stayed at his parent's home while the boys and I attended a church game night. In the open gym, the boys ran and played with their friends until late. On our way home, we stopped to say prayers with their daddy. Comfortable in a blue recliner, he planned to spend the night with his parents before returning home with us after church the next day.

Huddled around the chair, we sang familiar songs and recited our prayers. As we finished our nighttime routine, Jason began breathing rapidly again. When his body shut down in other distinct ways, we knew the end was near.

His dad got him comfortable on their fold out sofa bed while I called the doctor. Since Jason refused to go to the hospital and we weren't signed up for hospice, the on-call doctor agreed to order morphine that his sister, a nurse, could pick up. She returned with the medicine in the wee hours of the morning and started an IV. As she began to administer the drugs, he grew restless and tried to speak. He calmed down after she said, "You're trying to tell her you love her, right?"

I told him I loved him too and watched as he drifted into a morphine haze that helped him through to the other side.

Curled up next to him on the sofa bed, I slept till morning. My sister came to get the boys and as they kissed their daddy goodbye one last time, I told them, "Today is a very special day because we're going to find out if our daddy is going to be healed on earth or in heaven."

After several kisses, they headed off to play. My parents arrived and drove to my home to pick up some clean clothes. Alone in the living room, I opened my Bible and read all of our favorite healing scriptures. The passages brought comfort even as he labored to breathe.

> *"Praise our God, O peoples, let the sound of his praise be heard; he has preserved our lives and kept our feet from slipping. For you, O God, tested us; you refined us like silver, you brought us into prison and laid burdens on our backs. You let men ride over our heads; we went through fire and water, but you brought us to a place of abundance"* (Psalm 66: 8 – 12 NIV).

> *"Praise the Lord, O my soul; all my inmost being; praise his holy name. Praise the Lord, O my soul, and forget not all his benefits. He forgives all my sins and heals all my diseases; he redeems my life from the pit and crowns me with love and compassion. He satisfies my desires with good things so that my youth is renewed like the eagles"* (Psalm 103: 1 – 5 NIV).

> *"Then they cried to the Lord in their trouble, and he saved them from their distress. He sent forth his word and healed him; he rescued them from the grave"* (Psalm 107: 19 – 20 NIV).

When I ran out of scriptures, I sang. Kneeling beside my ailing spouse, I worshipped God. Jason would have wanted me to. The words anchored us to the divine—whether in sickness, sadness, doubt, or fear. Worship remained the only viable answer.

In time I walked the streets with my parents and discussed memorial service plans for the first time. Their support buoyed me so they stayed close, and I needed them.

Friends came and went, including a dear pastor who once prayed for dying people in Africa who came back to life. As a last ditch effort perhaps, I wanted him to pray that way again so Jason's body would fill with life and breath. Our pastor certainly prayed. But nothing changed. However, when he left, he stopped on the doorstep and said, "The presence of God is all over that room, Susan."

His affirmation mattered.

June and Brendon, friends from the new church, stopped by. Veterans to difficulty, they had pressed in when others stepped back, filling a void. As the evening sun sank into the horizon, I rambled with them in a cool breeze on the back porch. After years of believing for a miracle, we faced the precipice of change. My brain struggled to juxtapose Jason's current condition with the barrage of hope we'd clung to throughout the journey.

Had our faith really mattered? Had it made any difference at all?

They listened as I reminisced about the powerful presence that came over me in Brownsville and as I recalled the angelic light that showed up when we needed it most. I prattled on about the countless times God intervened when we'd reached our end, including our recent trip to the mountains that meant so much to me.

In time, my thoughts slowed and I concluded, "You know what? Either God is about to raise Jason up off that bed, or I have nothing to worry about. He's carried us this far. He won't leave us now."

With that, I headed back to where my husband labored. Strangely confident, I curled up next to my best friend and father of my children, ready to wait for the miracle to unfold—the miracle of life restored here or set free to eternity. Hunched over his lanky frame I felt as if his arms wrapped around me tight. A divine peace filled me and overflowed in prayer—fervent whispered prayers. As I prayed, the warmth of our love filled my heart, as if heaven orchestrated one last embrace.

Still huddled over his body, basking in the divine embrace, I heard a family member say, "I think he just took his last breath."

When I sat up, it was obvious the father of my children had slipped from here to eternity. And I was in awe. Honestly. The God of the Universe had waited for me all day to take him home—waited until I was confident I could go on no matter how our story ended. And then, as a bonus, he allowed me to sense the transaction as it occurred.

Our final goodbye assured me that heaven was real. Though absent from the body, Jason was very much alive with God.

So the countdown began; the thirty-minute countdown I'd promised. According to my calculations, Jason could still come back to life. So our families gathered in the living room, sang several hymns, and listened as my dad read:

> *"After this I looked and there before me was a great multitude that no one could count, from every nation, tribe, people, and language, standing before the throne and in front of the Lamb. They were wearing white robes and were holding palm branches in their hands. And they cried out in a loud voice,*
>
> *'Salvation belongs to our God, who sits on the throne, and to the Lamb...'*
>
> *...Then one of the elders asked me, 'These in white robes—who are they, and where do they come from?'*
>
> *I answered, 'Sir, you know.'*
>
> *And he said, 'These are they who have come out of the great tribulation; they have washed their robes and made them white in the blood of the Lamb. Therefore, 'they are before the throne of God and serve him day and night in his temple; and he who sits on the throne will spread out his tent over them. Never again will they hunger; never again will they thirst. The sun will not beat upon them, or any scorching heat. For the Lamb at the center of the throne will be their shepherd; he will lead them to springs of living water. And God will wipe away every tear from their eyes'"* (Revelation 7: 9 – 10 & 13 – 17 NIV).

When thirty minutes had passed, we closed in prayer. A physical healing had not occurred but a very real transformation prepared me to let him go. Hope alone allowed me to focus on God's goodness and to anchor my soul in His love. Without that assurance, I would have crumbled under the loss.

The next day, I stopped by our home to gather some things for the memorial service. After returning a few calls to let art directors know Jason wasn't available for work anymore, I started to cry. As I sorted through his art studio, I became overwhelmed by the thought that he died without feeling like a success.

As the thoughts grabbed hold, the phone rang. A reporter from the Atlanta Journal and Constitution had read his obituary in a smaller paper and wanted to run a half page story about him. The timely interruption stopped my negative flow. Whether Jason knew it or not, he had succeeded. His art work appeared on bill boards around town and in numerous publications. I promised to send her a copy of the last piece of art he did for the Farmer's Almanac.

As I searched for the copies, I opened a random journal. There, on a back page, I found these words. Poignant, bold, and true, they reassured me then like they do now.

> *"I sat in Sunday school the other day as we spoke about faith. Everyone was well at ease with the subject. We spoke of the need for it and when we had experienced it (sick child, job loss, etc.). But I had the distinct impression we really know nothing about it.*
>
> *The descriptions of faith in the Bible really have no resemblance to our anemic examples of faith. So often the church accepts our lifestyles as the norm; the spiritually expected and accepted. We sit around like Appalachian mountain people discussing mountains, refusing to see God's descriptions of mountains – Mt. Everest.*
>
> *When God says they are high, we nod and say, 'Absolutely, they are.' When God says they're difficult to climb, we agree saying, 'We've stumbled through the pines often.' When God says it's difficult to breath, we remember getting winded in our own ascents. We think we know what he's talking about when*

he says mountain, but we have no idea at all. And it grieves me to see how easily we talk about it—how common an experience it seems to be to us. We sit on our hilltop and reminisce about how great the climb was and how beautiful the view is, when we really know nothing at all and worse—we're satisfied.

I sit on that hilltop with everyone else. My faith is no greater. But I know I'm on the wrong mountain. I know there are higher places where the world stretches out into every horizon—above the clouds where the air is so thin it's hard to breathe.

I know this place exists, not from experience but just because God has said to me, 'Don't stop here. It's not enough. There are higher places. I'm an Appalachian man from birth. In my best times I've been at the crest of some Piney ridge. But I'm not satisfied because I've seen a photograph of Everest. God sent me a postcard of it. On the back he wrote, 'Wish you were here.''

Jason was there, with God, where he belonged. I was left behind—for a little while—to raise our boys, to fight my good fight, and to live the faith we learned.

Our journey may have taken us to the highest point in the Appalachian Mountains but there was much farther to go. In a blink of an eye, Jason had transitioned from a place of need to utter completeness, way beyond me. I was to look forward, not back. To press on through grief and embrace the new life God had given me.

"He sets aside the first to establish the second" (Hebrews 10: 9 NIV).

Forty-Five

It doesn't matter
What lies ahead
It doesn't matter
What the journey brings
I can lean into the wind
And let your Spirit
Sing over me

"LAY MY HEAD AND REST"

From my vantage point on the top level of the parking deck, I see medical buildings, a few trees, and grey clouds. The sun tries to peek through the heavy mist, but with little success. So I stand at the edge, gazing out over the view, hoping to hear from God, even if in the form of a faint rainbow. He must have something to say.

Jason had brain surgery eighteen-years-ago today in the hospital across the street—the one adjacent to the clinic where I saw an orthoptist[12] who prescribed my new prism lenses this morning. Throw in Sam's twenty-first birthday, and emotions collide.

When the eye clinic offered me their first available appointment on this poignant day months ago, I considered declining. But when the next available time was over a week later, I took the slot. Desperate, due to constant eye strain, I decided to walk down memory lane with my heart wide open.

A cool breeze blows, reminding me of the coming seasonal shift. I wait for tears as I peer over the familiar landscape, but none form. Even with a serious change in eyewear at hand, my emotions remain in check. The orthoptist suggested I undergo a surgical procedure at some point to correct my double vision. For now, I'll wear contacts to correct nearsightedness and glasses to help me see one image instead of two.

I stare into the mist, befuddled by the irony. Who would have thought both my former spouse and I would suffer a neurological decline? A jolt of mom-worry shoots through me and I force myself to let it go. God holds my boys. He knew the plan long before they were born. So I stand on my perch, overlooking the very paths I walked years ago, searching for a cosmic interpretation of events.

None appears.

While God has certainly brought me back from the brink, I haven't experienced a dramatic, spiritual event since Jason was sick. No angels or odd shaking. At some point, those encounters faded into a distant memory and didn't even feel real. So when life served up more than I expected, I stopped listening for the spirit's lullaby.

But I've been hearing the song again. I've even been writing songs again. And the music—His and mine—has brought me back to life; to life in Him. And while sometimes I still want more, my faith now rises up, reminding me that simple life in Him is the greatest miracle—

---

[12] An eye care specialist trained to evaluate eye movement disorders.

"God has chosen to make known among the Gentiles the glorious riches of this mystery, which is Christ in you, the hope of glory" (Colossian 1: 27 NIV).

False expectations led me astray and the power of cross grew dim. But today I remember when God spoke to my heart and asked, *"Is it not enough if I heal you?"*

My journey to a deeper, abiding awareness of His presence began in earnest that night so many years ago. The intangible became real and the veil between heaven and earth, permeable. Miraculously transformed by His divine assurance and love, I had been able to kiss Jason goodbye and begin life as a single mom with a confidence not my own.

A miracle occurred then and another is changing me now. Maybe not in this exact moment. But the miracle of the cross—His life given for mine—is awakening an acceptance, peace, and sense of purpose that allows me to look over the precipice with tired eyes and accept:

"Our light and momentary troubles are achieving for us an eternal glory that far outweighs them all so we fix our eyes not on what is seen, but on what is unseen, since what is seen is temporary, but what is unseen is eternal" (2 Corinthians 4: 17 - 18; NIV).

A light rain begins, sending me to my car. I back out of the tight space and wind down through the garage. In a way, it's just another day; just one more doctor's appointment in a long line of many. Thankful to leave the memories behind, I drive across town to a local eyeglass store and ask a receptionist if they make prism lenses. They do. So for the first time in twenty years, I search for new frames.

Since they need to be large enough to include progressive bifocals, personal vanity prolongs the process. I don't want to wear glasses on my face every day. Let alone big ones.

Unable to make a decision, I grow determined when a familiar face catches my eye across the store. I don't remember her name, but I recognize the tall, classy woman from our new church. With no one else to turn to, I ask her opinion.

The stylish woman and her son help me narrow down the choices. I almost choose a plastic pair with a light-blue hue but at the last minute another option pops out at me on the expensive rack. With streaks of variant browns, the coloring matches my hair. Silver adornments at the outer corners add a stylish touch. I hunt down my church friend and her son once more and they both affirm the expensive choice, assuring me the cost is worth the added flair.

Thankful for their help, I pay for my new glasses and drive home to rest. Hours later, I return. When I put the glasses on, their intellectual panache changes my appearance. Unsure about the new look, I leave insecure. But as I drive home, the pressure behind my eyes abates. I'll be able to work on my laptop again soon. Seeing the world through new lenses—literally and figuratively—stabilizes me for the next round.

While my altered appearance highlights the inner change, many won't notice. But I will. Every day.

My ankles hold together with cadaver tendons. My back is fused for necessary support. Now a big pair of glasses covers my face, helping my eyes do their job. I'm not the girl I was four years ago who crashed on the living room floor and numbed herself with crime TV.

Not even close. And that's a good thing.

My body is still unreliable. Clinical care remains a frustrating matter. But there's something big going on in the world around us that calls me to leave behind petty distractions and dig a deeper well in my soul. Because we all dry up at times. Our faith wavers when the bad seems to win. But if there's enough air for all of us to breathe—every minute of every day—then there's more than enough of God's love to satisfy our thirsty places and sustain our weary souls.

I simply had to believe it again.

I had to relinquish the wounds caused by the jagged edge sword of rejection and breathe in the life Jesus died for me to live. Crawling back from the dark place, the place of my undoing, callused my fingers and weak knees. But I'm getting there.

It's not that I've arrived or walk confident that I won't be thrown from my horse again. No, I just relish anew the quiet whisper that speaks life to my soul.

When I walk into church a few days later, Heather compliments my new glasses. I immediately give credit to my helpers and describe the woman in detail.

"You're talking about Nancy!"

"Yes," I reply. "Thank you! That's who it was. It was Nancy."

"Well, girl," she begins, "God was definitely looking out for you. If there's anyone I'd want helping me with a fashion choice, it's Nancy. She's got an eye for style and will tell you if something doesn't look good."

I enter the sanctuary, encouraged. Nerves abate, knowing I had the best consultant available while making my choice. Few comment on my four eyes, but as the music starts and I look to the screen, the words don't split in two.

Don and I sit side by side, ready to join with others throughout the world to offer praise to the God of Heaven. Back from the brink, I know God has done a deep work in me. Like a divine chemotherapy, the dark days allowed for a cleansing so that as I reemerge, cancerous beliefs have been replaced by truth.

As we sing, my mind drifts back in time to the day I stood on Jason's parent's back porch and stated, "God's either about to raise Him up off that bed or I have nothing to worry about."

The surge of confidence that filled me in that moment prepared me to say goodbye to my first spouse only minutes later. A similar overflow fills me today.

When I remember each tiny step that led to my restoration, I stand confident that no matter what's to come, He's got this. I have nothing to worry about. God will either heal me or give me what I need to make it through every symptom change and coming heartache. No matter where I am or what I've done, the miraculous can invade, assuring me of His grace.

Kevin, the energetic Irishman who attends our church, reiterated this point in a recent sermon. Using the story of Moses' life as an example, he explained God often moves our lives from the majestic to the mundane to the miraculous.

Saved as an infant when other babies were killed, Moses grew up in Pharaoh's household—the majestic. When the plight of his people became real and he murdered an Egyptian who was beating a Hebrew slave, he ran to the desert and lived as a shepherd, hidden away—the mundane. Then a burning bush invaded his quiet, safe life and he was never the same. As God's spokesperson, he confronted Pharaoh, demanded the Israelites release, and led the wayward people to the Promised Land—the miraculous.

My journey with Jason certainly felt majestic. God's constant presence made me better through the worse. But years of mundane wore me down. As I grab hold of the simple truth—that the power that raised Jesus Christ from the dead is available to transform me still—I open myself to the miraculous again.

If this is true, then I have to conclude that the mundane, the rejection, the years hidden away serve as part of a bigger plan. While the hurt has names and faces associated with it, perhaps the character God longed to grow in me matters more than the discomfort others caused.

> *"No discipline seems pleasant at the time, but painful. Later on, however, it produces a harvest of righteousness and peace for those who have been trained by it"* (Hebrews 12: 11 NIV).

When trained by discipline, the miraculous flows. For *"God disciplines us for our good that we may share in his holiness"* (Hebrews 12: 10 NIV).

Our adult reasoning belies this logic. *"For the message of the cross is foolishness to those who are perishing, but to us who are being saved it is the power of God"* (1 Corinthians 1: 18 NIV).

Stuck in the tight place between logic and freedom, I remember the words of Graham Cooke, *"Essentially what the Lord is saying to us is: How about you be powerless and happy at the same time; How about you be happy that I'm with you even though you feel powerless and weak; How about you be thrilled to be in Jesus right now. Because isn't it great to be going through this in Christ?"*[13]

---

[13]   Cooke, Graham, *Growing Up In God,* Brilliant Book House, 2014, CD.

The pain is real. The journey long. The miraculous may invade or Jesus may say, *Trust me. I'm at work. Be happy in me regardless of what you see.* While trapped in the confines of my human shell, I'll have to fight daily against the message of evil that ricochets around the world.

But the fight is worthwhile.

And I never want to give up again.

A salon hair dryer warms my scalp. Pulled through a cap, long strands of my mousy-colored hair with streaks of grey await change. Covered in a crown of chemicals, I sit still, letting the heat set the color.

Another client enters and I hear, "Your roots aren't nearly as bad as hers."

My hairdresser, Anita, points my way, "She refused to get her hair done until she finished her book."

It's true. My hair has remained untouched by scissors—and highlights—for over six months. My sixteen-year-old nephew jolted me into action when he recently stated, "Wait a minute! Your hair is as dark as my mom's. You're not a *real* blonde. I never knew that."

My cool status upended, I scheduled an appointment.

Anita pulls up the dryer, surveys my progress, and tells me to sit still a little longer. The other fake blonde with dark roots swings her rotating chair my way, "You're writing a book?"

"Yes."

"What's it about?"

Having melted into the soothing warmth of the dryer, I struggle to form words, "It's about my life," I start and then quickly realize how banal my explanation sounds.

"It's a then and now kind of thing," Anita announces like a proud mom. "She goes back and forth in time."

Trying again I share, "I lost my first husband a long time ago and then ended up in a hard place when my son and I were diagnosed with a genetic disorder."

Anita chimes in again, "She doesn't always walk this well. She's used a cane and even a walker sometimes."

She knows me well, having cut and highlighted my hair for years.

271

"I should be better at this," I contend, although I can't hear well due to the whirl of air blowing around my head. Talking loud I share about the video and Sam, and his life-changing question, *"What happened to you, Mom?"*

"I learned a lot about faith in God when my first husband died," I assert. "But when things got hard, I had to learn the lessons again."

The hairdresser who works beside Anita states the obvious, "It's hard to keep the faith sometimes."

No one argues—or even says a word. They don't have to. Terrorists wreaked havoc in Paris only days ago. Many lives were taken and now traumatized survivors struggle to live. Aware that evil longs to dismantle our way of life, our small group knows we're all targets. Throw in the vast array of health issues, family strife, and financial concerns plaguing society, and it's no wonder Jesus said,

> *"In this world you will have trouble. But take heart! I have overcome the world"* (John 16: 33 NIV).

Anita turns off the dryer. With my hair plastered thick with goop, I turn toward the others, "I guess that's why we share our stories. We need each other's faith when ours is lacking."

"That's profound," Anita says like she means it and then directs me to the oversized-sink where I crane my neck back for a wash.

My hair will soon look perky again. But the roots will grow, demanding money and time. Uncomfortable in the chair, a trite analogy forms in my mind.

Just as my grey, mousy-colored hair will continue to war with my desire to be a perky-blonde, the battle for my soul will continue much the same. The roots of sin and suffering, entrenched in the soil of this world, will inch forward every day, threatening to overtake my joy and peace. While finances may demand I give up my hair color fight someday, I firmly believe that of all the battles we fight on this earth, the battle to know the love of God on the best and darkest days is the battle that matters most.

The God of Heaven came to earth wrapped in a human shell to pay the price for our sin. He suffered on the cross, broke the power of sin and death, and then sent His Holy Spirit to shine in us, lighting a path through the darkness.

Belief fuels the light. And the enemy of our souls knows this well. The devil, who prowls around like a roaring lion, desires nothing more than for us to give up our faith and dwell in utter darkness.

Thus, to live in the light of love requires a constant choice, a daily battle, and a constant surrender of will to the Master Creator of the Universe. No matter the pain. No matter the suffering. He longs to cover us with His love, where guilt and shame bow to acceptance.

There on bended knees, the light grows strong, the peace that passes understand prevails, and His purpose overflows in us, igniting fires of love in the hearts of those around us.

It's not an easy choice. And I don't think it's going to get easier. But there is a way in the wilderness, a highway in the desert, a road that leads to all things eternal.

"What happened to you, Mom?"

I finally remembered the battle that counts. The love that sacrificed all. And the hope that does not disappoint.

So I will walk on toward heaven with the mass of humanity in the throngs of strife, eagerly awaiting the promise to come.

"For He who promised is faithful" (Hebrews 10: 23 NIV).

Artwork by Jason Schreer

Epilogue

Posted December 20, 2015 on Susan's Blog :
www.coffeefaithandchronicdisease.blogspot.com

Soon after I fill a cup with coffee in the morning, Eggs, our cat, follows me to where I sit on the floor. There, I savor caffeine while batting her with my free hand.

This morning was no different, except that as we played, I rehashed an odd dream. Still lost in the intense emotion that woke me, I tried to shake it loose as the kitty pounced and clawed.

It took time. Lots of time.

When I left to teach, a drizzly wet permeated the air. So I drove through a virtual pea soup, feeling emotionally lost in the same.

For some reason, I occasionally dream that my first husband never died, but instead, went to live somewhere else. Sometimes he moved in with a friend. Sometimes he retreated to a care facility to not be a burden. Either way, when he shows up after so many years, I fight to understand where he's been and how his reappearance reconciles with my present reality.

It freaks me out every time.

As I wake and push through the mental fog, I remember being at his side the day he died and slowly awaken to daylight... and reality. And by the time I roll out of bed, I normally move on without thought. However, the version I dreamed last night was so real and intense, it stayed with me most of the morning.

As I talked it through with Don, I was able to connect the feeling I had in the dream to what haunted me yesterday. For after two and half hours in a genetic doctor's office, every potential diagnosis I've had in the last five years had been tossed about and basically disregarded.

Medical pea soup, indeed.

It's too complicated to explain in detail. Let's just say Sam and I both had muscle biopsies and spinal taps by a reputable doctor that confirmed mitochondrial disease in 2009 and 2010.

Fast forward a few years and the reputable doctor fell out of favor with much of the mitochondrial disease medical community. Thus his science is no longer accepted in some circles and his diagnosis' now questioned.

As a result, my neurologist sent me for an entirely new genetic work up last spring. While a few more blood tests need to be completed to understand the results of my genome sequencing, when I left the office Wednesday, the geneticist proposed that I suffer with a hypermobility syndrome that cannot be confirmed with any testing. Since he has a patient who manages a similar disease by dancing, he suggested I exercise more.

And that's where I mentally derailed.

I had just walked through the halls of the Emory clinic with my walker to support a friend. By the time I reached my car, my right leg turned inward and my ankle felt like it hung loose like a rag doll.

Exercise more? Just dance? I left with whirling thoughts.

As many chronically ill can attest, living with an un-diagnosable illness creates a unique stress. Because doctors are like designers. They have their own medical tastes, preferred diagnosis', and background of experience that influences their opinion. If I detailed all the contradictory advice I've been given in the last ten years, it would make your head spin too.

While I worked to reconcile the latest information with my present reality, a call from my youngest son, Sam, saved me.

"Mom, I don't think he's right about the exercise," he began. "You've lived an active life and have gone downhill. You haven't just been a sedentary writer who doesn't move enough."

His acknowledgment pierced the crazy place.

"You're not just looking for a name for this thing," he continued. *"You want to know how to live."*

And those words, my dear friends, helped me breathe again. Because deep down, that's really all I want. I want to know how to keep living in the haze of medical oddness.

What about you? This world serves up a healthy dose of virtual pea soup every day. We swim through the thick muck posted in the news and experienced by friends and family alike. It's easy to feel crazy, unsettled, and quite confused by it all.

Like we're just living a bad dream.

A host of theories attempt to explain the discord. Opinions abound. But at times, the voices simply turn into a cacophony of babble.

Which is why I rest assured, knowing a baby was born, in a stable, at a most inconvenient time.

You could say my voice simply adds to the noise. But when I contemplate that baby's life given for mine, a supernatural exchange takes place in my soul.

Pea soup turns to crystal waters. Hope springs forth. And an eternal perspective transforms my momentary difficulty into a manageable annoyance.

I don't enjoy bad dreams. Or living with a seemingly un-diagnosable physical ailment. I don't like confusion, heartache, or facing unknowns.

But when I quiet myself, look to the manger, and sing *Silent Night*, I'm transformed by the miracle of Emmanuel, God with us.

"Arise, shine, your light has come" (Isaiah 60: 1 NIV).

Artwork by Jason Schreer

Acknowledgements

Without the encouragement of family and friends, I would never have had the courage to finish this manuscript. So there are many to thank.

First, thank you, Don for encouraging me to go ahead with the project—even without a publisher or promise of sales. You knew I needed to write and made adjustments to make it happen. Thank you for your sacrifice and faithful devotion. I love you very much.

Second, thank you, Nathan for acting as my first editor and pushing me to find vision beyond the status quo. Your insight and honest assessment proved invaluable—and always has. I'm awfully proud of you.

Thank you, Sam for allowing me to share our story and for reminding me of who I was—and want to be. Thank you, Courtney, for being my second amazing editor and for encouraging the stories when I wondered if they mattered. Your maturity and devotion to each other blesses me.

Thank you, Ann Nelson and Nancy Patton for reading my first draft and offering input that kept me writing when the days grew long and the stories hard to write. And thank you, Reva Austin, Anissa Shoemaker, and Renee Montgomery for perusing the final copy and offering requested input.

Thank you, McKenzie Crowe for writing me letters from prison and for making me feel accepted for who I am. Being your friend helped my words flow again.

Thank you, Mosaics (aka my Bible Study girls) for meaty discussions, a place for tears, and for just being who you are, a motley crew of Jesus followers trying hard to figure this thing out. And since our group has gone through some changes since we first met a few years ago, I want to also thank Lauri and Betsy for joining us and for bringing your God given color to our Monday Mosaic encounters. Lauri, your devotion to your unique family reminds us to live for what matters. And Betsy, your sweet spirit that transformed into spirited squealing delight made our video game night the best ever.

While I'm indebted to the Mosaics as a whole for allowing me to share their stories, I owe a special thanks to Bonnie Shaver and Luanne Atkins who proofread my final manuscript and found mistakes others did not. Knowing Bonnie's battle with ALS was nearing the end, their time and effort meant even more—especially since Bonnie left her earthly shell just over a month later, on January 29, 2016.

Thank you, Allen Levi, for letting me record and now share the song that gave me the courage to step out with my own music. *"So go into this hurting world with music for the day, the songs that God has given us, we were meant to give away."* (Levi, Allen, "Open Windows", 1995.)

Thank you, Rick Parker, for editing Jason's artwork on the fly, just when I needed it most.

Thank you Mom, Dad, Laura, Mark, George, Jess, Trey, Drew, Josh, Nana, Papa, and the Schreer gang for living life through the years and for pressing on as family. In the ups and downs. Good days and bad. Family matters much.

In the same vein, thank you, Davis clan for not giving up on me. It's been quite the journey. Not an easy one for any of us. May God continue to heal, reconcile, and draw us together in ways that far surpass all we can ask or imagine.

Lastly, thank you Sanctuary Church—Craig Bowler, Sonny Lallerstedt, and those who let me share their stories—Bonnie and Lu, Sherrie, Somer, Isabel, Ken Johnson, MA, LPC (www.eastwestpsyche. com), Kevin Daly, MA, LCC, BCPC (www.brokenchainsintl.com), and Carl, Olivia, and Makayla—and the congregation as a whole who embraced us, loved us, and encouraged us when the times got tough. I wouldn't be where I am without the body of Christ in action, forgiving, growing, and striving to reflect more of him in our earthly, tainted shells. I'm honored to be on this journey with you all.

About the Author

Susan Schreer Davis is a songwriter, blogger, and mother of two adult sons. She lives outside of Atlanta, Georgia, with her husband, Don, and tabby cat, Eggs. To listen to her songs and read more about her story, visit her at susanschreerdavis.com.

Printed in the United States
By Bookmasters